READING
SPEED AND STRATEGY
for
the Business and
Professional Man

Prentice-Hall, Inc.
Englewood Cliffs, N.J.

READING
SPEED AND STRATEGY
for
the Business and
Professional Man

KENNETH P. BALDRIDGE
Director, Baldridge Reading Skill Development, Inc.

PRINTED IN THE UNITED STATES OF AMERICA

76212 — B & P

How to Gain the Most
Profitable Change in Your
Reading Habits Since You
First Began to Read

At the end of an executive reading program I conducted a few years ago, one of my students came to me with a wry comment. He said that the course had been a great help to him, and that he had profited from it, but if only someone had taught him the same skills years earlier, he might now be the company president instead of a regional manager.

It is an axiom in business that time is money *and* success; yet many executives waste many hours through inefficient reading habits. How often have you wished that you had the extra time to find out more about some neglected aspect of your field and yet been forced to fall back on someone else's knowledge? How often have you looked at a stack of newspapers, journals, and reports, promising yourself to get through them all, only to discover a month later that you had fallen even further behind?

Several years ago, a corporation called me in to help with a management trainee program. All the candidates chosen for this program had completed six to ten years with the company and had been rotated through operating positions, doing well enough until they were faced with *nine feet* of books, pamphlets, procedures, and journals covering broader phases of management responsibility. These men had been selected on the basis of exceptional achievement; yet, most of them couldn't begin to cope with the quantity of reading their company deemed essential to full participation in upper-level management decisions.

I know that if you have taken the time to pick up this book, you are aware of the vast amount of reading you have to do. Of course, reading skills alone, no matter how well developed, will not guarantee success in management and professional spheres; yet, without extensive and productive reading, the best qualities of imagination, personality and old-fashioned drive may be cancelled by sheer ignorance.

There is no point in mincing words. If you are unfamiliar with developments in your field, in related fields, and with major trends in the world around you, you are the victim of a special sort of ignorance, characteristic of our time, which has resulted from phenomenal increases in new information available in all fields. Reading today requires efficient location, storage, and subsequent retrieval of relevant information drawn from millions of irrelevant words. Word-by-word reading in this search for vital information simply will not work.

Reduction of the overwhelming volume of available information can be achieved in an effective manner by following the steps proposed in this book. The first step is to learn to *locate quickly the information you need*. The second step is to *organize this information* in such a way that the third step, *future recall and use of the information* will present no problem.

In this book *location of information* is emphasized in Skill I ("Skim-Reading") and Skill II ("Phrase Reading"); *organization and recall* in Skill III ("Paragraph Analysis"), Skill IV ("Structuring Ideas"), and Skill V ("Concentration"). And an *advanced technique* is found in Skill VI ("Critical Reading"). In addition, the final two chapters ("A Test of Your Skills . . ." and "Extending Your Skills") serve as a *review and extension* of all the skills.

This book is not a magic formula. No magic formula will work with an activity as complex as reading. However, I can tell you that employing the skills presented here can make the most profitable change in your reading habits since you first began to read, a claim made on the basis of fifteen years' experience in the reading-improvement field. The techniques you are about to cover have been successfully used in programs given for Western Electric, TIME, NBC, General Electric, IBM, and other major corporations. They have been perfected in the Baldridge Reading and Study Skills Programs which have been conducted in more than 350 schools, colleges and universities in the United States.

Among the unique features of this book is the high degree of direct application to the business and professional man's reading material. The exercises are taken from the kind of reading you must do every day of your professional life. This application begins in the first chapter with the reading material that most business and professional men encounter at the beginning of the day: their newspapers.

This immediate application is consistent with the assumption that the readers of this book are individuals who do not have any difficulties serious enough to warrant remedial help. For this reason, we have not included in the first part of our book the intensive diagnostic tests and analyses that are frequently included in books designed for students in academic difficulty.

Virtually all of the skills in this book can contribute to the speed with which you can complete your reading. As you master the specific skills and tactics, you can evolve specific strategies for each type of reading you do.

Look through the book. Plan a program that will carry you right through it, or if you prefer, jump ahead to the chapters that seem to apply most directly to your needs (except for Skill VI). The only warning we would like to make is that whatever section you do read, *you must apply the skills in this book, and, more importantly, you must apply them to your own reading,* if you want them to work. Reading skills, like any other skills, improve through use, and direct application of these skills to your own materials leads to the greater reading proficiency necessary for your professional field.

It is a pleasure to share with you what we have learned.

K.P.B.

Table of Contents

tail • Accuracy Statements • STRUCTURING: ADVANCED APPLICATION • Structure Statements • STRUCTURING: INDEPENDENT APPLICATION • STRUCTURING: FURTHER INDEPENDENT APPLICATION • Structure and Accuracy Statements • STRUCTURING: CORRESPONDENCE APPLICATION • SUMMARY • Skill Reminder

What the Skill Is • What Concentration Does • How to Use It • QUESTIONING • ANTICIPATING • VISUALIZING • SUMMARIZING • CONCENTRATION: BASIC APPLICATION • Close-Reading for Concentration • Reading for Purpose with Variable Rate • Summarizing While Reading • CONCENTRATION: FURTHER APPLICATION • Close-Reading Exercise • CONCENTRATION: ADVANCED APPLICATION • SUMMARY • Skill Reminder

What the Skill Is • What Critical Reading Does • How to Use It • CRITICAL READING: BASIC APPLICATION • Critical Evaluation • CRITICAL READING: FURTHER APPLICATION I • Similarities and Differences • Critical Evaluation • CRITICAL READING: FURTHER APPLICATION II • Similarities and Differences • Critical Evaluation • CRITICAL READING: ADVANCED APPLICATION • Skim-Read for Structure • Fill in the Loopholes • SUMMARY • Skill Reminder

SKILL QUESTIONNAIRE • Skill 1: Skim-Reading • Skill II: Phrase Reading • Skill III: Paragraph Analysis • Skill IV: Structuring Ideas • Skill V: Concentration • Skill VI: Critical Reading • NOW ANSWER THE FOLLOWING QUESTIONS ON THE SELECTION • TYPICAL READING PROBLEMS AND THEIR SOLUTIONS • A REVIEW OF THIS CHAPTER AND BOOK

SUGGESTED READINGS • Business and Economics • The Classics • Fine Arts • History • Modern Life • Philosophy and Religion • Psychology and Medicine • Poetry • Science

*READING
SPEED AND STRATEGY*
*for
the Business and
Professional Man*

SKIM-READING

To get at the FACTS that count . . . FAST

Skill

I

What the Skill Is: The ability to extract the main points without getting bogged down in details by a systematic survey of the material.

What Skim-Reading Does: Enables you quickly to determine the substance, difficulty level, importance and organization of the material to be read.

How to Use It: Skim-Reading is a procedure for gathering essential facts about what you are going to read *before* a thorough reading. This fact-gathering is accomplished by a planned examination of significant sections of the material to be read: in newspapers, the summaries, headlines, and initial paragraphs; in correspondence, the name of the sender, the date, and the decision words; in periodicals and books, the titles, subtitles, and first and last paragraphs.

The skim-reading technique takes advantage of the organization each writer builds into his material. A writer's organization is similar to that used by a man making a speech. A speaker begins with a core of ideas, adds illustrations and anec-

1

dotes to his ideas, and arranges the whole in an order that will interest or convince the people he is addressing. If you had an advance copy of the speaker's notes, you would be better able to follow his argument, assess his ideas, and remember what he said. You might even decide not to hear his speech, or send someone else. In any case, an outline or précis of the speech would certainly make it easier for you to understand what the man was trying to communicate. Skim-reading is designed to give you just that kind of help with the mass of printed matter you must, or would like to, get through every day.

Skim-reading also takes advantage of the structure that is inherent in many kinds of printed materials: newspapers, correspondence, magazines, and some books. The same elements occur in a predictable place day after day in any given newspaper, journal, report, or correspondence. Of course, the organization of a letter differs from that of a newspaper article, but the structural constants in each make the reader's task much simpler, *once he knows what to look for.*

This chapter will present information about the structures typical of most of the material you are likely to encounter in your daily reading. You will use this information to skim-read samples of many different kinds of reading material. Most important, this chapter will encourage extended application of skim-reading to all materials you are currently reading, including this book.

Start now to determine the benefits of skim-reading. Take two minutes to examine the rest of this chapter and a few minutes to skim-read the rest of the book. In this and succeeding chapters, note particularly the sequence of main points and the summary at the end of the chapter.

To develop the skill of skim-reading, it is essential that you be aware of elapsing time, that you go right to work and, above all, *keep moving.* Therefore, use a clock or watch with a sweep second hand in order to time yourself exactly. Keep on the move by reassuring yourself that this is skim-reading. Later, you can go back and read thoroughly those sections most relevant to your interests and your needs. But for skim-reading, every time you start to pause or slow down, remind yourself that skim-reading is the warm-up, the dry-run, the exploratory sampling technique that allows you to invest your later, extended time commitment more wisely and with a greater return on your investment.

How long did you spend skim-reading this chapter? _____ minutes, _____ seconds

How long did you spend skim-reading this book? _____ minutes, _____ seconds

The skim-reading technique is designed to give you the core of meaning from all the material you read so that you may read with maximum efficiency and judgment. On the basis of a skim-reading you can determine four basic factors:

1. The essentials of the material to be read.   *"What is it really about?"*

2. The importance of the material at this time.   *"Should I read this thoroughly now, later, not at all, or pass it on?"*

3. The difficulty and complexity of the material.   *"How much power must I turn on to get what I want from this?"*

4. The structure of the material.   *"What is the organization of the material?"*

1. "What Is It Really About?"

You might look to the title to learn the subject, but the title of a piece of printed material does not necessarily tell you its substance and purpose. A newspaper headline may jubilantly announce the end of a strike; yet a skim-reading of the article might indicate that the settlement was disastrous for one side. A book or chapter title may claim that the contents are an impartial history, when a skim-reading will tell you that the material is a polemic for a particular political party. With the diversification of products by many traditional industries, the corporate title on a letterhead may give no indication of the product being offered. Don't buy the label! The reader must be as careful as the buyer. *Caveat lector.* Reader beware!

A systematic skim-reading of the material gives you an opportunity to make a decision about the content rather than having to accept what may be a misleading title; or having to become more and more dependent upon assistants, secretaries, and other processors. One executive of a major corporation found that the amount of mail reaching his desk gradually lessened as his secretary made more and more decisions about the importance of items or their relevance to his responsibilities. After he developed the skill of skim-reading, the executive was able to skim over the entire body of his mail in order to control abstracting and indexing done by assistants and secretaries. In several instances his skim-reading turned up possibilities that only he had sufficient information to recognize.

Once you have discovered the basic content of material, you are both able to make a preliminary decision about it, and you can understand the material better in less time if you read it thoroughly later. Through the familiarity provided by skim-reading you will have time to organize your own thoughts, to raise questions, and to assemble data before beginning your close reading.

2. "Should I Read This Thoroughly Now, Later, Not at All, or Pass It On?"

Your skim-reading makes it possible for you to categorize material, decide upon its immediate or ultimate importance, or decide who in your organization would be best equipped to deal with it if you wish to delegate it.

3. "How Much Power Must I Turn On in Order to Get What I Want From This?"

There can be a considerable waste of energy in grappling with a news story that you have read earlier in the day, have heard discussed on your car radio, and have seen analyzed on a TV special. Your skim-reading should warn you when there is little new in the article so that you may approach it with some of your power reduced, looking only for the significant changes since you last encountered the story. The reduced expenditure of power for easy material permits you to have reserves of intensity when your skim-reading alerts you to an item of considerable difficulty and complexity.

4. "What Is the Organization of the Material?"

After skim-reading the material, you will have an awareness of the content and also an awareness of the organization of the material. A subsequent close reading will be far more effective. The order of presentation can be anticipated, and conclusions can be sampled before you become involved with supporting evidence. You are now able to proceed through the unfamiliar territory, following the route skim-reading has marked out for you.

APPLICATION

This section of the chapter will give you a chance to apply skim-reading to various newspapers, correspondence, periodicals, and a book. You will find specific tactics for the adaptation of skim-reading to each of these forms. These exercises will help you to begin to make skim-reading a part of your repertoire right now. However, this is just the first step. You must use your new skill as often as you can and as widely as you can on your own reading. Information about skilled reading techniques, even confidence in their probable usefulness, will not be of much benefit unless you make a conscious change in your reading habits. In the area of reading improvement, "practice makes perfect" is a truth rather than a truism.

HOW TO SKIM-READ NEWSPAPERS

Skim-reading can be your most important newspaper reading tool when you want both broad coverage and a thorough understanding of the items you may find of special interest and sometimes of profit as well. In short, an efficient reading of a good daily paper can keep you oriented to the world around you, informed of developments in your own field, and aware of significant activities in other fields.

If you observe newspaper readers on the train or subway, you know that each approaches his paper with a system of some kind, regardless of the organization of the paper. One reader may follow this sort of pattern: headlines, weather, the financial pages; another may turn to the comics, sports, editorials; while a third may go over the obituaries, advice to the lonely, and the television page.

Newspaper editors have spent a good deal of effort arranging their contents in a way that is easy to read for all of their readers. Since you are keenly interested in efficient reading procedures—procedures that will give you maximum coverage of your areas of interest—it is only logical that you should be aware of every one of these built-in aids. Let's make it even stronger. If you want to know your way around in the newspaper, *you cannot afford to ignore these aids.*

The three newspapers we have chosen for practice application of skim-reading are three of America's best known newspapers for businessmen:

The New York Times, The New York Herald Tribune, and *The Wall Street Journal.* They also assist their readers through summaries, headings, and subheadings. For papers less well-structured, of course, you will have to apply skim-reading even more consciously to dig out the important facts.

BASIC SKIM-READING: *THE NEW YORK TIMES*

The New York Times is arranged in a way that makes it very easy for you to find out what is in each issue with just a couple of minutes of skim-reading. A "News Summary and Index" appears daily on the lower half of the first page of the Second Section. By skim-reading the "News Summary and Index," you will be prepared with a grasp of the whole before you begin to select items for intensive reading later on. In addition, a quick survey here will prevent the very common accident in newspaper reading that occurs when a reader—usually a highly interested reader—pursues one story from the front page to an inner page and in the process misses whole pages that may be of great interest to him.

TACTIC 1: To skim-read well, you must move your eyes rapidly down the page, searching for the pattern of presentation rather than emphasizing the content. While you will become somewhat familiar with the information, you should avoid attempting to read whole sentences or to develop ideas. Now turn to Figure 1A and glance over the entire "News Summary and Index" by letting your eyes run down the columns to see what you can learn about its physical organization. (Disregard the grey guide lines at this time.)

What you should have noticed:
The first two left-hand columns are headed "The Major Events of the Day." Page and column references follow each story summary. The three right-hand columns contain two-line summaries with page references only.

By noting headings in the "News Summary and Index," you should have seen that the major news events were classified in a funnel from *International,* to *National,* to *Metropolitan.* You should also have noted that "The Other News" was classified topically as: *Industry and Labor, Health and Science, Religion,* and so forth. In addition, you probably noticed the "Quotation of the Day" space.

TACTIC 2: Having skimmed for overall organization, you are now ready to skim for some specific content. Run your eyes down the two columns headed "The Major Events of the Day," following a pattern similar to that of the guide lines on page 8. Note in the *International* just the localities mentioned but in the *National* and *Metropolitan* get some idea of the specific items.

> *What you should have noticed:*
> INTERNATIONAL: Algeria, France, Peru, Britain, Netherlands, Indonesia, Laos.
> NATIONAL: Federal judge ordering reopening of schools; a voter registration rally for Negroes in Georgia; failure of a Thor missile in a high altitude nuclear test; President signs Welfare Reform Bill; Ways and Means discusses tax cut; Senator Goldwater discusses campaign.
> METROPOLITAN: Rejection of Justice Keogh's retirement request; Congressional district line said to be discriminatory; lower deck of George Washington Bridge to open August 29th.

TACTIC 3: Following the guide lines, continue skim-reading the section headed "The Other News." Select one story from the category of greatest interest to you—the one that you will be most inclined to follow up for a thorough reading. Also note which category has the greatest number of references on this day.

> *What you should have noticed:*
> Whatever story caught your interest.
> *Government and Politics* has the most references.

TACTIC 4: Return to page 9 and glance at the "Quotation of the Day." Read it rapidly and note with what news story it is associated. This is often a means *The New York Times* uses for emphasizing what it feels to be an especially significant story or situation.

will be opened and golf ball, five s,
closed to prevent or minimize of salmon eggs, a fishing reel, He was sentenced to sixty
tie-ups when volume gets very fish hooks, two steak knives, days in jail on the vagrancy
heavy. one fork, a lady's pin, three charge.

News Summary and Index

FRIDAY, JULY 27, 1962

The Major Events of the Day

International

The power struggle in newly independent Algeria, which had threatened to erupt in civil war, moved yesterday toward peace and compromise. A concerted effort seemed to be in progress to minimize the casualty figures in Wednesday's fighting in Constantine. New estimates put the number of dead at no more than four and the wounded at ten, in place of earlier reports of twenty-five dead and as many wounded. Leaders of the dissident faction led by Vice Premier Ben Bella plan to send an advance party to Algiers today to prepare for the arrival of Mr. Ben Bella's new political bureau. [Page 1, Column 8.] The struggle was said to stem from rivalries of individuals and clans rather than from ideological differences. [2:5-7.]

The French Government views the Algerian power struggle with sadness but also with a determination to avoid, if possible, any direct involvement. [1:8.]

A week after the coup d'état in Peru, the military junta was master of the political situation without resorting to terror. Most Peruvians were apparently giving tacit consent to the military take-over. [4:1.]

After more than six hours of debate in the House of Commons, Prime Minister Macmillan's Government defeated a censure motion with a majority of ninety-eight. But the response of Conservative backbenchers to his new program indicated that he might have only one more chance to lead Britain out of her economic troubles. [1:5.]

Britain's Court of Appeal rejected a plea for the release of Dr. Robert A. Soblen from detention by British authorities. [5:1.]

Talks in Washington between the Netherlands and Indonesia on the future of Netherlands New Guinea were near collapse. Informed officials said that the snag was over Indonesia's insistence on a modification of the peace proposals advanced by Ellsworth Bunker, a retired United States diplomat. [1:7.] Diplomatic activity in Washington also involved a dignified welcome to Prince Souvanna Phouma, the new Laotian Premier, whom the United States helped to drive out of power almost two years ago. [1:5-7.]

National

A Federal judge in Richmond, Va., ordered the reopening of public schools in Prince Edward County next September "without regard to race or color." The schools have been shut down for three years in a controversy over desegregation. [1:2-2.]

A voter registration rally attended by thirty-eight Negroes and two whites in Terrell County, Ga., was interrupted by three police officials. As the county sheriff warned the participants that "we want our colored people to go on living like they have for the last hundred years," his chief deputy swaggered back and forth fingering a black leather cartridge belt and a revolver. [1:2-3.]

A United States attempt to conduct a high-altitude nuclear test over Johnston Island in the Pacific failed when a Thor rocket burst into flames on the launching pad and had to be destroyed. The failure, the third in the long-delayed test program, presented the Administration with a dilemma on whether to cut short the tests or exceed a Presidential deadline for concluding the series. [1:6.]

President Kennedy announced that he had signed a sweeping welfare reform bill. The new law ended a year of turbulent debate over the direction of welfare programs. [1:1.]

The House Ways and Means Committee began closed hearings to determine whether the national economy needs a speedy tax cut. The meetings are scheduled to continue through next week. [1:3-4.] In a free-swinging attack on Administration policies, Senator Barry Goldwater expressed the view that the economic "slide" would be the dominant issue in the coming campaign. [5:5-6.]

Metropolitan

The Board of Estimate unanimously rejected the retirement application of Justice J. Vincent Keogh, who was convicted last month of accepting a bribe to fix a Federal court case. Keogh, who has served twelve years as a state Supreme Court justice, is expected to go to court to seek a city pension. [1:1.]

The state government was accused of discriminating against Negroes and Puerto Ricans in redrawing Congressional district lines in Manhattan. The charge against the Republican-controlled Legislature was made in a suit filed in Manhattan's Federal court by nine Democratic residents, supported by the county Democratic committee. [1:4.]

Finishing work on the lower deck of the George Washington Bridge is being pushed for the scheduled opening on Aug. 29. The new deck will make the bridge the world's only fourteen-lane suspension bridge. [27:2.]

Figure 1A

Figure 1A (Cont.)

The Other News

International

U. N. backs admission for Rwanda, Burundi.   Page 2

Belgian business men fear Katanga violence.   Page 2

British move step closer to Common Market.   Page 3

Famous London mansion sold to developer.   Page 3

United States craft buzzed by Soviet fighter.   Page 3

Red youth festival draws friend and a foe.   Page 3

Soviet bloc to coordinate electricity movement.   Page 3

O. E. C. D., Common Market plan aid increase.   Page 3

Vietnamese balk at U. S. plan on forts.   Page 4

Government and Politics

Senators start hearing on school prayer.   Page 5

Senate foes of satellite bill win a round.   Page 6

Ribicoff opens Connecticut drive for U.S. Senate. Page 6

U. S. denies it played politics on drought.   Page 6

Ex-Representative is held in counterfeiting.   Page 7

G. O. P. backs Kupferman for City Council.   Page 7

State G. O. P. appoints platform advisory unit. Page 8

Stratton and Samuels fight McKeon parley.   Page 8

Conservative party names Senate candidate.   Page 8

Pacts to end job bias are disclosed.   Page 9

No. Carolina G.O.P. chief quits; admits double life.   Page 10

Goldberg presses Eastern Air Lines' peace bid.   Page 10

City to sell park land to Westchester.   Page 26

Roadblocks for drinkers held legal in Jersey.   Page 27

General

Post Office plans $70,000,000 modernization here.   Page 1

Albany, Ga., Negroes warned on new violence.   Page 9

City is cracking down on rooming houses.   Page 15

Writer sues True magazine over editing.   Page 22

Udall is assailed over Fire Island.   Page 22

Pact reached with U. N. on hydrants.   Page 27

Westchester stand on parkway tolls scored.   Page 27

Two steelworkers are killed by cable.   Page 49

Industry and Labor

Rail unions threaten strike over rules.   Page 10

Port Authority takes over the H. & M.   Page 27

Waterman Lines denied an operating subsidy. Page 48

Health and Science

Virus of German measles is isolated and grown. Page 1

3 babies born deformed here; mothers took drug. Page 12

Religion

Catholic Bishop consecrated in Rockville Centre.   Page 22

Amusements and the Arts

Two directors of Fox quit board.   Page 13

Tchaikovsky night at Lewisohn Stadium.   Page 13

Ford grants awarded for "internship" in arts. Page 14

Britain to celebrate Shakespeare anniversary. Page 14

"Come on Strong" switches producers.   Page 15

"The Notorious Landlady" stars Jack Lemmon. Page 15

"The Premise" opens in London's West End.   Page 15

Steinbeck's "Travels With Charley" reviewed. Page 23

Jose Quintero directing television plays.   Page 49

British do-it-yourself series proves popular.   Page 49

"Superfluous People" shown on Channel 3.   Page 49

Fashions and Home

Dior's collection is shown in Paris.   Page 11

Home products undergo testing for safety.   Page 11

Obituaries

Raquel Meller, Spanish singer in the Thirties.   Page 25

Christie MacDonald, musical star 1910 to 1920. Page 25

Mrs. Esther G. Friedman, former Socialist leader. Page 25

Gabriel Salgado, ex-Spanish Cabinet member.   Page 25

Matt Cvetic, former F. B. I. counterspy.   Page 25

Financial and Business

Stock market stages a moderate advance.   Page 29

U. S. monetary gold stock at 23-year low.   Page 29

Union Pacific reports decline in earnings.   Page 29

Eastern Gas and Fuel plans share exchange.   Page 29

American Home Products sets sales, profits marks. Page 29

Jersey Standard profit rose 10.4% in half.   Page 29

United Nations to help Thais in rice research.   Page 29

Treasury announces financing terms.   Page 29

Chrysler reports profit for 3d successive quarter. Page 29

Simmons cuts dividend to 40 cents from 60.   Page 29

Bethlehem Steel increasing capital outlays.   Page 29

	Page		Page
Adv. News	28	Grains	31
Amer. Exch	34	Money	33
Bond Sales	31	Mutual Funds	35
Bus. Records	36	N. Y. Stk. Exch.	30
Commodities	31	Out-of-Town	34
Cotton	31	Over the Counter	35
Dividends	31	Sidelights	30
Foreign Exch	34		

Sports

Yankees whip Red Sox, 13—3, with 8-run third.   Page 16

Mets bow to Braves, 6—1, for 11th loss in row.   Page 16

Humm's 68 wins medal in L. I. amateur golf. Page 17

Ghezzi, Ellis, Lumpkin share Jersey P.G.A. lead. Page 17

Henry T. Adios takes Empire Pace at Yonkers.   Page 18

Fox, Reed, Bond, Holmberg advance in tennis. Page 19

Man in the News

M. A. MacIntyre, head of Eastern Air Lines. Page 10

Analysis and Comment

Atkinson comments on leisure in United States.   Page 22

Reston discusses our Latin-American ties.   Page 24

ing t... would Tubes er rail...

The ... and p... stores, and n... Legisla... Author... bined H... ter ente... this spr... New J...

Abou... men of... and vo... sit in, vent t...

Abi
Ple
To

Park Morris recomm... more plann... Abin...

He grou... lead... par... arou...

Th cerne... propos... the sit... comfort... tion of Bleecker agreed th... cluded.

The park, Hudson, Bl West Eleven... nounced in C... liminary sk... area and b... ball courts

The Vill... yesterday... fer a par... with benc... surface ... They cited... for older cl... Horatio St...

Mr. Morr... a plan for... pared by th...

Among conference William F... Philip W... the Park Greenwich Anthony I... the Green... nity Plan... Jane Jac... Save the... tee.

Quotation of the Day

"We want our colored people to go on living like they have for the last hundred years."—Sheriff Z. T. Mathews of Terrell County, Ga., warning Negroes at a voter registration rally. [1:2-3.]

---

* AUTHOR'S APOLOGY: This sample from *The New York Times* is now considerably outdated. I regret that this and all other newspaper selections in the book will become more a part of history than current events and trust that you will recognize time precludes inclusion of real "news" but does not prevent application of a skill to an old piece of news and then application to your today's newspaper.

KPB

What you should have noticed:

The quotation is related to the second item under *National* news: a voter registration rally for Negroes. Sheriff Matthews of Georgia made the statement.

WHAT WAS THE PURPOSE OF THESE FOUR SKIM-READING TACTICS? HOW LONG WILL A SKILLFUL SKIM-READING USUALLY TAKE?

The purpose of the skim-reading tactics you have just practiced is to allow you to size up the day's news rapidly with your own prior knowledge for support and your special interests as a directing agent. Without being forced to accept the newspaper's judgment of what is most important, you can survey the whole and make your own decisions about what you should and should not spend time on. As you skim-read the "News Summary and Index," you can distinguish between the actual *news* (i.e., that which is new) and those running stories on items that broke some time ago.

With practice, a skillful skim-reading will usually take you *no more than one or two minutes.*

TACTIC 5: For those days when you have no more than the time over your morning coffee for the paper, skim-reading of the summaries will keep you up-to-date. More importantly, this skim-reading will keep you from missing that especially important bit of information (the kind that adds so much in a conference or interview) that you might miss in an unsystematic once-over. If you always read the paper right through, skim-reading the summaries will serve as an alerting device and will make it possible for you to react to the news rather than simply absorb it.

When you have more time after your skim-reading of the summary, go back to the beginning of the "News Summary and Index" columns and read closely each of the summaries under *International* and *National*. If you are a New Yorker—or an interested suburbanite—read the *Metropolitan* summaries as well. In the "Other News" section, examine more carefully the items that fall into the areas of your special interests. Both the initial skim-reading tactics and this more thorough reading of the summaries should take you *no more than five to ten minutes* if you are a daily reader of the paper. If you read the paper less often, of course, it will take you a little longer because follow-up stories will be new material as far as you are concerned.

What you should have noticed both during and after your skim-reading:

1. *"What is it really about?"*—Your skim-reading of the "News Summary and Index" in the exercise you have just done (and, for best results, applied to your own paper today) should be giving you a good grasp of the *substance* of the news.

2. *"Should I read this thoroughly now, later, not at all, or pass it on?"* —Your skim-reading of the "News Summary and Index" allows you to *decide which stories you intend to follow up*. Once again, if you regularly read everything in your paper, skim-reading will allow you to determine which stories ought to be read first. In addition, a sampling of each story will increase your interest and improve your understanding of the story when you get to it.

3. *"How much power must I turn on to get what I want from this?"* —Skim-reading will tell you how much of today's news is *really news*. It will prepare you for those stories with background or personalities so unfamiliar to you that you will be ready in advance to give them every bit of attention you possess. In the same way, it will prepare you to recognize familiar stories, so you can proceed more quickly with your reading.

4. *"What is the organization of the material?"*—For an intensive reading of those stories you select, the principles of skim-reading will once again be applied. Whether you want to read a particular story in its entirety or want just to pick up some details not presented in the summary, you should *always begin with a skim-reading* of the article itself. Anticipation of the organization of the article through skim-reading will help you to read with full alertness, and with your background information in sharp focus.

Up to this point, the skim-reading tactics in this chapter were applied to the "News Summary and Index" of *The New York Times*. Now the same principles will be adapted to the skim-reading of an entire news story in *The Times*. Later in this chapter you will apply skim-reading techniques to *The New York Herald Tribune* and *The Wall Street Journal*.

TACTIC 6: The most important news story in *The New York Times* is usually found in the far right column on page one. By reading the story heading, subheadings, and the first two paragraphs, you can grasp the main ideas in the article and notice a sequence of events. Now turn to Figure 1B and skim-read by following the guide-lines and then continuing to skim just down the center of the column.

York Times.

LATE CITY EDITION

U. S. Weather Bureau Report (Page 46) forecast:
Sunny with low humidity today; fair
and cool tonight. Fair tomorrow.

Temp. range: 77—60; yesterday: 85—65.
Temp.- Hum. Index: 68; yesterday: 75.

FIVE CENTS

RK, FRIDAY, JULY 27, 1962.

10 cents beyond 30-mile zone from New York City
except on Long Island. Higher in air delivery cities.

New Premier of Laos Is Welcomed to U. S. by Rusk

WHO >

DID WHAT >

WHEN >

ALGERIANS SEEK
TO HEAL DISPUTE
IN WAKE OF CLASH

Reports of Constantine Fight
Are Termed Exaggerated
by Ministers in Algiers

FACTIONS IN CONTACT

Ally of Ben Bella Plans Trip
to Capital to See Aides of
Provisional Government

WHERE >

WHAT NEXT >

WHY >

WHO >

By THOMAS F. BRADY
Special to The New York Times.

ALGIERS, July 26—The Al-
gerian political pendulum
swung back toward peace and
compromise today impelled in
part by the fear of civil war
that gripped the country during the previous twenty-four
hours.

Ministers of the Algerian
Provisional Government here

Secretary of State Rusk greeting Prince Souvanna Phouma at National Airport reception

Figure 1B © 1962 by The New York Times Company. Reprinted by permission.

By MAX FRANKEL
Special to The New York Times

WASHINGTON, July 26 — The United States today a dignified welcome today to Prince Souvanna Phouma, the new Laotian Premier, whom it helped to drive out of pow-

were seeking a compromise solution to the leadership crisis.

They were in telephone contact with the backers of Vice Premier Mohammed Ben Bella in Oran, with the anti-Ben Bella camp in Tizi-Ouzou and with the forces supporting Mr. Ben Bella that seized Constantine yesterday after a brief clash with Government troops.

Minister of State Rabah Bitat, who flew here today from Constantine, and other ministers said first reports of twenty-five dead there and as many wounded were exaggerated. New estimates put the number of dead at two or four and the wounded at ten.

Minister Is Freed

Lakhdar Ben Tobbal, another Minister of State, who had been arrested by the Ben Bella troops in Constantine, arrived in Algiers with Mr. Bitat. He was reported to have been freed late yesterday, reportedly at Mr. Bitat's demand.

Abdel Hafid Boussouf, Minister of Armament and Liaison, who was visiting his family in the Constantine region during the violence there, also returned to Algiers. He stopped en route in Tizi-Ouzou, the capital of the Kabylia region, to see Mr. Ben Bella's chief antagonists, Vice Premiers Belkacem Krim and Mohammed Boudiaf.

There was no word of the 1,200 Kabyle troops who, according to an announcement from Tizi-Ouzou last night, were marching to the relief of Constantine and should have reached that city by dawn.

The only warlike words of

Continued on Page 2, Column 4

3d Atom Test Fails; U.S. Faces Dilemma On Friendship Series

By JOHN W. FINNEY
Special to The New York Times

WASHINGTON, July 26 — The United States failed again today in an attempt to conduct a high-altitude nuclear test over Johnston Island in the Pacific.

A Thor rocket burst into flames and was destroyed on the launching pad.

The rocket failure was to have carried a nuclear device to an altitude of about 100 miles.

Conservatives Rally Behind Him, but Rank and File Are Cool to His Program

By SYDNEY S. KING
Special to The New York Times

LONDON, July 26 — Prime Minister Macmillan rallied the Conservative members of the House of Commons behind him today...

Indonesia's Demands Lead to Deadlock With Dutch — Subandrio Sees Kennedy

By E. W. KENWORTHY
Special to The New York Times

WASHINGTON, July 22 —

ALGERIANS SEEK TO HEAL DISPUTE

Continued From Page 1, Col. 8

the day came tonight from Mr. Boudiaf. He said:

"Even if tomorrow those people [the friends of Mr. Ben Bella] should occupy nine-tenths of Algeria, even if only one-tenth of the national territory remained to us, we would still go on fighting."

Mr. Boudiaf denounced the dissident faction as "demagogues." He added that the accords signed in March between the nationalists and the French, guaranteeing the future of Europeans in this land, would be respected even if "a revolutionary committee is set up to fight against dictatorship."

This was the first that had been heard of such a "revolutionary committee." It suggested the possibility that the Tizi-Ouzou group was preparing a counter-organization to the seven-man political bureau proclaimed Sunday night by the Ben Bella faction.

A dispute over membership in the political bureau to head the National Liberation Front, the nationalist organization, was one of the main causes of the present factional rift. The discord broke out last month at a meeting of the National Council of the Algerian Revolution, the movement's parliament, in Tripoli, Libya last month.

Another cause was Premier Benyoussef Ben Khedda's attempt June 30 to discharge the nationalist army's General Staff for "criminal activities." The General Staff remains in control of the forces previously stationed in Morocco and Tunisia and is allied with Mr. Ben Bella.

Boudiaf Named to Bureau

Mr. Boudiaf was named a member of the political bureau set up by the Ben Bella group, but Mr. Krim was not, and Mr. Boudiaf would have found himself faced with a strong Ben Bella majority.

In Algeria, the command of the capital's autonomous military zone prepared to greet "fraternally" Minister of State Mohammed Khider, Mr. Ben Bella's stanchest supporter, who announced earlier that he would arrive here tomorrow.

The autonomous zone had been hostile to the dissident group, but declared last night that it was "neither for nor against anybody."

The Provisional Government ministers who appeared ready to compromise included Mr. Boussouf, Mr. Ben Tobbal, Minister of State Hocine Ait-Ahmed, Information Minister M'hammed Yazid and, particularly, Mr. Bitat, who is known as a close friend of Mr. Ben Bella.

Mohammedi Said, also a Minister of State, was already in the Ben Bella camp at Oran. The situation now appears to have reversed, with a majority of ministers either supporting Mr. Ben Bella or preparing to compromise on his terms and a minority of two resisting such a compromise in Kabylia.

Amar Mohammed, the new police prefect in Algiers, announced that twenty-three Europeans would be liberated by the autonomous zone command as a gesture of "appeasement." The Europeans had been arrested after charges had been compiled against them, he said.

As for the rash of kidnappings, he said the zone command and the city administration "condemn them" and are opening an inquiry with the aim of punishing "the harmful elements seeking to change the relations between Europeans and Moslems."

Figure 1B (Cont.)

14

What you should have noticed:

The story begins with the most important and most recent facts for that day. This inverted pyramid construction makes it possible for you to stop reading the news story at that point where older material or elaboration upon less important material begins to show up.

important . . . . . . facts

less . . . . important

even . . . . less

The danger of missing the new or significant information is thus considerably reduced. You should also have noticed that the opening paragraphs contain the *who, what, why, how, where, when* of the story, along with a prediction of *what next*.

WHO—The Algerian provisional government
WHAT—seeks leadership compromise
WHY—to avert civil war
HOW—by conferring with all sides
WHERE—in Algiers
WHEN—after Ben Bella had seized Constantine
WHAT NEXT—peace may follow.

TACTIC 7: For this exercise we shall assume that you elected to go on to read the article in its entirety. Start with the opening paragraphs once again and continue through to the end of the news story. Look for any new information, criticizing the story as you read and being certain that you have clearly in mind the *who, what, why, how, where, when,* and *what next* structure presented above.

What you should have noticed:

While there was no new information to be picked up after your skim-reading of the "News Summary and Index" and your initial skim-reading of the story itself, the story does contain a good deal of *background information*. Also, you should have been able to criticize the article—the prediction of peace to follow, made in the first paragraph of the news story, is an *interpretation and not a fact*. Did you agree with the interpretation? You should also have been able to fix in your mind the structure of *who, what, why, how, where, when,* and *what next* so that you could remember the news story more easily and accurately.

THE IMPORTANCE OF APPLICATION

Now that you have tried skim-reading on the "News Summary and Index" and on a news story, you ought to have this extremely valuable reading tool pretty well in hand. But before you can have complete confidence in the technique, and before you can be sure that you have made a consistent change in your approach to the newspaper, *you must consciously apply what you have learned to your daily reading.* The increased alertness, improved recall, and time saved by regular application of skim-reading will convince you of its worth much more quickly than any further words from this book.

So right here, take a short break. Apply what you have learned to your own newspaper and the current news, then come back for some further work. When you are ready for more exercises, you can continue with the remaining applications on *The New York Herald Tribune* and *The Wall Street Journal.* If you are in doubt so far about skim-reading, glance back over the chapter, rereading each tactic to get its main ideas fixed firmly in your mind.

ADVANCED SKIM-READING: *THE NEW YORK HERALD TRIBUNE*

Now that you have followed the detailed specific directions for basic skim-reading and have practiced on your own newspaper, you are ready to do some more advanced skim-reading—this time on *The New York Herald Tribune.* Here you are going to combine several of the basic skim-reading tactics into fewer, more comprehensive steps—first on the news summary and then on a news story.

TACTIC 1: Run your eyes rapidly down the summary column headed "In the News This Morning" (found on the far left side of the front page of the *Tribune*) and note the order of presentation. Turn to Figure 1C and read only the subheadings and the first few words of each paragraph (follow the marginal arrows).

Friday, July 27, 1962

IN THE NEWS THIS MORNING

[FROM THE HERALD TRIBUNE'S OWN WORLD-WIDE SOURCES. FULL COVERAGE OF ALL IMPORTANT EVENTS IN THIS EDITION.]

TOPIC A—

Senate standstill. A squabble within the Democratic party, led by 16 or 17 liberal Democratic Senators, broke into the open as Oregon Sen. Wayne Morse began a filibuster. Morse and his followers bitterly oppose President Kennedy's House-passed communications satellite bill. *Upshot: The filibuster may tie up the Senate for perhaps as much as three weeks, seriously imperil the Administration's bills on taxes, trade, defense funds.*

IN THE WORLD—

Algeria. Insurgent Deputy Premier Ben Bella's troops were reported ready to enter Algiers. Girding to meet Bella in the threatened civil war: Interior Minister Krim, who is supported by fierce Berber troops. *On the sidelines, at least for the moment: 300,000 French troops, whom President de Gaulle has reportedly threatened to use to protect Frenchmen still in Algeria.*

Soblen. A British appeals court refused to release convicted, runaway Red spy Dr. Robert A. Soblen on a writ of habeas corpus. *Next step: His lawyers already have asked the Home Secretary for asylum, are considering a petition to the appeal committee of the House of Lords. The Israeli cabinet is expected to decide Sunday on still another Soblen move (a request for admission) to avoid returning to the U. S. and a life prison sentence.*

IN THE NATION—

Taxes. The House Ways and Means Committee opened closed-door hearings to determine whether a tax cut is needed now to stimulate the nation's economy. First witness: U. S. Chamber of Commerce president H. Ladd Plumley, who refused to discuss his testimony in compliance with the strict security rules laid down by committee chairman Wilbur Mills. *But it was learned that Plumley stuck by his recent public proposal for an immediate personal and corporate income tax cut.*

Failure. For the third time in four tries the U. S. failed to explode a nuclear device between 30 to 60 miles above Johnston Island in the Pacific. A Thor rocket carrying a submegaton-size warhead had to be destroyed when it refused to rise from the launch pad. *Big question: Will the President extend his vague cut-off date (already passed) and end U. S. nuclear tests?* Top U. S. disarmament advisers met to consider the possibility of offering easier terms to the Soviet for policing a nuclear test ban treaty. *They reached no clearcut decision.*

Desegregation. A Federal judge directed the Prince Edward County (Va.) school board to re-open its public schools—on a non-racial basis. Rather than integrate, Prince-Edward County closed its schools in 1959. *Note: The county figured in the U. S. Supreme Court's historic 1954 school desegregation order.*

Racial strife. Georgia Gov. Vandiver threatened to send 3,000 National Guardsmen into Albany to remove integration leader Dr. Martin Luther King jr. and other "agitators" if there is further violence in the troubled city. *Albany police chief Pritchett brushed the Governor's statement aside, said the troops weren't needed.*

Rail work rules. Five railroad operating brotherhoods asked a Federal Court for an injunction to prevent the nation's railroads from changing work rules (as recommended by a Presidential commission). *At stake: Eventual elimination of 41,000 firemen, who, the railroads claim, are unneeded in diesel locomotives.*

IN THE CITY—

Expanding. Postmaster General Day announced a record $70 million building program which will add three new major facilities to the city's postal system. *The three units will be put up in midtown Manhattan, will be the biggest single undertaking in Post Office history.*

Keogh. The Board of Estimate unanimously rejected a retirement application from convicted Supreme Court Justice J. Vincent Keogh pending a court decision. *Big question: Did Keogh automatically lose his job on June 16, when he was found guilty of accepting a bribe?*

Car deal. A Queens County grand jury indicted two officials (a father and son) of a Queens auto dealer and a salesman. The charges: The men conspired to defraud two Brooklyn men into buying "new" cars which actually were used, and doctored "used cars to make them appear as new." *One way the cars were "doctored": They were sprayed with a "new car" smell.*

IN BUSINESS AND FINANCE—

The economy. Treasury Under Secretary Roosa reported there are "ample" funds available, urged lending institutions and business men to put it to use now. He also urged cities and towns to borrow money now for schools, sewers, other public works. *Behind it all: The Administration's effort to spur the lagging business boom.*

". . . Camera. Action." Newly-elected president of 20th Century-Fox, Darryl F. Zanuck, won another round in his bid for complete control. Two major Wall St. opponents resigned from the board of directors. *The two reportedly were instrumental in ousting Spyros Skouras as president of 20th Century last month. This aroused Zanuck's ire and moved him to fight for the job himself.*

IN SPORTS—

Death in the ring. Featherweight Sonny Nunez, 22, making his professional debut, was knocked out in the 4th and final round, by Roderigo Conterras in Phoenix, Ariz., died during brain surgery. *Note: It was the eighth death in amateur and professional bouts this year.*

Esc

As Briti Soblen's Interior bar the ing to the full to take Sunday.

By R
A S

The Br yesterday convicted A. Soble corpus. however 61 - ye chances sentence United
In Isi of Int passed Cabinet decidin enter t migrant quest, placed Sunday Soblei ton Pri British clear th to the
More

T
By W

Hu dicts yestei the si and Boha first. It fiesta peopl rich, com thir. or si calle lets skirt

Figure 1C

What you should have noticed:

The news items are once again divided into a funnel arrangement similar to that of the *Times.* The *Herald Tribune*'s categories are: *In the World, In the Nation, In the City, In Business and Finance, In Sports* (except for the first category, *Topic A*). You should have noticed that each item is preceded by a single word or single phrase description of the paragraph to follow: Senate Standstill, Algeria, Soblen, Texas, etc. The italics at the end of the paragraphs are used for interpretative commentary or significant details.

TACTIC 2: With the structure well in mind, you are now ready to survey the content. Skim-read rapidly down the column again, following the guide lines, noting especially *Topic A* (Senate Standstill), which the editors of the *Tribune* consider the most important item of the day. For this and all other topics bear in mind the familiar questions:

1. "What is it really about?"
2. "Should I read this thoroughly now, later, not at all, or pass it on?"
3. "How much power must I turn on to get what I want from this?"
4. "What is the organization of the material?"

What you noticed:
1. Record significant facts from *Topic A:*

_____

_____

_____

_____

2. List topics important to you and significant facts from them:

_____

_____

_____

_____

TACTIC 3: Now that you have completed your skim-reading of "In the News This Morning," you are ready to apply an advanced skim-reading approach to an entire news story in the *Tribune.*

Turn to Figure 1D and read only the headlines and the first several paragraphs of the news story referred to under *Topic A*. You can use the guide lines to help you skim-read. With your reading of the paragraph from "In the News This Morning" for support, summarize the story after your skim-reading by noting major personalities involved, the major issue, and unclear issues.

What you noticed:
1. Major personalities involved:

   _____

   _____

2. The major issue:

   _____

   _____

   _____

3. Is there anything else you need or want to know about it?

   _____

   _____

   _____

TACTIC 4: If you are unclear about the background of the story or if you want to explore all the details, continue reading to the bottom of the column, following the remaining guide lines. You will note that background material is identified by the subheading "Basis for Battle" and that the article ends with a prediction.

What you noticed:
1. The background:

   _____

   _____

2. Your prediction of what will happen next:

   _____

   _____

   _____

Tribune

on Is Published Daily in Paris

1962   © 1962, New York Herald Tribune Inc.   10c in areas 50 miles from New York City except on Long Island

Democrats Filibuster Democrats

> WHO

> WHAT

> TO WHOM

> WHERE
> WHEN

By Rowland Evans Jr.
A Staff Correspondent

WASHINGTON.

A bitter family fight within the Democratic party set the Senate on a filibuster trail yesterday with no respite in sight for at least three weeks.

The issue is President Kennedy's communications satellite bill. If Telstar, the first successful privately-owned relay station to operate in outer space, could have glimpsed the scene on the Senate floor at noon yesterday it might have asked to come on back down.

The filibuster tactics of about 16 or 17 liberal Democrats got under way when Sen. Wayne Morse, D., Ore., demanded that the entire journal of the Senate's preceding day be read in a loud and clear voice.

The Oregon Republican-turned-Democrat said he was "astounded" and "embarrassed" that the President would urge upon Congress a "giveaway" bill like the communications satellite proposal.

His demand, coupled with some "amendments" he will offer to the journal, was the first in a series of intricate parliamentary moves to delay a vote on the bill. The last time the Senate saw so much fuss and feathers was in 1946 when the late Sen. Clyde Hoey, D., N. C., tied up the Senate for two weeks with a proposal to amend the Senate prayer. The issue then was civil rights, and at the end of the two weeks Sen. Hoey withdrew his "amendment."

The Kennedy satellite measure passed the House May 3, 354 to 9. If Sen. Mike Mansfield, Mont., the Democratic Senate leader, could get it to a vote in the Senate it would pass by about 85 to 15, according to Senate experts.

Sen. Mansfield has flatly refused to set the bill aside for other major legislation that must go through the Senate before adjournment. It already

More on DEMOCRATS—P 10

Facing Us: A Decision On A-Tests

> HOW

WASHINGTON.

The United States failed yesterday for the third time in four tries to explode a nuclear device high over Johnston Island to the embarrassment of the country and the President.

The usually reliable Thor rocket refused to rise from the launching pad and was destroyed along with its nuclear warhead. There were no injuries or radiation hazard from the incident, the government announced.

At least two and possibly more high altitude shots were originally planned by the Atomic Energy Commission and the Defense Department. To conduct them, the President will have to extend the deadline.

Defense officials huddled all day in Washington following the failure, but no decision was reached as to precisely the next step to be taken. One official said:

"President Kennedy has been

More on A-TEST—P 2

Democrats vs. Democrats

(Continued from page one)

has been set aside once He has laid his prestige squarely on the line to keep the Senate's nose to the grindstone of the satellite bill until it is passed. That may take three to four weeks.

According to last night's plans, the only interference that will be permitted is the compromise farm bill. All other high-priority legislation will pile up.

Basis for Battle

The substance of the fight, led by Sen. Morse and Sen. Albert Gore, D., Tenn., is this:

The bill sets up a private corporation, with half the stock owned by communications companies, the other half by the public, to launch and maintain message-bouncing satellites. Telstar was the first. Rates charged by this new corporation would be regulated by the Federal Communications Commission. The liberals think the Federal government itself should own and operate the satellites and the monopoly they will represent.

So virulent has the liberal Democratic campaign become against the bill that some Administrative strategists think it should be abandoned until the end of the session and taken up again next year if not passed. President Kennedy himself, with an eye on his tax, trade, farm, appropriations and other major bills, reportedly would not be too unhappy if that course had been chosen.

But Sen. Mansfield, who was

once caught in an embarrassing signal switch by the White House on the timing of legislation, is said to be adamant. He is described as angry at suggestions that the bill be laid aside again. He counts on public support of the Administration to help break the filibuster, no matter what the cost elsewhere.

What the Morse-Gore platoon wants, of course, is to prevent the bill from coming to a vote at all. The tactic of forcing the journal to be read, and then tying the Senate up in a week of debate on Sen. Morse's "amendments," prevents the Senate from taking up the bill itself. Then, once the bill formally becomes the pending business, other delaying tactics will be employed. More than 40 amendments have been filed.

The Democratic leaders, and virtually the entire Republican contingent, possibly could force an end to the debate by applying cloture under Rule XXII. This requires an affirmative vote of two-thirds of all Senators present and voting. Whether the leaders would resort to this has not been decided and will depend on the course of events.

Revolving in the struggle are wheels within wheels. Sen. Robert S. Kerr, D., Okla., for example, is the chief advocate of the bill. He is also the President's main ally on the Senate Finance Committee for moving the President's tax and trade bills. If the Administration showed an inclination to give up on the satellite bill, Sen. Kerr might be less persistent in the President's behalf on the tax and trade measures. Accordingly, in the words of one highly placed Senate leader last night, the Senate is "in the soup" for the next several weeks, with unpredictable consequences.

Kupferman's Choice Ratified

Members of the Republican County Committee from the 1st, 6th and 9th Assembly Districts

INDEPENDENT SKIM-READING: *THE WALL STREET JOURNAL*

Tactic 1: Glance rapidly over the "What's News" section by reading the subheadings. This section is found on the front page of *The Wall Street Journal* and is illustrated in Figure 1E in this book. Follow the marginal arrows and note:

1. The order of presentation.
2. The specific items covered.
3. The extent of the coverage.

Then choose those summary paragraphs that you plan to read thoroughly.

What you should have noticed:

There are two major news divisions: "Business and Finance" and "World Wide." The first words of paragraphs are in heavy print for rapid identification of the item. The paragraphs are more complete than those of the *Times* or the *Herald Tribune*. Italics are used for dramatic illustration. Unfortunately, there are no page references, but you can use the index to help search out the articles you want to pursue.

Tactic 2: While your selection would be based on your own business, professional, and personal interests, we have arbitrarily chosen the story that appears as the first item in the summary section, "The Treasury." Turn to Figure 1F and skim-read by reading the heading, the first two paragraphs, and the subheadings. Use the guide lines to help you skim-read. Then glance at the last paragraph and go back and read the article thoroughly for those points you wish to cover.

What you noticed:

1. Information in addition to the "What's News" summary:

_____

_____

_____

2. Interpretations not included under "What's News":

_____

_____

_____

THE WALL STR

Copyright 1962 by Dow

r ★ EASTERN EDITION FRIDAY, JULY 27, 196

What's News—

* * * * * *

Business and Finance

THE TREASURY announced plans for replacing nearly $7.5 billion of old debt that matures next month and raising $1 billion in new cash. Subscription books will be open for one day, next Monday, for the sale of three new securities, including a bond with a final maturity 30 years hence. Under Secretary Roosa said the $1 billion of new cash to be raised in the current operation will conclude borrowing totaling $3 billion to $3.5 billion in the July-September quarter. An additional $6.5 billion to $7 billion in new cash will have to be raised in the October-December quarter, Mr. Roosa added.

◦ ◦ ◦

Bethlehem Steel directors declared the regular quarterly 60-cent dividend on the common stock. The company reported its second quarter earnings declined to 46 cents a share from 53 cents a share a year earlier. This brought first half net to $1.27 a share, up from 67 cents a share in the initial six months last year. First half earnings covered Bethlehem's dividend rate by seven cents a share. Arthur B. Homer, chairman, said he expected third quarter shipments to run "slightly below" the second quarter, indicating the company is unlikely to cover the 60-cent dividend rate in the current period.

◦ ◦ ◦

Building contracts awarded in June climbed to nearly $3.9 billion, according to F. W. Dodge Corp. This was 8% above the like 1961 period, the sixth consecutive monthly increase from year-earlier levels, the construction industry statistical concern reported. However, the rate of gain was smaller than in any of the previous four months and contracts for single-family homes eased 1%, the first year-to-year decline since last August.

◦ ◦ ◦

Chrysler Corp.'s profit in the second quarter rose 71% on a sales increase of only 1.5%, George H. Love, chairman, and Lynn A. Townsend, president, reported. As a result the auto maker wound up the first half with earnings of $1.31 a share, compared with a $15.7 million loss in the initial six months last year. Mr. Town-

World-Wide

PRINCE EDWARD COUNTY in Virginia was ordered to reopen public schools.

A Federal judge in Richmond directed the county school board to make plans for the admission of pupils to the schools "without regard to race or color," and reopen schools by Sept. 7. The schools were closed three years ago to avoid court-ordered racial integration. The county's 1,400 white children have been attending private segregated schools. The county's 1,700 Negro school children have, in the main, been without formal education.

Prince Edward is the only locality in the U.S. to have closed its schools rather than integrate.

◦ ◦ ◦

A BEN BELLA AIDE went to Algiers to prepare the way for Ben Bella's entry.

Mohammed Khider, chief assistant to Vice Premier Ben Bella, said Ben Bella's forces would move into Algiers and take it over "in the next few days." Ben Bella's troops two days ago captured Bone and Constantine in Eastern Algeria from forces loyal to Premier Ben Khedda of the moderate provisional government. Ben Bella's troops also control Oran in western Algeria. Two of Ben Khedda's ministers have set up headquarters in the interior to combat Ben Bella. Ben Khedda remained in Algiers.

French sources said France's 400,000-man army in Algeria would intervene only if Europeans were endangered.

◦ ◦ ◦

A defense budget calling for record peacetime spending of $48.1 billion in fiscal 1963 was approved by the House. The compromise measure, representing a $229 million increase from the $47.9 billion recommended by the Administration, may be passed and sent to the White House today. The bill supports the broad outline of Administration planning.

◦ ◦ ◦

Kennedy's disarmament advisers were said to have agreed in a State Department meeting that new scientific findings justify scaling down U.S. demands on a nuclear test ban treaty with Russia. However, the Associated Press said, the advisers believe the U.S. should continue to insist on some sort of inspection system inside the Soviet. Reason for the possible easing: Improved equipment that can detect nuclear blasts at a greater distance than earlier supposed.

◦ ◦ ◦

Welfare legislation that increases Federal welfare costs by $300 million in fiscal 1963 was signed into law by Kennedy. However, officials say the measure eventually will save the Government money by stressing rehabilitation and self-support of the needy and by simplifying welfare administration. The legislation basically follows Administration pro-

NOTE: Columns continue on facing page.

22

Figure 1E

send was named president of Chrysler a year ago following the resignation of L. L. Colbert, who had been under fire from dissident stockholders for more than two years. Mr. Love was made chairman last September.

* * *

Rail operating unions filed suit in U.S. district court at Chicago seeking to prevent the railroads from drastically overhauling work rules on August 16. The court was asked to declare that an attempt to change the work rules unilaterally would violate the Railway Labor Act. The five brotherhoods threatened a nationwide rail strike if the carriers put the revisions into effect.

* * *

U.S. gold stocks fell $90 million in the week ended Wednesday, Federal Reserve figures showed. This carried the outflow so far this year to $682 million. In the like 1961 period, gold losses totaled $240 million.

* * *

Auto assemblies this week are slated to drop to 137,703 cars, down 7% from last week, as the industry moves closer to winding up 1962 model production. Next week's volume will drop sharply. Indicated output this week is 84% above the like 1961 period, when most plants had already closed for model change-over.

* * *

Twentieth Century-Fox's election of Darryl F. Zanuck as president was criticized by John L. Loeb and Milton S. Gould in resigning yesterday from the film company's board of directors. The two men joined the board last year to represent securities firms holding over 300,000 of the nearly 2.5 million Fox shares outstanding. They had been pressing for reforms to halt the company's financial slide.

* * *

Standard Oil Co. (New Jersey) first half profit increased to $1.96 a share from $1.78 a share a year earlier. M. J. Rathbone, president, said the earnings gain reflected increased production and sales in all areas, particularly abroad.

* * *

Markets—
   Stocks – Volume 2,790,000 shares. Dow-Jones industrials 579.61, up 0.86%; rails 121.86, up 0.21%; utilities 115.17, up 1.09%.
   London – Financial Times common share index 265.3, up 4.3.
   Bonds – Volume $3,610,000. Dow-Jones 40 bonds 85.30, up 0.04; high grade rails 79.24, up 0.08; speculative rails 82.84, up 0.03; utilities 86.89, up 0.14; industrials 92.24, off 0.10.
   Commodities – Dow-Jones futures index 143.92, off 0.22; spot index 146.06, up 0.13.

* * *

Earnings—

	Net Income —		Per Com. Shr.	
Quarter June 30:	1962	1961	1962	1961
American Brake Shoe ..	$2,026,112	$1,169,021	$1.24	$.72
American Motors	12,161,123	7,689,174	.66	.42
Anaconda Wire	687,840	514,899	.81	.60
Atlantic Refining	9,406,000	6,779,000	.98	.71
Chrysler Corp.	10,600,000	6,200,000	1.17	.69
Houdaille Industries ...	842,682	1,031,962	.50	.63
Motorola, Inc.	3,230,032	2,259,552	.80	.56
Zenith Radio	2,253,815	1,947,214	.25	.22

posals. The $300 million increase is $110 million more than Kennedy requested.

* * *

Robert Soblen's hopes of escaping a life prison term in the U.S. on charges of spying for Russia were dealt successive blows yesterday. The British court of appeals rejected his request that he be freed from British custody. This followed refusal by Israel's interior ministry to admit Soblen to Israel. There is to be a review Sunday by Israel's cabinet of the ministry's decision.

* * *

Criminal charges against some officials of Commercial Solvents Corp. are being considered by the state of Texas in connection with the company's fertilizer dealings with Billie Sol Estes. Yesterday, the state won a legal skirmish and began a hearing into the matter. In May, Texas filed a civil antitrust suit against Estes, Commercial Solvents and others, charging they tried to corner the West Texas fertilizer market.

* * *

Dutch-Indonesian talks on peaceful settlement to the Netherlands-Indonesian dispute over rights to Dutch New Guinea were said to be nearing collapse. Indonesian Foreign Minister Subandrio made a hasty visit yesterday to the White House and conferred with Kennedy on the talks, which are taking place near Washington. Subandrio is to leave Washington tomorrow, but he indicated that talks with the Netherlands would continue.

* * *

Prime Minister Macmillan of Britain unveiled a broad program designed to strengthen the government's voice in British economic affairs. Later yesterday, his Conservative Party defeated a move by the Labor Party to censure the government and force a general election over Macmillan's recent cabinet shakeup. Among other things, Macmillan's new program would examine the merits of workers' wage claims and restrain "any undue growth in profits which might follow from restraint in wages and salaries."

* * *

The U.S. will ask Canada to impose a voluntary quota on its rapidly growing lumber exports in the U.S., President Kennedy said. The quota is one of several Presidential proposals designed to relieve Northwest lumber producers hard-pressed by Canadian competition. Canada's lumber prices are lower than those of the U.S. and its share of the U.S. market now is about 17%.

* * *

A U.S. Thor missile and its nuclear device were intentionally destroyed Wednesday night at Johnston Island in the Pacific in a test that was to have set off another high-altitude nuclear explosion. There were no injuries and no danger from radiation. The missile was blown up when it burst into flames on its launch pad.

* * *

Laos' premier, Prince Souvanna Phouma, arrived in Washington from Geneva to meet with Kennedy and discuss the possibility of U.S. aid to Laos. Foreign ministers of 14 nations last Monday signed in Geneva a treaty guaranteeing Laos' neutrality.

* * *

The state of the economy and the possible need for an income tax cut was looked into by the House Ways and Means Committee in the start of an eight-day closed-door session. Among those testifying yesterday was Ladd Plumley, president of the U.S. Chamber of Commerce and a vigorous advocate of a speedy tax reduction.

23

Figure 1E (Cont.)

Treasury to Raise $1 Billion in New Cash, Sell 30-Year Bond in $8.5 Billion Financing

By a WALL STREET JOURNAL Staff Reporter

WASHINGTON — The Treasury announced plans for replacing nearly $7.5 billion of old debt that matures next month and raising approximately another $1 billion in new borrowed cash.

The three-part financing plan includes the sale of a new bond with a final maturity in 30 years—an offer to which the Treasury attached great symbolic significance.

Government bond dealers said the inclusion of the 25-to-30-year bond in the Treasury financing probably would act to suppress prices of long-term Government bonds and corporate issues at this morning's opening. (See story below.)

The Treasury said its subscription books will be open for one day on Monday for the cash sale of the following new securities:

About $6.5 billion of a new one-year 3½% certificate maturing Aug. 15, 1963.

About $1.5 billion of a new 6½-year 4% bond maturing Feb. 15, 1969.

Up to $750 million of a new bond callable after Aug. 15, 1987, with a final maturity date of Aug. 15, 1992. The 25-to-30-year bond will carry a formal interest coupon of 4¼% but the Treasury will charge a $1 premium for each $100 face value, reducing the buyer's actual yield to 4.19%.

Treasury Under Secretary Roosa said the $1 billion of new cash raised in the current operation will be the final major part of a borrowing totaling $3 billion to $3.5 billion in the July-September quarter.

Another part is $1.4 billion being raised piecemeal, through borrowings of $200 million each week, at the Treasury's regular auctions of short-term bills. Four such weekly borrowings already have occurred since July 1, a fifth has been announced for next Monday, and Mr. Roosa said it is a "reasonable expectation" that two more will be scheduled.

Also to be received by the Treasury in the July-September quarter is about $600 million of cash from foreign sources. Most of it will be the previously announced early debt repayments by France and Italy. The rest will be cash invested in Treasury securities by European governments that are receiving dollars in a series of currency exchange agreements with the U.S. Government.

Mr. Roosa said the Treasury will need to borrow between $6.5 billion and $7 billion in new cash in the October-December quarter. An announcement of terms of a big part of this borrowing will be made in late September, he said.

The Treasury's chief debt manager said the over-all borrowing target of "$10 billion-plus" in the last six months of calendar 1962 will hold good whether or not a deficit develops in fiscal 1963, which ends next June 30. At no time during his press conference did Mr. Roosa concede a deficit will occur, but the Kennedy Administration informally has abandoned hope of achieving the balanced budget projected in January. A deficit due solely to failure of the economy to expand as predicted could be made still deeper if President Kennedy decides to seek an immediate anti-recession tax cut from Congress.

Entry Into Long-Term Market

Mr. Roosa said he doesn't expect orders for the new 30-year bond to come up to the $750 million "outside limit" of the offer. But despite the relatively small amount of money involved, he sees the offer as a definite signal to investors that the Treasury won't limit itself to selling purely short-term securities in the months ahead.

The 1992 issue is the longest-term bond yet offered for direct cash sale to investors by the Kennedy Administration. The Treasury had confined its direct sales of securities to relatively early maturing issues. Instead of selling big amounts of long-term bonds outright, the Treasury has issued them in "advance refunding" exchanges for existing bonds.

But Mr. Roosa said it's probable the Treasury has exhausted major potentialities of the advance refunding technique as a way of keeping part of the Federal debt in the hands of long-term investors. The offer of the new long-term bond for direct cash sale, he said, is a sign that the Treasury "must begin making a direct entry into the long-term market."

Though small in amount, the new bond sale meets a prescription offered recently by Federal Reserve Board Chairman Martin for proper anti-inflationary handling of Government budget deficits. Mr. Martin has argued the sale of long-term bonds finances deficits out of cash savings, creating no new money. In contrast, the repeated sale of short-term securities is believed to add to the potential money supply.

That's because banks prefer to buy short-term issues, and they make their purchases by setting up new deposits, which are counted as part of the money supply.

Message for Private Borrowers

Mr. Roosa remarked that talk about financing deficits through savings sometimes "gets pretty glib." But he agreed good debt management does require Treasury willingness to borrow in all ranges of maturities, long-term as well as short-term, and the current bond offering is intended as a symbol of that willingness.

Debt management policies aside, Mr. Roosa said there was another reason for the decision to sell the 1992 bond. A detailed Treasury canvass of the long-term securities market showed some private borrowers of long-term funds have been uncertain whether new issues would be attractive to investors at present interest rate levels.

Mr. Roosa said the Treasury's studies found an ample supply of investment funds available in the long-term market. Appearance of the Treasury's new bond at a yield of 4.19% is intended to prove to private borrowers that similar issues of their own will be successful. "We're hoping to stir things up a little in the long-term market by showing that money can and does move at this level of rates," he said.

Besides raising about $1 billion in new cash, the current financing is intended to replace $7.5 billion of old debt maturing next month. This consists of more than $7.3 billion of 3½% notes and $158 million of 4% notes maturing Aug. 15.

The Treasury is replacing this debt by allowing any investor to buy the three new securities, whether or not he owns the old notes. This is an alternative to the traditional debt refunding technique in which replacement securities can be obtained only by trading the maturing ones.

The Treasury said commercial banks can pay for both the new 1969 and 1992 bonds by entering a bookkeeping credit to deposits of funds they maintain for the Government. This payment technique, however, can't be used in buying the new one-year certificate.

The payment date for buying all three new securities is Aug. 15. However, the Treasury said such "savings-type" investors as pension funds, insurance companies, credit unions, and savings and loan associations can pay for the new 1992 bond in instalments through Oct. 15.

24   **Figure 1F**

HOW TO SKIM-READ CORRESPONDENCE

Many business men spend several hours a day reading and replying to correspondence, and all professional people find that a greater and greater amount of their time is devoted to this particular form of written material. Fortunately, the same principles of skim-reading that you applied to newspapers can be adapted to the reading of correspondence. With a little practice you will find that you can get through your mail faster and, at the same time, *have a much better grasp of what is and is not important to you.* Once again, the key principle lies in a quick look at the whole before studying the parts. That principle, plus the use of structural constants, should make your correspondence more manageable.

Skim-reading of correspondence must be action-oriented—"Who wants what from me, and what am I going to do about it?" The goal of efficient skim-reading here is to get through as many letters as possible in as short a time as possible; *but always with a full awareness of what has been requested and what action you must take.* In this variety of skim-reading, you may have to set aside some letters for a later, more thorough analysis, or you may need to gather some background information before making a decision. In any case, the bulk of your correspondence can be handled promptly and decisively if you will make skim-reading an automatic response when you start to work on the mail.

TACTIC 1: Follow the guide lines which have been marked on the sample letter (Figure 1G-a). Begin at Point A on the letter and proceed through B, C, and D.

> *What you should have noticed:*
> Proper skim-reading of correspondence should reveal the following order:

   A. Letterhead.
   B. Title and signature of sender.
   C. Background or previous correspondence cited.
   D. Action requested.

Moving from the letterhead to the signature may appear to be working backward. However, there is no point in beginning with your name or the name of your company—they are both familiar enough. Instead, you want to find out as soon as possible who wants what from you and what previous contacts you have had with the sender.

MORRIS, MORRIS, & MURPHY
Attorneys and Counselors at Law
Patent, Trade Mark and Copyright Causes
45 West 57th Street
New York 17, New York

Cable Address
Mormor, New York

July 27, 1965

Mayfair Productions, Inc.
Farley Street
Stamford, Connecticut 203605

Attention: Mr. John Zipf

Dear Mr. Zipf:

We have received and gone over the three copyright applications prepared by you and enclosed in your letter of June 29.
We have some suggestions being set forth below:

1. On all three forms in paragraph numbered 1, your name and
address should appear on the lines provided therefor as indicated
by us in handwriting. In other words, if there is more than one
copyright claimant, each claimant should be listed separately as
indicated.

2. On all three forms in paragraph number 11, the affidavit should
be set up as indicated in handwriting. The reason for this is that
you were signing both as one of the copyright claimants and as the
agent for the other copyright claimant.

3. The word "by" does not belong in the copyright notice. It
appears in the specimens for two of the three applications. There
is no need to change this for these present applications. We mention this matter for your future guidance.

4. The charge mentioned in the second paragraph of your letter is
for copyright services, not forms.

5. In answer to the last paragraph of your letter, the cost of the
usual preliminary patentability search is $50.00 plus disbursements
for patents or publications which usually comes to a few dollars more.
As to copyrights, we charge $25.00 for services plus the filing fee
which is $4.00 or $6.00, depending upon the class. Class A is $4.00.

We trust the foregoing answers your questions. We are returning
the documents enclosed in your letter of June 29 with the suggestion
that they be redone and resubmitted to us for filing.

Very truly yours,

Morris, Morris & Murphy
Morris, Morris, & Murphy

BY *Harold Murphy*

HM/rw

Figure 1G-a

TACTIC 2: Skim-read the same letter a second time and this time note especially the action requested and the references and the decisions that have been indicated in pencil on the following annotated copy (Figure 1G-b).

What you should have noticed:

Murphy, of Morris, Morris and Murphy, has requested a resubmission of copyright forms. He has tabulated the specifics of revision, both to indicate subordination of detail to the main request and to isolate each item he wishes corrected. A note at the bottom of the letter would effectively delegate your decision to a secretary or an assistant. Furthermore, you will have your original decision recorded on the letter itself for future reference. According to the annotation, the recipient of the letter has passed it on with suggested action to another department. It is very important that decisions made and recollections inspired by a letter be recorded *immediately* on the letter itself. Your early decisions, though tentative, may be very valuable.

For those especially complicated letters which require the gathering of file data and the careful reading of several pages of text, skim-reading must be applied in full intensity. Your initial skim-reading serves as a preparation. A systematic skim-reading may reveal that the complexity is only apparent and that an ordering of the contents indicates that there are just a few basic ideas present among the details. Or, although the letter may be too complicated for immediate decision, preliminary decisions can and should be recorded before you forget them or become involved with other matters. When you come back for a more thorough reading, you may find that something you have learned in the meantime will be of help to you. And if nothing else, you have had the chance to turn the problem over in your mind.

By all means, use skim-reading to establish priorities for all your mail; use it to get the routine letters out of the way. Save your mental energy for those letters where you have to concentrate to your utmost.

HOW TO SKIM-READ PERIODICALS

Specialized periodicals you subscribe to as a professional necessity and even your more general magazines tend to pile up unread. You may plan to get to them on a business trip, or even to take some along on a vacation.

MORRIS, MORRIS, & MURPHY
Attorneys and Counselors at Law
Patent, Trade Mark and Copyright Causes
45 West 57th Street
New York 17, New York

Cable Address
Mormor, New York

July 27, 1965

Mayfair Productions, Inc.
Farley Street
Stamford, Connecticut   203605

Attention: Mr. John Zipf

Dear Mr. Zipf:

We have received and gone over the three copyright applications prepared by you and enclosed in your letter of June 29. We have some suggestions being set forth below:

1. On all three forms in paragraph numbered 1, your name and address should appear on the lines provided therefor as indicated by us in handwriting. In other words, if there is more than one copyright claimant, each claimant should be listed separately as indicated.

2. On all three forms in paragraph number 11, the affidavit should be set up as indicated in handwriting. The reason for this is that you were signing both as one of the copyright claimants and as the agent for the other copyright claimant.

3. The word "by" does not belong in the copyright notice. It appears in the specimens for two of the three applications. There is no need to change this for these present applications. We mention this matter for your future guidance.

4. The charge mentioned in the second paragraph of your letter is for copyright services, not forms.

5. In answer to the last paragraph of your letter, the cost of the usual preliminary patentability search is $50.00 plus disbursements for patents or publications which usually comes to a few dollars more. As to copyrights, we charge $25.00 for services plus the filing fee which is $4.00 or $6.00, depending upon the class. Class A is $4.00.

We trust the foregoing answers your questions. We are returning the documents enclosed in your letter of June 29 with the suggestion that they be redone and resubmitted to us for filing.

Very truly yours,

Morris Morris & Murphy
Morris, Morris, & Murphy

BY *Harold Murphy*

HM/rw

Jane,
Please
respond changing
documents in
accord with
#'s 1 and 2.

Yet you know how rarely you ever do. A skim-reading of these periodicals *as soon as they arrive,* along with the mastery of the structural constants that appear in each, will make it possible for you to distill from the mass of print exactly what will be of greatest value or what you wish to read. Magazines without articles of significance to you can be covered quite adequately in the skim-reading, so that your deferred reading pile will be a much smaller and more carefully selected one.

TACTIC 1: Now turn to Figure 1H and skim-read the titles of the articles listed in the table of contents of the *Harvard Business Review*. Note the subjects covered by the articles. You are to relate similar articles into groupings, like those used in newspaper summaries.

    What you should have noticed:

        Six general areas of coverage, although you may have grouped them differently:

1. *International*—Common Market; Foreign Opportunities.
2. *National*—Labor and Business; National Purpose.
3. *Research and Marketing*—PERT; Research and Marketing.
4. *Personnel*—De-Emphasized Wage Incentives.
5. *Finance*—Corporate Debt Policy; Stock Options; Private Financial Institutions; Capital.
6. *Editorial*—Election at Zenith Life.

TACTIC 2: Skim-read the titles once again, looking to see if any of the authors are familiar to you. Decide which articles you would plan to skim-read and put a check beside them.

TACTIC 3: The article we have selected for your skim-reading is "How to Plan and Control with PERT" (Figure 1I). Within a brief time (no more than a few minutes), read the italicized overview and the first few paragraphs, including the black-dotted items, to find out what PERT means and what the article is going to tell you about it. Then read the conclusion of the article, noting only the fundamental recommendations to management.

    What you should have noticed:

        PERT is spelled out as "Program Evaluation Review Technique" in two places: in the italicized overview and also in the second paragraph of the article. Five items that are to be covered in the article

H B R / in brief

Edward C. Bursk, EDITOR • JOHN F. CHAPMAN, *Associate Editor*; VIRGINIA B. FALES, *Managing Editor*; DAVID W. EWING, *Assistant Editor*; JOHN FIELDEN, *Assistant Editor*; STEPHEN

Big Business and the National Purpose   49

No longer hostile to big business, the American public looks to corporation executives for leadership in an era of frightening change. Specifically, the businessman must rise to four challenges if he is to be worthy of the public's trust in him.

PETER F. DRUCKER *is Professor of Management and the Chairman of the Management Area at the Graduate Business School of New York University. Equally respected as an international management consultant and as a scholar and teacher, his widely read books and articles on business exert a continuing influence on management practices.*

Analyzing Foreign Opportunities   60

All that glisters abroad may not be gold. Management's evaluation of foreign business opportunities must go beyond judgments of market growth. The *opportunity analysis* technique given here helps top management make sounder decisions on where and if to move.

RAPHAEL W. HODGSON *is on the staff of the Management Services Division, Arthur D. Little, Inc., specializing in international business problems.* HUGO E. R. UYTERHOEVEN *teaches the management of foreign operations at Harvard Business School and is Program Director of the International Marketing Institute's Program in International Business for U.S. Managers.*

Conservative Labor/Radical Business   80

Openly conservative in his social and political thinking, unconsciously radical in his technical and entrepreneurial actions, the businessman must recognize his responsibility for easing the social unrest caused by the technological revolution he implements.

BENJAMIN M. SELEKMAN *is Kirstein Professor of Labor Relations Emeritus, Harvard Business School. He is author of* A Moral Philosophy for Management *(McGraw-Hill, 1959),* Power and Morality in a Business Society *(McGraw-Hill, 1956), and other books. His last HBR article ("Businessmen in Power," September–October 1961) won a 1961 McKinsey Award.*

HARVARD BUSINESS REVIEW   *March–April 1962, Vol. 40, No. 2.*   *Published bimonthly by the Graduate School of Business Administration, Harvard University.*

30   **Figure 1H**

Figure 1H (Cont.)   31

• *Program Evaluation Review Technique is the full name of one of the newest, most talked about, and least understood techniques for managing operations.*

How to Plan
and Control
with PERT

By Robert W. Miller

The last three years have seen the explosive growth of a new family of planning and control techniques adapted to the Space Age. Much of the development work has been done in the defense industry, but the construction, chemical, and other industries have played an important part in the story, too.

In this article we shall consider what is perhaps the best known of all of the new techniques, Program Evaluation Review Technique. In particular, we shall look at:

1. • PERT's basic requirements, such as the presentation of tasks, events, and activities on a network in sequential form with time estimates.

2. • Its advantages, including greatly improved control over complex development and production programs, and the capacity to distill large amounts of data in brief, orderly fashion.

3. • Its limitations, as in situations where there is little interconnection between the different activities pursued.

4. • Solutions for certain difficulties, e.g., the problem of relating time needed and job costs in the planning stage of a project.

5. • Policies that top management might do well to adopt, such as taking steps to train, experiment with, and put into effect the new controls.

Leading Features

The new techniques have several distinguishing characteristics:

(1) They give management the ability to plan the best possible use of resources to achieve a given goal, within over-all time and cost limitations.

(2) They enable executives to manage "one-of-a-kind" programs, as opposed to repetitive production situations. The importance of this kind of program in the national and world economy has become increasingly clear. Many observers have noted that the techniques of Frederick W. Taylor and Henry L. Gantt, introduced during the early part of the century for large-scale production operations, are inapplicable for a major share of the industrial effort of the 1960's — an era aptly characterized by Paul O. Gaddis as the "Age of Massive Engineering." [1]

(3) They help management to handle the uncertainties involved in programs where no standard cost and time data of the Taylor-Gantt variety are available.

(4) They utilize what is called "time network analysis" as a basic method of approach and as a foundation for determining manpower, material, and capital requirements.

Current Efforts & Progress

A few examples may serve to indicate for top management the current status of the new techniques:

❧ The Special Projects Office of the U.S. Navy, concerned with performance trends in the execution of large military development programs, introduced PERT on its Polaris Weapon Systems in 1958. Since that time, PERT has spread rapidly throughout the U.S. defense and space industry.

[1] See "Thinking Ahead: The Age of Massive Engineering," HBR January–February 1961, p. 138.

93

Figure 1I

for many programs, either in terms of its shape or dollar value, should be obvious. But it is significant to note that in certain industrial applications such utility cost data have already been developed, typically in the form of "outage" costs or loss-of-profit opportunities, and used as the basis for improved decision making. Further, in the military area, utility cost is the converse of the *benefit* concept in the *benefit-cost* ratio of a weapon system; this factor varies with the time of availability of a weapon system, even though judgments of benefit are made difficult by rapidly changing circumstances in the external world.

Conclusion

It is clear that there are difficulties yet to be overcome in advancing the new management controls — particularly in the new areas into which PERT is being extended. Yet it is equally clear that significant progress has been made during the last few years. Assuming that developments continue at the rate at which they have taken place up to this time, what position should top management adopt *today* with regard to its own internal policies on the new management controls? Here are the most important steps:

(1) Management should review its present planning and scheduling methods and compare their effectiveness with that of the PERT system. (I refer here to time networks only — not time-and-cost networks.) If the company has no direct experience with PERT, it will certainly want to consider training and experimentation programs to acquaint the organization with the technique. Management may even decide to install PERT on all of its development programs (as some companies have done), even though it has no contractual requirement to do so.

(2) Management may wish to enter directly into research efforts on the new management controls or, if such efforts are already underway in the organization, place them on a higher priority basis. As a minimum, it will probably want to assign someone in the organization to follow the numerous developments that are taking place in the field.

(3) Executives should consider carefully the problem of organization to make the most effective use of the new management controls. They should consider the responsibilities of the level of management that actually uses PERT data in its working form, and the responsibilities of the levels of management that review PERT in its various summary forms. Clearly, the usefulness of the new management controls is no greater than the ability of management actually to act on the information revealed. It should be realized that problems of "recentralization" will probably accompany the advent of the new tools, particularly when applied to the planning and control of large projects throughout an entire organization.

(4) Finally, management may wish to assess the longer range implications of the new management controls, both for itself and for the entire industrial community, since the forces calling for centralization of planning and control within the firm can apply equally well outside it. In the Age of Massive Engineering, the new controls will be utilized to an increasing extent in the nation's defense and space programs, which are in turn increasing in size and complexity. It seems clear that the inevitably closer relationships between government and industry will require the establishment of new guidelines for procurement and incentive contracting where these management control techniques are used.

APPENDIXES

Readers interested in applying PERT may find it helpful to have a more precise formulation of certain calculations mentioned earlier in this article. The mathematics involved is basically simple, as the following material demonstrates.

Appendix A. Expected Time Estimate

In analyzing the three time estimates, it is clear that the optimistic and the pessimistic time should occur least often, and that the most likely time should occur most often. Thus, it is assumed that the most likely time represents the peak or modal value of a probability distribution; however, it can move between the two extremes. These characteristics are best described by the Beta distribution, which is shown in two different conditions in the figures that follow.

are black-dotted just below the second paragraph. The conclusion of the article sums up the progress that has been made in the last few years and then sets off typographically (listing from 1 to 4) specific recommendations for management.

Thus, by skim-reading the first few paragraphs and the last few, and noting especially the black-dotted and numbered items, you can get a good idea of what the article has to say, *spending no more than a couple of minutes in the process.*

Now that you have had some practice, apply the same skim-reading tactics to one of your own periodicals. Skim-read the table of contents, checking off the articles you will want to go through right away. Skim-read one of these checked articles and decide whether you ought to read it thoroughly now, later, or not at all. At the beginning of the article write a one-sentence description—perhaps just a phrase—that sums up the article's importance to you. Go on to skim-read other articles of interest to you and index them in just the same way as a means of digging out the important facts or as a preparation for a more thorough reading.

HOW TO SKIM-READ BOOKS

What about reading a whole book in one hour? Is it possible to *read* a book of 300–500 pages from your professional reading material within one hour—and still comprehend it?

The answer is no, of course, if you plod through the book reading each word. A normal adult reader would slog through at 200 words per minute. It would then take him 450 minutes—or $7\frac{1}{2}$ hours—to finish a book of 90,000 words or approximately 300 pages.

However, you could *skim-read* the whole book in one hour—and make intelligent comments about it—

if you are roughly familiar with the area the book covers.

if you are willing to let a heavy percentage of the details go by in favor of the major ideas in the book.

if you recognize that some portions must be read thoroughly later on.

Experiment by following these four tactics on Peter F. Drucker's book, *The Practice of Management:*

TACTIC 1: Examine the *title page* (Figure 1J).

THE
PRACTICE
OF
MANAGEMENT

By PETER F. DRUCKER

HARPER & ROW, PUBLISHERS

NEW YORK AND EVANSTON

Figure IJ

CONTENTS

Figure 1K

What you should have noticed:

The title creates an analogy between management and the practices of medicine and law, so that this book will probably present responsible, professional advice to management people. You may have recognized the author's name from business sources or magazines (Have you ever read anything else by him?). Harper and Brothers is a well known publishing house. No date of publication is given here, but this is usually found on the back side of the title page. (For your information, this book was copyrighted in 1954.)

TACTIC 2: Examine the *table of contents* (Figure 1K), noting the main parts and then the subdivisions.

What you should have noticed:

The book is divided into five parts, plus an introduction and a conclusion. Drucker seems to move from the general to the specific and back to the general. He begins with managing a business, then managing managers, then managing workers and the work, and then back to the overall picture of the meaning and responsibilities of management.

Drucker uses at least three large corporations as examples of management: 1. Sears, under "Managing a Business," 2. Ford, under "Managing Managers," and 3. IBM under "The Management of Worker and Work."

TACTIC 3: Read the *preface* (Figure 1L), noting the particular emphasis or reason for the book.

What you should have noticed:

The aim of the book is to disperse information from the background of a few outstanding leaders in the management field to the average or non-managerial person. It is meant to be a practical guide to help the less successful improve their own work. Therefore, references and other scholarly appendages have been avoided.

On the basis of these three skim-reading tactics, you could come to a quick, reasonably sure judgment of the book's value for you. Depending upon your interest and need, you can next either single out one chapter of special interest or you can skim-read the entire book chapter by chapter. Skim-reading only one chapter will, of course, take less time than for the entire book, but, with practice on the following skim-reading tactic, the entire book should take no longer than one hour.

PREFACE

We have available today the knowledge and experience needed for the successful practice of management. But there is probably no field of human endeavor where the always tremendous gap between the knowledge and performance of the leaders and the knowledge and performance of the average is wider or more intractable. This book does not exclude from its aims the advancement of the frontier of knowledge; it hopes, indeed, to make some contribution to it. But its first aim is to narrow the gap between what can be done and what is being done, between the leaders in management and the average.

Though not concerned with techniques this is a practical book. It is written out of many years of experience in working with managements—managements of small companies as well as managements of large and very large companies. And it aims at being a guide for men in major management positions, enabling them to examine their own work and performance, to diagnose their weaknesses and to improve their own effectiveness as well as the results of the enterprise they are responsible for. For younger men in management—and for men who plan to make management their career—this book should provide both a vision of what management is and concrete guidance in the knowledge, performance and discipline that are needed to quality for a major management position.

But this book is written fully as much for the citizen without direct management experience. He, perhaps more than anyone else, needs to know what management is, what it does and what he can rightfully expect from it. For the ignorance of the function of management, of its work, of its standards and of its responsibilities is one of the most serious weaknesses of an industrial society—and it is almost universal.

Footnotes, acknowledgments and other references have been avoided throughout this book except where necessary to identify a direct quotation, or where likely to be helpful to the reader by guiding him to books that give full treatment to important subjects only touched upon in this text. Readers familiar with the work of

Joseph A. Schumpeter will recognize without special reference how much the author owes to this most fruitful of modern economists; to others a footnote acknowledging the debt would be neither helpful nor meaningful. Readers interested in organization theory need no "X" to mark the spot where the author falls off the tightrope of organization orthodoxy. All my readers, I am sure, will assume that this book, like any other, has a long and mixed intellectual ancestry. And all, I trust, are more concerned with what is right than with who is right, and, accordingly, are neither assuaged by appeal to authority nor alarmed by its absence.

But I want to acknowledge the special debt I owe to some friends in American management: to Charles R. Hook, Jr., now Deputy-Postmaster General of the United States (formerly with the Chesapeake and Ohio Railroad); James C. Worthy, now Assistant Secretary of Commerce (formerly with Sears, Roebuck and Company); Frank C. Householder, Jr., John E. Kusik and Vernon C. Mickelson of the Chesapeake and Ohio Railway Company; Fred J. Borch, L. Byron Cherry, Russell Colley, M. L. Hurni, T. M. Linville, P. E. Mills and Moorhead Wright of General Electric; Donaldson Brown, Chester E. Evans, Walter G. Morris, L. N. Laseau, Alfred P. Sloan, Jr., and the late Henry G. Weaver of General Motors Corporation; Kendrick Porter of Lester B. Knight and Associates; Ewing W. Reilley, Bernard Muller-Thym and Robert K. Stolz of McKinsey & Company; Leo Cherne, David Emery, Aaron Levenstein, Jack Livingston and Auren Uris of The Research Institute of America; Clarence B. Caldwell of Sears, Roebuck and Company. To a greater extent than any number of footnotes could express, this book rests on their thought and on their work on management problems in which they allowed me to share. And I am in debt to Hermine Popper, Roxanne Wright Smith, John Fischer, Eldridge Haynes and Daniel Maue for generous help in the writing and editing of this book.

Above all I wish here to acknowledge the debt this book and I owe to Harold F. Smiddy of the General Electric Company. Despite misgivings and dissents he gave to this book of his counsel, advice and help, freely and far beyond the call of friendship. He is truly the book's Godfather; and I can only hope that the Godchild will prove itself worthy of the care he bestowed on it.

Montclair, New Jersey   PETER F. DRUCKER
March 1, 1954

Figure 1L   Copyright 1954 by Peter F. Drucker. Reprinted with the permission of Harper & Row, Publishers, Inc.

TACTIC 4: Skim-read Chapter VIII, "Today's Decisions for Tomorrow's Results" (Figure 1M), from Drucker's book. Read the *title,* the *subtitles* directly beneath the title, and the *first three paragraphs.* Glance at topic sentences on the five pages between the first page and the last page and read the *last three paragraphs.*

C H A P T E R 8

TODAY'S DECISIONS FOR TOMORROW'S RESULTS

Management must always anticipate the future—Getting around the business cycle—Finding the range of fluctuations—Finding economic bedrock—Trend analysis—Tomorrow's managers the only real safeguard.

AN OBJECTIVE, a goal, a target serves to determine what action to take today to obtain results tomorrow. It is based on anticipating the future. It requires action to mold the future. It always balances present means and future results, results in the immediate future and results in the more distant future.

This is of particular importance in managing a business. In the first place, practically every basic management decision is a long-range decision—with ten years a rather short time-span in these days. Whether on research or on building a new plant, on designing a new marketing organization or a new product, every major management decision takes years before it is really effective. And it takes years for it to be productive, that is, to pay off the invest-ment of men or money.

Management has no choice but to anticipate the future, to attempt to mold it and to balance short-range and long-range goals. It is not given to mortals to do either of these well. But lacking divine guidance, business management must make sure that these difficult responsibilities are not overlooked or neglected but taken care of as well as is humanly possible.

Predictions concerning five, ten or fifteen years ahead are always

88

Figure 1M

"guesses." Still, there is a difference between an "educated guess" and a "hunch," between a guess that is based upon a rational appraisal of the range of possibilities and a guess that is simply a gamble.

Getting around the Business Cycle

Any business exists as a part of a larger economic context; a concern with "general business conditions" is mandatory to any plan for the future. However, what management needs is not the "business forecast" in the usual sense, that is, a forecast that attempts to read tomorrow's weather and to predict what business conditions will be like three, five or ten years ahead. What management needs are tools that enable it to free its thinking and planning from dependence on the business cycle.

At first sight this may look like a paradox. Certainly the business cycle is an important factor; whether a decision will be carried out in a period of boom or in a period of depression may make all the difference in its validity and success. The standard advice of the economists to make capital investments at the trough of the depression and to refrain from expansion and new investments at the peak of a boom seems to be nothing but the most elementary common sense.

Actually it is no more useful and no more valid than the advice to buy cheap and sell dear. It is good advice; but how is it to be followed? Who knows in what stage of the cycle we are? The batting average of the economists has not been impressive—and the forecasting success of businessmen has not been much more so. (Remember the all but general prediction back in 1944 or 1945 of a major postwar slump?) Even if it were sound, to play the business cycle would be unusable advice.

If people could act according to this advice, we would not have boom and depression to begin with. We have extreme fluctuations only because it is psychologically impossible to follow such advice. In a boom almost everybody is convinced that this time even the sky will not be the limit. At the bottom of a depression everybody is equally convinced that this time there will be no recovery but that we will keep on going down or stay at the bottom forever. As long as businessmen focus their thinking on the business cycle they

will be dominated by the business-cycle psychology. They will therefore make the wrong decision no matter how good their intentions and how good the economists' analytical ability.

Moreover, economists doubt more and more whether there is a real "cycle." There are ups and downs, no doubt; but do they have any periodicity, any inherent predictability? The greatest of modern economists, the late Joseph A. Schumpeter, labored mightily for twenty-five years to find the "cycle." But at best, his "business cycle" is the result of so many different cyclical movements that it can only be analyzed in retrospect. And a business-cycle analysis that only tells where the cycle has been but not where it will go, is of little use in managing a business.

Finally, the business cycle is too short a period for a good many business decisions—and for the most important ones. A plant expansion program in heavy industry, for instance, cannot be founded on a forecast for the next four or five or six years. It is a fifteen- or twenty-year program. And the same is true of a basic change in product or marketing organization, of a decision to build a new store or to develop a new type of insurance policy.

What business needs therefore are tools which will enable it to make decisions without having to try to guess in what stage of the cycle the economy finds itself. These tools must enable business to plan and develop for more than the next three or even the next seven years, regardless of the economic fluctuations to be expected over the cyclical period.

We have today three such tools. In managing a business all three are useful.

In the first place, we can assume that there will always be fluctuations, without attempting to guess what stage of the cycle the economy is currently passing through. We can, in other words, free decisions from cyclical guesswork by testing the business decision against the worst possible and the sharpest possible setback that past experience could lead us to expect.[1]

This method does not indicate whether a decision is right or

[1] For most American manufacturing industries this was not the "Great Depression" of 1929-31, but the much shorter "recession" of 1937-38. The rate of decline during the eight months of that depression was the sharpest ever witnessed in an industrial country other than the collapse following total defeat in war such as that of Germany or Japan.

Figure 1M (Cont.)

40

not. It indicates, however, the extremes of cyclical risk involved. It is therefore the most important forecasting tool in the determination of the minimum necessary profit.

The second tool—more difficult to handle but also more productive—consists of basing a decision on events which are likely to have heavy impact upon future economic conditions but which have already happened. Instead of forecasting the future, this method focuses on past events—events which, however, have not yet expressed themselves economically. Instead of attempting to guess economic conditions, this method tries to find the "bedrock" underlying economic conditions.

We have mentioned before the case of the company which decided during World War II to turn to the production of fuse boxes and switch boxes after the war. This decision was based on such an analysis of the bedrock underlying the economy, namely, the pattern of family formation and population structure that had emerged in the United States between 1937 and 1943.

By 1943 it had become clear that something fundamental was happening to population trends. Even if the population statisticians had turned out to be right in their forecast that the high birthrate was a wartime phenomenon and would come to an end with the conclusion of the war (one of the most groundless, if not frivolous, forecasts ever made), it would not have altered the fact that from a low point in 1937 the rate of family formation had risen to where it was significantly above the rate of the depression years. These new families would need houses, even if the rate of family formation and the birthrate were to decline again after the end of the war. In addition, there had been almost twenty years of stagnation in residential building, so that there was a tremendous pent-up demand for houses. From this it could be concluded that there would be substantial residential building activity in the postwar period. The only thing that could have prevented it would have been America's losing the war.

If the postwar period had brought a sizable depression, this housing activity would have been a government project. In fact, population trends and the housing situation indicated that housing would have to be the major depression-fighting tool of governmental policy. If the postwar period were to be a boom period, as it turned out to be, there should be substantial private housing activity. In other words, housing would be at a high level in depression as well as in boom. (In fact, building would probably have been on a higher level than the one we actually experienced

in the postwar period, had the much-heralded postwar depression actually come to pass.)

It was on the basis of this analysis of a development that had already happened and that could be expected to shape the economy regardless of business conditions, that the company's management decided to move into its new business. Management could justifiably claim that, even though it planned long-range, no forecast regarding the future was actually involved.

Of course, population structure is only one of the bedrock factors. In the period immediately following World War II it was probably a dominant factor in the American economy. In other times, however, it might well be secondary, if not irrelevant.

However, the basic method used is universally applicable: to find events that have already occurred, events that lie outside of economic conditions, but in turn shape those conditions, thus basing a decision for the future on events that have already happened.

But though the best tool we have, bedrock analysis is far from perfect. Exactly the same bedrock analysis of population trends with the same conclusion for a postwar housing boom could have been made in 1944 for France. The analysis would have been right; but the French housing boom never occurred. Of course, the reasons may be totally outside of the economic system proper. Perhaps they are to be found in strangulation by rent controls and by a vicious tax system. The boom may only be delayed and may still be "just around the corner." And the lack of any appreciable postwar residential building in France may be a major cause of the French political and economic sickness, and therefore should not have been allowed to happen. This would have been cold comfort to the businessman, however. In France the decision to go into fuse boxes and switch boxes, though based on rational premises, would still have been the wrong decision.

In other words, one cannot say that anything will "inevitably" happen in the future. Even if the inevitable does happen, one does not know when. Bedrock analysis should therefore never be used alone. It should always be tested by the third and final method of limiting the risks of making prediction: Trend analysis—the most widely used of the three tools in this country today. Where bedrock

Figure 1M (*Cont.*)

analysis tries to find the "why" of future events, trend analysis asks "how likely" and "how fast."

Trend analysis rests on the assumption that economic phenomena —say, the use of electric power by a residential customer or the amount of life insurance per dollar of family income—have a long-term trend that does not change quickly or capriciously. The trend may be confused by cyclical fluctuations; but over the long run it will reassert itself. To express it in the terms of the statistician: the "trend line" will tend to be a "true curve" over a ten-, fifteen- or twenty-year period.

Trend analysis thus tries to find the specific trends that pertain to the company's business. It then projects them in such a form that decisions can be taken for the long term without too much attention to the business cycle.

As a check of the results of bedrock analysis, trend analysis is invaluable. But it, too, should never be used by itself lest it become blind reliance on the past or on a rather mythical "law of social inertia." In fact, though quite different in techniques, the two analyses are really the two jaws of the same vise with which we attempt to arrest fleeting time long enough to get a good look at it.

Despite their shortcomings, the three methods sketched here, if used consistently, skillfully and with full realization of their limitations, should go a long way toward converting management decisions from "hunch" into "educated guess." At least they will enable management to know on what expectations it founds its objectives, whether the expectations are reasonable, and when to review an objective because the expected has not happened or has happened when not expected.

Tomorrow's Managers the Only Real Safeguard

But even with these improved methods, decisions concerning the future will always remain anticipations; and the odds will always be against their being right. Any management decision must therefore contain provision for change, adaptation and salvage. Management must with every decision make provision for molding the future as far as possible toward the predicted shape of things to come. Otherwise, despite all technical brilliance in forecasting, management

decisions will be merely wishful thinking—as all decisions based on long-range prediction alone inevitably are.

Concretely this means that today's managers must systematically provide for tomorrow's managers. Tomorrow's managers alone can adapt today's decision to tomorrow's conditions, can convert the "educated guess" into solid achievement. They alone can mold tomorrow's conditions to conform to the decisions made today.

In our discussions of manager development we tend to stress that provision must be made for managers capable of making the decisions of tomorrow. This is true; but systematic manager development is first needed for the sake of the decisions made today. It must, above all, provide for men who know and understand these decisions and the thinking behind them, so that they can act intelligently when the decisions of today will have become the headaches of tomorrow.

In the last analysis, therefore, managing a business always comes back to the human element—no matter how sound the business economics, how careful the analysis, how good the tools.

Figure 1M (Cont.)

What you should have noticed:

The title and subtitles provide a topical overview of the entire chapter: decisions of today provide for results of tomorrow; therefore, management must always anticipate the future by knowing the business cycles and economic factors but, most importantly, must provide for tomorrow's managers.

The beginning paragraphs set up the problem of the chapter: how can management anticipate the future? The final paragraphs summarize the argument of the chapter and supply the solution: management anticipates the future most importantly by developing new managers.

It has taken you only a few minutes to learn the major ideas in this chapter. In the same way, it would take you only an hour, or possibly less time, to learn the major ideas in the whole book. Knowing this, you could then make further informed decisions about it: you could assign it or recommend it to others who might profit from it; you could set aside time for a more intensive study of the book; you could decide that you object so thoroughly to its point of view that you will not waste any more time on it; or you could decide that you agree with its arguments and are so familiar with its thesis and proofs that you do not have to go through a detailed reading. No matter what you decide, your decision will be based on a systematic examination of the whole book, *with a minimal expenditure of time.*

Without your skim-reading and subsequent decision, it is entirely possible that you could struggle through the entire book, only to discover at the end of a week that it was completely irrelevant to your purposes. It is even more likely that you might abandon the book in the second chapter when what you needed to know or wanted to know was actually in Chapter III or Chapter XIII.

For independent practice, take a book you have bought or borrowed and never gotten around to reading. Now, give yourself a time limit—an hour or perhaps only a half hour. Follow the skim-reading tactics you have just gone over with the Drucker book. Learn as much as you can in the shortest possible time from the title, the table of contents, the preface (if included), and the beginning and end paragraphs of the chapters. *Consciously seek to avoid details.* Then see if you can summarize the book—its main points and its value to you—in just one page.

SUMMARY

You have now read a general description of the skim-reading skill and have applied the skill specifically to newspapers, correspondence, periodicals, and a book. Your success in gathering essential facts before a thorough reading on the exercises in this book is an important measure of how well you have converted a theory into a skill. Yet, success with the exercises still cannot take the place of day-to-day application of skim-reading to your own materials. As you consistently practice the skill, you will find skim-reading just as natural to you as your careful, thorough reading—yet, with an extraordinary increase in speed to get at the facts you want and need.

The next chapter will deal with an equally important, though rather different skill, that of phrase reading. But before you go on, quickly skim-read the table of contents once more to decide if phrase reading is really highest on your list of priorities. If you feel that concentration will help you more immediately, by all means, skip ahead. Remember that in reading—practically all reading—your needs, your interests, and your time come first.

SKILL REMINDER

To skim-read, do this:

1. Read key selections, such as titles, beginning and end paragraphs, topic sentences, and summaries before reading closely.
2. Avoid details.
3. Keep moving.
4. Decide on the material's value for you.

PHRASE READING

For high COMPREHENSION and high SPEED

Skill

II

What the Skill Is: The prompt recognition of words in meaningful groups, rather than the recognition of only one word at a time.

What Phrase Reading Does: Reading a whole phrase at a glance makes for better understanding of the material and frees you for expansion of rate beyond that possible in word-by-word reading.

How to Use It: The skill of phrase reading can be considered a continuation of basic reading skills begun at an early age. Young children are, quite properly, taught the fundamental skill of recognizing a single word at a time. The child who recognizes one word at a time will recite words aloud and, through this "oral reading," will assemble the individually recognized words into phrases and sentences. For the child, then, comprehension is achieved through two distinct stages: recognition and combination. Adults, on the other hand, have a capacity for recognizing the meaning of a group of related words. For the adult, sense often can be derived at once from the meaningful group. Just as the child has progressed from word parts to the whole word, the adult can progress from individual words to the understanding of an entire phrase. Since it is impossible to pronounce more than one word at the same time, but it is possible to derive meaning from more than one word simultaneously, phrase reading is essentially a silent-reading process.

However, most adults have not converted this capacity for phrase reading into a skill; they continue to read one word at a time in an oral reading pattern which could have been abandoned after elementary school. The persistence of this oral, one-word-at-a-time pattern is usually caused by *fear* of missing something of importance in the reading material; hence, the unskilled adult reader does not dare to alter the pattern that gave him success in his first years of schooling.

The exercises that follow will be designed to remove or reduce this fear. We will ask you to read beginning selections in the chapter twice, so that a second reading immediately after the first will provide you with a check on your understanding of the material. There will be practice in identifying word groups to assure you that you can recognize the kinds of phrases you should be reading as units of meaning. You will also have an opportunity to explore at higher rates once you have overcome a strictly oral reading pattern.

Essentially, then, phrase reading makes it possible for the adult reader to increase his speed *and* understanding by reading in meaningful units rather than by reading individual words and then assembling them into phrases and sentences. Through phrase reading, you can take advantage of the familiar word combinations accumulated by adults in reading and speaking. In addition, as a result of intellectual maturation, adults are better equipped than children to *sustain* this process of abstracting ideas from multiple word groupings. This chapter provides you with the opportunity to utilize this phrase reading capacity. Once you have mastered the phrase reading technique, you will be able to achieve higher rates of speed, no longer held down to a speaking rate. And, best of all, phrase reading actually improves comprehension at higher rates, since reading in meaningful units puts you more closely in touch with the author's own thought processes.

PHRASE READING: BASIC APPLICATION

This is the first of three applications of the phrase reading technique to the type of material you will encounter in your business and professional reading. The first application will give you many directions; then, as you gain confidence, the directions will be reduced. The purpose of the first selection is: to test the rate at which you normally read; to test the rate at which you reread the same selection; to compare your rate variation in the two readings; and to measure the comprehension you usually derive from your reading. Later in this chapter, you will be given an opportunity to check your recognition of natural word groupings of phrases, and you will also be given an opportunity to explore at a rate of speed higher than your usual pace.

Tactic 1: Comparison of Reading and Rereading Rates

READING-RATE COMPARISON: FIRST READING

Read the selection from *Business Week* in Figure 2A at your usual reading pace. Note your start and end time, then compute the total time elapsed. For accuracy, it will be a great help if you can use a clock or watch with a sweep second hand.

Start time: _____ minutes; _____ seconds

End time: _____ minutes; _____ seconds

READING TIME: _____ minutes; _____ seconds

READING RATE TABLE

READING TIME (min.; sec.):	0:30	0:40	0:50	1:00	1:10	1:20	1:30	1:40	1:50	2:00
WORDS PER MINUTE:	1030	768	620	515	440	387	343	308	281	258

RECORD YOUR WPM SCORE: _____

READING RATE COMPARISON: SECOND READING OF THE SAME SELECTION

Now go back to the selection and reread it to provide a basis for comparing two reading rate scores derived from the same materials. You should be able to read it considerably faster since you have already read it once. Again, record your start and end times. After your second reading you can compare your reading rates, and you will be asked to evaluate these rates.

Start time: _____ minutes; _____ seconds

End time: _____ minutes; _____ seconds

READING TIME: _____ minutes; _____ seconds

RECORD WPM SCORE FOR SECOND READING: _____

Call it the cheerful science

Economists always have taken a certain glum pride in Carlyle's description of them as "respectable professors of the dismal science." Traditionally, moroseness has been the mark of sound forecasting—for the very good reason that in a highly cyclical economy the man who forecasts trouble will be right before long even if he is wrong at the moment.

In the past couple of years, however, a mood of sustained optimism has begun to creep through the profession. And when the step-up in military spending was announced early this summer, it was remarkable how many forecasters seized the opportunity to mark up their estimates of business in 1966.

So striking is this new optimism that some economists have turned to another Victorian author to find a name for it. They call it "the Micawber effect" —after Charles Dickens' eternal optimist who always had the feeling that something would turn up. When the Micawber effect is working, forecasters assume that something will happen to give the economic system more of a lift than a cold calculation of the visible trends would indicate.

In part, the Micawber effect probably results from the simple fact that the economy has been in the midst of a great expansion that already has continued longer than any other period of peacetime growth in history. The dismal prophets have been proved wrong so often in the past four years that they have lost faith in the virtues of pessimism.

But beyond that are the forecasting implications of what we have learned about fiscal policy in recent years. The manifest success of the 1964 tax cut has demonstrated that the U.S. economy will respond strongly to well-designed stimulative measures. Although economists cannot know in advance exactly what new steps will be taken, they now can be reasonably sure that each new legislative year will bring a package of measures specifically designed to offset the fiscal drag that otherwise would be imposed by the growth of federal revenues.

It is significant, too, that the private sector of the economy—business and labor—has shown a remarkable ability to avoid the kind of excesses that carry a boom out of bounds and set the stage for a painful correction. Industry, by and large, has kept its inventories in line. And over the past four years, collective bargaining agreements, in general, have resulted in wage gains moderate enough to avoid upward pressure on prices.

There is no guarantee, of course, that all this will continue unchanged in the future. Indeed, there already is one serious cloud on the horizon—in the form of a tendency for this year's wage settlements to creep up out of line with productivity increases. Much will depend on what happens in the steel negotiations, even now coming down to the deadline. If good sense prevails in steel and elsewhere, however, it may well turn out that the new Micawber effect is not misplaced optimism but realistic recognition of the fact that we have learned something from our past mistakes and need not repeat them in the future.

Figure 2A   Reprinted from the August 28, 1965 issue of *Business Week* by special permission. Copyrighted 1965 by McGraw-Hill, Inc.

Answer the following comprehension questions on the selection you have just read and reread (Figure 2A).

1. Economists have been described as "respectable professors of the dismal science" because

_____a. Moroseness has been the mark of sound forecasting.

_____b. The person who forecasts trouble will be right before long due to the highly cyclical economy, even if he is presently wrong.

_____c. The tendency for wage settlements to bypass production leads to pessimistic outlooks.

2. The more recent "Micawber effect" results from

_____a. Great expansion of the economy.

_____b. Legislation such as the 1964 tax cut to offset fiscal drags.

_____c. Both a and b.

3. This editorial reflects the basic idea that

_____a. The cheerful science is misplaced optimism.

_____b. The cheerful science may be a realistic recognition of past mistakes which do not need repeating.

Answers: 1. b
2. c
3. c

Answer the following questions *on your reading processes.*

1. Was your second reading of the material faster than 400 WPM?
_____Yes; _____No.

● If your answer is yes and you had all items correct, then you are probably reading groups of words simultaneously and have broken through the oral reading barrier. If, however, you were reading at less than 400 WPM, you are probably following a word-by-word pattern. In subsequent applications and in your own reading, see if you can cut your time by half in a *second* reading in order to boost yourself into the phrase-reading area. You might even reread the last selection a third and possibly a fourth time, seeking to explore a rate exceeding your first two rates.

2. Did you find that your second reading was unnecessary, since you had

grasped not only the main idea of the selection but all the details on the first reading?

    ____Yes; ____No.

> ● If your answer is yes, you are probably reading too slowly on your first reading. For experiment, advance your rate until you are getting just the main idea the first time through. Assure yourself that you will find the details on a second reading. When you have learned to identify main ideas quickly, you will be ready for rapid phrase reading.

3. Did you find that your second reading gave you both the main idea of the selection and the details? In other words, did you fail to get anything out of your first reading?

    ____Yes; ____No.

> ● If your answer is yes, you are probably reading too rapidly for adequate comprehension. You should adjust your speed in order to grasp the main idea on your first reading. After more successful comprehension, you can begin to advance your speed once again.

Tactic 2: Phrase Recognition

The first paragraph of the selection you have read is reprinted here with an indication of how phrases might have appeared had you been reading in meaningful units rather than word-by-word. Continue the encircling yourself. Decide what groups would be visually possible and meaningfully related at one eye glance.

> Economists always have taken a certain glum pride in Carlyle's description of them as "respectable professors of the dismal science." Traditionally, moroseness has been the mark of sound forecasting—for the very good reason that in a highly cyclical economy the man who forecasts trouble will be right before long even if he is wrong at the moment.

When you have finished encircling phrases, reread the above lines, looking *slightly* above the words, rather than focusing sharply on any one word. This will help you to see groups of words more easily and will help to utilize more fully your peripheral, or side, vision than looking directly at the individual words. Use the line you have drawn around these groups of words to help you grasp the meaning of a whole phrase at one glance. Think constantly of the meaning to avoid reverting to a word-by-word level of understanding.

On a paperback book or a wide-columned magazine, practice selecting and encircling phrases. Encircle phrases on several pages each day, rereading the material afterward. This will help you become a consistent phrase reader. The number of days necessary for this training is impossible to determine because your progress depends upon your initial method of reading, your type of reading material, your amount of practice, and your confidence in using a new skill to replace the old habit. However, a detectable change will very likely occur within one week, after consistent, daily practice.

The basic phrase-reading application just completed should have helped you to analyze your present phrase reading skills and may have emphasized the need for rate exploration. The succeeding applications will give you additional practice in the change from word-by-word reading to phrase reading, or reinforce and solidify your present phrase-reading skill.

As you practice with these applications—*and on your own day-to-day reading*—you must constantly remind yourself that phrases are, in most cases, the smallest meaning units that deserve your time and attention. The single word exists meaningfully only in the relation it establishes with the words around it. Occasionally, you must analyze the parts of a phrase, just as the beginning reader must analyze the parts of an unfamiliar word; but your aim is immediately to reassemble the recognized words into a meaningful phrase unit.

You can prove the importance of phrase reading to yourself in two ways: first by noticing the speech patterns that lead most effectively to meaning, and second by noticing those eye-movements that reflect the most efficient phrase reading pattern.

Listen to people talking—and to yourself. Notice that meaning is conveyed in phrases, not isolated words. Meaning comes from the combinations of spoken words. Try reading aloud the separated words below and imagine how much like this dull performance is the reading pattern when meaning is taken from the printed page one word at a time.

If	you	were	to	speak	to	anyone	one	word	at	a
time,	you	would	probably	not	be	understood,	and
even	if	you	were,	you	would	be	*very*	boring!

Children can accept this word-by-word pattern because they still focus on the excitement of recognizing individual words. Adults, on the other hand, must break the word-by-word habit to be freed for the more rapid and effective understanding of which they are capable.

Experiments with eye-movement photography show that a reader does not sweep his eyes smoothly along the page, but that the eye makes a series of stops along the line. The eye sees a single word or phrase at a stop and then shifts along the line to another position. The eye does not see effectively during the shifts—only during the stops. Speed can be increased by reducing the duration of the stop and, more importantly, by reducing the number of stops by means of reading idea units.

To check your own eye movement, hold a book or magazine high enough so that your eye movements can be seen by someone else; then ask the observer to count the number of fixations or stops you make on a line. You can use this exercise to determine if you are stopping once—or possibly more than once, through repetition—on each word, as opposed to making fewer stops than there are words on the line, which would indicate some degree of phrase reading.

To further your skill in phrase reading, proceed with the advanced application, which continues the pattern of rate exploration and expands into more detailed tactics of phrase reading. As you continue this skill, do not concentrate on the eye-movement process itself. While there is an advantage in recognizing the patterns of different eye movements, excessive stops on a line are usually *symptoms* of poor reading skills, rather than *causes*. Therefore, it is more important to combine the skill of skim-reading (described in Skill I) with this skill of phrase reading through rate exploration to improve your understanding and speed; your eye movements will then be dependent upon your understanding, rather than any arbitrary mechanical process.

PHRASE READING: ADVANCED APPLICATION

READING RATE COMPARISON: FIRST READING

Read the selection illustrated in Figure 2B at a pace faster than your first reading of the previous selection. Remember that you will be reading this selection twice, so that you do not have to worry about details on your first reading. As you read, consciously note the phrases in the selection.

Start time: _____ minutes; _____ seconds

End time: _____ minutes; _____ seconds

READING TIME: _____ minutes; _____ seconds

READING RATE TABLE

READING TIME (min.; sec.):	1:00	1:15	1:30	1:45	2:00	2:20	2:40	3:00	3:30	4:00	5:00
WORDS PER MINUTE:	1000	800	666	572	500	429	375	333	286	250	200

RECORD YOUR WPM SCORE: _____

Before you go on to the second reading of the selection, write below one or two of its main points or premises. Imagine, for a moment, that the title resolves the problem posed by the selection. Ask yourself what exactly the problem is, and what is an expanded version of the title-solution?

_____

_____

_____

Regularly practiced, this very simple exercise can be of enormous help to your memory. You can evaluate your own answers after the second reading. Furthermore, your second reading will supply any necessary details for these main points.

Phrase Recognition

Before you go on to your second reading, complete the following exercise. A few lines from the selection you have just read are reprinted below; go through these lines and encircle groups of words that you would expect to read at a single glance in a fairly rapid reading.

> The motion picture projector might be considered the "pioneer" electronic audio-visual aid, since it has been in use for three decades. In 1950, the Office of Education reported: "Five out of six (84 percent) of the public high schools in the United States have 16 mm. projectors, and these schools contain 96 percent of the public high school students of the country."

Read over the phrases you have encircled. In order to be certain you are reading the phrases, look slightly above the line. Focusing on the top of the loop you have used for each phrase, notice whether your encircling gave you meaningful phrases that can easily be taken in at one glance. If you find that

Needed Now: Asst. Supt. for Technology

A new staff member to handle new administrative tasks

By Al Renfro

Mr. Renfro is chief engineer for the Alabama Educational Television Commission in Birmingham.

Figure 2B

THE MOTION PICTURE PROJECTOR might be considered the "pioneer" electronic audio-visual aid, since it has been in use for three decades. In 1950, the Office of Education reported: "Five out of six (84 percent) of the public high schools in the United States have 16mm sound projectors, and these schools contain 96 percent of the public high school students of the country."

But the increase in electronic a-v aids has kept pace with expanding enrollments. Today, types of equipment in common use in schools include: tape recorders with headsets and microphones; phonographs for individual and multiple use; still and motion picture projectors; programmed-learning machines; testing and grading devices; classroom radio and television receivers; and language-instructional adaptations with a combination of units and computers.

What does this tremendous expansion in equipment mean in terms of personnel? It means that, as electro-mechanical devices handle more and more administrative and classroom work, the need for technicians, engineers, technical supervisors, and, above all, a special administrator on the staff will grow.

Technicians will be needed to repair and maintain all kinds of a-v equipment. Learning-lab equipment, for example, needs regular care, and "teachers should not be expected to perform the maintenance and repair work," says Joseph C. Hutchinson in *The Language Laboratory.* Of the 240 colleges and universities known by the Office of Education to have laboratories for use in foreign language study in 1957–1958, six already had full-time laboratory directors, and four had full-time technicians in charge of the laboratory. One had a half-time technician and one a technical director. The director of another college laboratory was a former commercial radio operator and radar officer.

For educational television, Martin J. Maloney and Stanley T. Donner, in their study of personnel and training needs in educational television, estimate we shall probably need to produce two or three thousand engineers during the next decade. "The principal problem," they say, "is one of sheer quantity. How do we get enough competent technical personnel? One of our respondents, an ETV station manager, says, in effect, 'I can have my pick of directors and producers, but where do you find a good engineer?' This question is likely to grow more pointed as time passes. The need for engineers in ETV will probably increase out of porportion to the need for most other kinds of personnel, since the most probable technical developments in ETV (a network operating with relay transmitter, for example) tend to be economical of production personnel and performers, but prodigal of equipment and, inevitably, of engineers."

Also needed will be technical su-

pervisors for educational television studios, stations, production centers, and closed-circuit systems. There are, presently, more than seventy-eight open-broadcast ETV stations on the air and 500 closed-circuit campus ETV systems, and these are considered only buds in a pending field of systems which will one day blanket the United States. The recently passed legislation compelling all TV-receiver manufacturers to produce all-channel sets as of April, 1964, is expected to boost ETV far beyond its present rate of growth (Sept62 OverVIEW p27).

But who is going to answer such questions as: "What equipment is needed?" "How much should we spend?" "What should we spend it on?" "Whom should we hire?"

At the present time, the average administrator "has probably had little instruction in the use of audio-visual aids other than possibly one course," says Donald G. Tarbet in *Television in Our Schools*. (Only five of fifty states even require this one audio-

visual or instructional-materials course of their teachers, though the number is expected to increase to seven in 1964.) This hardly qualifies the average administrator to answer the complicated questions posed by the expansion of a-v facilities. We are going to have to hire a special administrator—an "Assistant Superintendent for Technology." We have broken out administrative functions before; administrative posts have been established for the feeding, transporting, accounting, and community relations tasks. We are going to have to break out those tasks which have to do with the new educational technology. Most larger school systems will need and be able to support an assistant superintendent for technology. Universities will be able to use a "Director of Educational Technology." If we are to administer modern schools, we will have to have the staff for it.

A commercial-broadcast transmitter engineer who is tired of working erratic schedules, reading meters, and

keeping hourly records, or one who feels he has reached his peak with his organization, may be an excellent prospect for a technical supervisor's job. He might even be willing to take a cut in salary in order to get a position with regular hours.

As for the assistant superintendent for technology, he will have to be someone with enough competence to specify, order, inspect, operate, and maintain the electromechanical devices needed for the modern school or college. But, more than that, he will have to be someone who understands (1) the full potential of electronic audio-visual aids, (2) the real purposes of education, and (3) all the ways in which the former can be used to further the latter.

Such a man, working full time for an educational system or institution, would save it both time and money by consolidating services, devising new ways of using electronic teaching aids, and, in general, facilitating and expediting the educational process.

Figure 2B (Cont.)

55

you encircled phrases too large to take in at one glance, or if you had some difficulty deciding just what groups to encircle, go back to pages 54 and 55 and encircle your way through more of the selection.

With the phrasing of the selection well established by your first reading and the exercise just completed, you should be able to move through your second reading at a speed advanced over your first. Since you have already found the main points in the selection, you are free for some rate exploration. *Push* yourself along in this second reading for as high a word-per-minute score as you can manage.

READING RATE COMPARISON: SECOND READING

Start time: _____ minutes; _____ seconds

End time: _____ minutes; _____ seconds

READING TIME: _____ minutes; _____ seconds

READING RATE TABLE

READING TIME (min.; sec.):	1:00	1:15	1:30	1:45	2:00	2:20	2:40	3:00	3:30	4:00	5:00
WORDS PER MINUTE:	1000	800	666	572	500	429	375	333	286	250	200

RECORD WPM SCORE FOR SECOND READING: _____

Answer the following comprehension questions on the selection you have read and reread.

1. The most important idea in the selection is that

_____a. The use of electronic audio-visual aids is increasing in our schools.

_____b. Technicians to handle the electronic audio-visual aids—in particular, educational television—are not numerous enough to fill the increasing demands.

_____c. A new administrator is needed to handle major decisions about audio-visual aids, an increasingly important aspect of our educational systems.

2. A possible implication is that

_____a. We must carefully assess our needs in the school systems and meet the needs on the administrative level.

_____b. Even basic and secondary education are being influenced by expanding technology.

_____c. Technology seems to be obscuring the basic essentials of teaching and administrations.

3. Other solutions to the problem the author outlines might be

_____

_____

Answers: 1. c
2. b
3. Check the selection to be certain your suggestions fit the problem.

Answer the following questions on your reading processes:

1. Was your second reading of the material slower than 400 WPM?
_____Yes; _____No.

● If your answer is yes, then you are probably still reading one word at a time instead of reading phrases. You might even try to boost your speed by reading the preceding selection a third time to further explore higher rates and conscious phrase reading. However, the next selection will give you another opportunity to break the word-by-word pattern.

2. Did you find that your second reading was unnecessary, since you had grasped not only the important idea of the selection but also the details on the first reading.
_____Yes; _____No.

● Again, as in the earlier exercise, if your answer is yes, then you are probably reading too slowly. Your first reading should have been directed only to the important idea, leaving details for a second reading. It is through focusing on main ideas that you can be freed for rapid phrase reading.

The next application will have two readings of a single selection as did the previous two applications. But before going on, assess your progress thus far.

If you have been reading the selections consistently at more than 400 WPM, you are doing *very well* and you may wish to move on to Skill III, Paragraph Analysis. You can save the remaining applications in this chapter for additional rate exploration when you have mastered the succeeding skills.

If you began by reading the selections at less than 350 **WPM**, but are now above 400 **WPM** on your second reading, you are making *good* progress, but you should continue with at least the next application to reinforce your success.

If you are reading the selection consistently below 350 WPM for both readings, you should continue through the remaining applications in this chapter. You should also begin to time your business and professional reading: as you pick up a report or any fairly lengthy article, try to estimate its length and notice the time it takes you to read it. This constant self-monitoring will be a considerable help. Practice in a light novel will assist you as well. Phrase encircling in a wide-columned magazine or paperbound book, suggested earlier in the chapter, is an excellent training aid for efficient phrase reading.

PHRASE READING: INDEPENDENT APPLICATION

READING RATE COMPARISON: FIRST READING

Push your speed along in your first reading of this selection (Figure 2C). If you find yourself slowing down, *remember that you will be able to read it again.*

Start time: _____ minutes; _____ seconds

End time: _____ minutes; _____ seconds

READING TIME: _____ minutes; _____ seconds

READING RATE TABLE

READING TIME (min.; sec.):	1:00	1:20	1:30	2:00	2:30	3:00	4:00	5:00
WORDS PER MINUTE:	1000	750	600	500	400	333	250	200

RECORD YOUR WPM SCORE: _____

The first paragraph of "The Inactive Lawyer" is reprinted here again. Organize words into phrases, but this time, instead of encircling phrases, simplify the procedure by inserting a slash between phrases.

There seems / to have developed / a gray area / in the practice / of the law / where one / who has been admitted / to the bar, / and perhaps may have practiced law for a time, on

The Inactive Lawyer

The author writes about the problems created by persons who are licensed to practice law but whose inactivity makes them dangerous counsellors. An inactive lawyer, the writer says, should be known exactly for what he is—no lawyer at all. Mr. Mooney offers suggestions directed at curbing those inactive lawyers who attempt to advise persons on legal problems.

by William E. Mooney • *of the Nebraska Bar (Omaha)*

THERE SEEMS to have developed a gray area in the practice of the law where one who has been admitted to the Bar, and perhaps may have practiced law for a time, on occasion gives legal advice to persons who are not aware of his equivocal status as a lawyer. This is the inactive lawyer who has abandoned the profession of the law, perhaps for business opportunities, but whose license to practice is still current.

The Bar spends much time and money on continuing the legal education of its practicing members, so that they may render better service to their clients and be a credit to the legal profession itself. On the other hand, the inactive lawyer has usually read no legal decisions in years, is not an active member of a bar association, has not kept abreast of state and national legislation, and knows little about the development of tax problems or current legal concepts. Frequently, his services are rendered voluntarily, with little or no fee exacted. He may actually be a menace to unsuspecting clients.

A check of members of the Bar in several states indicates that from 35 per cent to 40 per cent of those who have licenses to practice law are inactive. It would be impossible to determine if this is a national average. The figures do not, of course, indicate the problems that arise when the inactive lawyer attempts to advise persons on legal problems. Be it said on behalf of most of these, that they do not attempt to practice law, or give legal advice.

It does appear, however, that there are many inactive lawyers who are giving erroneous legal advice and preparing legal documents to the detriment of the profession, and frequently to the injury of their clients. The active lawyer is concerned not about any competition from this work, but because he is too often called upon to remedy and correct what the inactive lawyer has initiated. He finds that from a bad result there is often no remedy and no point of return. It is unfortunate that legal advice by inactive lawyers is not confined to one class of persons, so that it might be attacked more successfully.

It is to the credit of most inactive lawyers that they soon realize their complete inadequacy concerning the advice they might give on legal matters. But some of those who do give legal advice or render legal service do not fully realize the harm that they may be doing. Others possibly do not care. The very fact that they possess licenses to practice law tempts some of them to undertake this work.

In active lawyers will not admit they are no longer qualified to act as lawyers. Perhaps this is due to egotism. In talking with other lawyers I find that they have had experiences of their own that point out the problem. Preparing wills, making tax returns, drawing long-term leases and the like are some of the common things that some inactive lawyers are found to do.

Defining an Inactive Lawyer Complicates the Solution

Committees on unauthorized practice of the law are already burdened in dealing with those lay persons who attempt to practice law. But here we have persons who are licensed to practice law, but whose inactivity in the profession makes them dangerous counsellors. The very fact that it is not easy properly to define what an inactive lawyer is makes it difficult to solve the problem. Should we say that abandonment of the practice for five or ten years is sufficient to indicate that a lawyer is inactive and should either resign or treat his license as a historical document only?

Some integrated bar associations provide for a distinction between active members and inactive members, and prohibit the inactive members from the practice of the law. However, the difference in status is purely a matter of the amount of the annual dues, and some inactive members often retain their status as active members, or may become active members upon mere request and the payment of the difference in the dues. This cost of division between the active and inactive lawyers may eliminate a few inactive lawyers, but in many cases the mispracticing lawyer enrolled in the active membership group.

Perhaps local bar associations may approach the problem with better information and accordingly with better judgment. Lawyers in their local communities who have abandoned the practice of the profession are doing a distinct injury to their clients by holding themselves out as still qualified to practice law. A general letter might be sent to all the inactive lawyers in the community. Thereafter any inactive lawyers who were suspect could be invited to appear before a bar association committee, which would point out that they were undertaking legal matters which they were not qualified to handle. This in itself may well constitute a breach of professional ethics. If some particular inactive lawyer in the community had some local dominance, the local bar committee might let a committee of the state bar association take over.

To a lawyer there is pride in the fact that people will approach him for the solution of a legal problem. Some inactive lawyers doubtless feel they may be deflating themselves by stating that they are not in the active practice of the law. Every successful business man who has been admitted to the Bar takes great pride in his legal education, training and experience. He likes to be known in the community as a lawyer or as a lawyer and a business man. Fortunately, most of them would never hesitate to say that they would not handle legal matters, or that they have been out of touch with the study of law for so long a time that it would be folly for them to do so. There is, however, the small percentage who relish the thought of undertaking a legal problem that they think they could surely solve. But only active lawyers should engage in legal problems. An inactive lawyer should be known exactly for what he is—no lawyer at all.

Figure 2C (Cont.)

occasion gives legal advice to persons who are not aware of his equivocal status as a lawyer. This is the inactive lawyer who has abandoned the profession of the law, perhaps for business opportunities but whose license to practice is still current.

READING RATE COMPARISON: SECOND READING

Now read rapidly over the article again.

Start time: _____ minutes; _____ seconds

End time: _____ minutes; _____ seconds

READING TIME: _____ minutes; _____ seconds

RECORD WPM SCORE FOR SECOND READING: _____

Complete the following comprehension statements:

1. The inactive lawyer is a lawyer who _____.

2. Problems often associated with an inactive lawyer's services are: _____

_____.

3. A method of dealing with the inactive lawyers suggested in the selection is _____

_____.

> *Answers:* 1. Has been admitted to the bar and may have practiced law but has abandoned the profession of law for business and other opportunities.
> 2. Erroneous, out-of-date legal advice and improperly prepared legal documents.
> 3. Local or state bar associations to seek out inactive lawyers and warn them against occasional practice.

PHRASE READING: FURTHER INDEPENDENT APPLICATION

In the previous selections, you have been reading at an initial exploratory rate, followed by a second reading to build confidence in your initial

Labor Row Anchors Nuclear Ship Savannah, Reflecting Woes of Kennedy Maritime Plans

◇

By LOUIS M. KOHLMEIER
Staff Reporter of THE WALL STREET JOURNAL

WASHINGTON—The nuclear ship Savannah, once envisioned by the White House as a champion in the global race with Russia for atomic prestige, has become an $80 million embarrassment to the Government.

Her power plant halted by a labor dispute, she stands at a dock in Galveston, silent as a sailing vessel in a marine museum, a symbol of the frustration of a Kennedy Administration effort to eliminate, or at least ease, the billion-dollar burden of the merchant marine on the Federal budget.

The Savannah, namesake of the first ship to cross the Atlantic under steam propulsion, is the world's first nuclear-powered merchant vessel. When President Eisenhower announced in 1955 that the U.S. would build an atomic ship, he declared that, "visiting the ports of the world, it will demonstrate to people everywhere this peacetime use of atomic energy, harnessed for the improvement of human living."

Delivered in May of last year, the sleek white ship contained not only a reactor that would permit her to sail for years without refueling but also the latest in cargo handling gear, 746,000 cubic feet of cargo capacity and accommodations for 60 passengers. A year later, she has yet to cross an ocean, has carried amost no cargo and few passengers and will remain tied to the Galveston dock four to six months more at least.

Labor Pains

Her labor pains started when she was on sea trials before delivery. The deck and radio officers and unlicensed personnel staged what a Government official says was in effect a sitdown strike. Their gripe: The engineers were getting more pay than they.

The engineers' income ranged between $14,000 and $22,000 on an annual basis, about 20% more than deck officers were getting. The pay scale was based on the extra training the engineers received—up to 18 months at Government expense—to operate the reactor.

The crew went back to work after their gripe was submitted to arbitration, as required by the contract between the Masters, Mates and Pilots Union and States Marine Lines, which operated the Savannah as the Government's general agent. The arbitrator ruled that the ship's captain, a deck officer, should receive $200 more annually than the chief engineer, while other deck personnel pay should be lower than engineer pay although pegged to it.

At this the engineers balked. The ship had been touring U.S. ports, so Americans could see her, but last November the engineers refused to sail her from Long Beach, Calif. So the world's first nuclear ship was ignominiously towed up to Los Angeles. Ultimately, they agreed to go back to work when States Marine and the Government jointly tried to have the arbitration award changed and eventually went to court to have the arbitration award set aside.

The Savannah sailed from the West Coast to Galveston for alterations to her air conditioning and other equipment, not including the reactor. She was to sail May 7 for New York and other East Coast ports, and in mid-June she was finally to sail for Europe. Early in May the Galveston work was finished, but on May 6—with the arbitration award still pending in the New York Supreme Court—the engineers halted the reactor as well as such conventional facilities as water and lighting, galley and refrigeration. That forced the deck officers and the rest of the crew to abandon ship and find living quarters ashore. Early this week States Marine and the Government fired the Savannah's 29 engineers.

To Seek New Company

Now the Government needs four to six months to train more engineers so they can obtain qualification certificates from the Atomic Energy Commission. And while that goes on, the Government will hunt ways to end the labor problem altogether. First it is going to search for an operating company that has a single labor contract covering both deck and engineering officers; the States Marine engineers belonged to the Marine Engineers Beneficial Association. If that fails, the Commerce Department says it might have its own Maritime Administration operate the Savannah. And, failing that, the Navy might take it over.

Whether or not the Savannah gets going on her "Atoms for Peace" mission even in six months, the dispute clearly illustrates the difficulties faced by the Kennedy Administration's whole merchant marine program.

"The Savannah is a battleground for a fight that has been going on ever since we furled our sails and started stoking boilers," says one official.

In the days of sail there were no marine engineers. And even with the beginning of steam, engineers were regarded as little more than grease monkeys. Over the years, engineers have achieved substantial pay parity with deck officers, but the captain remains master of the ship and usually is paid a bit more than the chief engineer. In the Savannah, the Government official continues, engineers see a new opportunity to further their argument that today's ships are essentially mechanical devices operated mainly by buttons and levers for engineers, not deck officers, to handle.

But the buttons-and-levers argument takes on quite a different meaning in the broader context of the Kennedy merchant marine program.

The President told Congress in 1962 that more research is needed "for developing ways and means of increasing the competitive efficiency of our merchant marine." The Savannah itself, aside from being a propaganda instrument, was part of a research effort to make the U.S. merchant fleet more competitive and less costly to the Government. Since 1955 the Government has spent more than $5 million on research into ship automation, cargo handling devices and other matters, and Mr. Kennedy has asked $2.5 million for this research in the new fiscal year, as a starter. But Congress hasn't yet voted the funds.

Says another Federal maritime official: "When one talks about automation or about increased productivity across the piers, there is a tendency on the part of shipping labor to bristle"

The Government, since it started handing out shipping subsidies in 1936, has spent nearly $1.5 billion to subsidize ship operations and $512 million to subsidize ship construction. In both cases, the Government outlays are used to make up the difference between foreign construction and operation of a vessel and costlier U.S. buildup and operation. Despite the handouts, U.S. shipping lines have continually lost ground to foreign competitors. Many Federal officials share with Mr. Kennedy the belief that the only hope of stemming the subsidy flow is to increase the efficiency, mainly through automation, of U.S. vessels so they will have some competitive advantage over foreign flags.

Figure 2D

rate. Now read Figure 2D just once and then answer questions on it. Try to make no more than two fixations or stops on a line. Read this selection as rapidly as you can while still understanding it. Do not be afraid to shift your speed several times while reading the article.

Start time: _____ minutes; _____ seconds

End time: _____ minutes; _____ seconds

READING TIME: _____ minutes; _____ seconds

READING RATE TABLE

READING TIME (min.; sec.):	1:00	1:15	1:30	1:45	2:00	2:20	2:40	3:00	3:30	4:00	5:00
WORDS PER MINUTE:	1000	800	666	572	500	429	375	333	286	250	200

RECORD YOUR WPM SCORE: _____

Answer the following comprehension questions:

1. The most important idea for the general reader is that the Savannah's woes
    _____a. Illustrate technological change.
    _____b. Indicate the capriciousness of labor.

2. The Savannah was built
    _____a. To demonstrate the U.S.'s peaceful uses of atomic energy.
    _____b. As part of a research effort to improve merchant marine procedures.
    _____c. Both a and b.

3. The way to solve the problem is to

    _____

    _____

Answers: 1. c
            2. c
            3. Check your selection to ensure that your selection meets the problem posed.

SUMMARY

In addition to skim-reading, you have read a description of the phrase-reading skill and have applied the skill through rate exploration and encircling of phrases. As a general rule, both the last two tactics should be continued if you find that you are still reading everything word-by-word. The goal is to remove the low ceiling imposed by a word-by-word rate. Remember that what seems a maximum may only be a temporary plateau— after reading for a considerable time at an apparent maximum, you may find it possible to explore and succeed within an even higher speed range.

SKILL REMINDER

To phrase read, do this:

1. Explore at different rates.
2. Encircle meaningful units or phrases.
3. Look for familiar word combinations.
4. Look slightly above the line of print.

PARAGRAPH ANALYSIS

To grasp large blocks of MEANING

What the Skill Is: An examination of paragraph units, *while reading,* to determine both their *meaning* and their *function* in terms of the organization of the entire article or chapter.

What Paragraph Analysis Does: Allows you to deal with large units of meaning rather than with individual words or sentences. You are thus able to increase your overall reading speed and to improve your understanding of the material you must cover.

How to Use It: You have probably been aware of paragraphs since your early school years. The indentions that mark them give the printed page a little bit of variety and also offer your eyes a moment's rest as you read. Perhaps you remember a junior high school or a high school composition course in which you learned a definite use for paragraphs, especially in writing letters and essays. Perhaps you also studied the elements of style during college. In any case, we would now like you to recall that past training and put it to work as an adult reader rather than as a writer or student of literature.

Skill

III

For successful paragraph analysis, you must look at paragraphs in two ways. One, of course, is for meaning. We will return to that aspect in just a moment. The other way to look at a paragraph is for its function as part of the architecture of a written selection. A building has its foundation, its walls, its roof, its chimney. All these are quite evident and their function hardly needs review. Now, think of any written selection as a building-like structure—some well built, some poorly built, but almost all of them composed of elements that are themselves made up of lesser elements. The chimney has its bricks; the paragraph has its words in sentences. Both bricks and individual words are, as a rule, not of great significance until they are combined in a more substantial unit. For your purposes as a reader, the unit should be the paragraph.

Paragraph units serve many functions. For instance, you might find a selection made up of an introductory paragraph containing the first assertion, two paragraphs for development and illustration, a qualifying paragraph, a digressive paragraph, a second paragraph of assertion, a third paragraph of assertion, one more illustrative paragraph, a summary paragraph, and a conclusion.

Architecturally, the selection just described seems quite well-balanced and convenient to read. However, once you develop the habit of constant paragraph analysis, you may observe that some material is made up almost entirely of assertions, with no proof whatever. Other authors may rely on illustrations and anecdotes so much that they never do get around to making much of a point or rendering a conclusion, while you, reading critically for paragraph analysis, may be able to tell just where they have failed and to supply what is missing.

There are no firmly established categories that will type the function of all conceivable paragraphs. However, we will suggest a few that you might use as guides under the three general categories:

INTRODUCTION	DEVELOPMENT	SUMMARY
Background	Assertion/Statement	Conclusion
Definition	Qualification	Prediction
Theme	Illustration	Admonition
	Anecdote	
	Transition	
	Digression	

(Include more in your analysis, if you can handle them.)

Paragraph analysis stressing *function* apart from *sense* is an enjoyable game, but not one you are liable to have much time to practice. You want meaning more than anything else. Therefore, at the same time that you are grasping of the logic and the architecture of the author's paragraphs, you will be gathering sense from within the paragraphs themselves. To check yourself on comprehension, learn to summarize on the run. At the end of each paragraph, and preferably with no more than a fraction of a second to do it, review what the author said; organize the paragraphs covered in relation to the importance of all the points he has made thus far, thereby preparing for the meaning of the paragraphs to come.

Let's see just how reading by paragraphs works in practice. Suppose you were to run across the following:

> Although poor weather conditions and a heavy investment in new equipment adversely affected the earnings picture for last year, under the aggressive new leadership of Trumbull and Snark, J&D Industries should show a healthy advance in 1967. On the other hand, any prediction in this field must be made with the firm warning that a cutback in government spending could well cause an overnight disaster. Should a major cutback occur, we have to advise that J&D Industries is presently in the weakest position of any firm in its area.

Note, first of all, that the paragraph combines the functions of at least three possible paragraphs. Two of these—background and prediction—are on our list. The third—a warning paragraph—is a less common type. You must be prepared for condensations of this sort, especially in financial writing. In this case, for a good general understanding, you should re-member: PAST—Negative . . . , FUTURE—Positive, because of new manage-ment . . . , WARNING—Company highly sensitive to government spending.

Almost all intelligent readers would understand the paragraph if allowed to read it several times. But you must understand, condense, and be ready for what will come next, preferably by pressing forward without the time cost of rereading. The surest way to reach this efficiency is to make up your mind that you will be able to *summarize to yourself as you read*. The habit of asking, "What does it say?" is the best device known for sharpening your summary skills and for overall paragraph comprehension.

There is still another considerable aid to your analytical procedure. Be on the lookout for *guide words and phrases* that can help to alert you to the structure of sentences and ideas before you finish reading them. In the excerpt you just read, notice "although" and "on the other hand." When you come across "although," you should not only read what follows, but mentally leap ahead to the words after the comma. It is after the introductory clause that you are most likely to find a significant fact or the author's real feelings about his subject.

For practice, try completing the following sentences. Supply main clauses for our subordinate clauses.

Although the Yankees showed up well in their pre-season training, _____

_____ .

Although many men claim that they hate injustice, _____

_____ .

Although Australia is still almost virgin land, in the next few years _____

_____ .

Now go back to our paragraph. The guide phrase, "on the other hand," alerts you to a major change of thought or substantial qualification. Here the author tells you about a possible situation that may completely negate what has gone before. If the author had written at greater length, this phrase might well introduce a paragraph of its own. As it is, several ideas are held within a single paragraph, making it even more important for you to recognize and follow the direction given by guide words and phrases.

There are a great many of these guide words and phrases. We will note just a few, but remember: the more sensitive you are to them and their use, the more readily can you anticipate what the author will say.

however	in spite of	let us assume	in short
nevertheless	thus	many people think	conversely
whereas	on the other hand	the future holds	look for
yet	in the first place	in the past	to sum up

These are some of the words and phrases that serve as road signs in reading. They tell you to slow down, to watch for a turn ahead, to be ready for all sorts of special situations before you actually reach them. Just as a skilled driver watches the signs to avoid being caught off guard, so you can become alert to the direction a sentence will take before you have finished reading it. Hence, you will have a greater comprehension of the paragraph through anticipation, as well as recognition of the paragraph's function.

PARAGRAPH ANALYSIS: BASIC APPLICATION

Skim-read the selection that follows in Figure 3A-a, giving special attention to the guide words that will help you anticipate developments in the article before they actually occur. After you have completed your skim-reading, go back over the selection. *Bracket the guide words* you noticed in your skim-reading (and any you may have missed). Also, *underline the key words*—words like "tension" and "limitations," which are essential to the argument. At the same time, in the margin, make a *note* by *each paragraph, stating its function* in terms of the architecture of the essay. You may want to glance back at the list of some paragraph functions on page 66.

There are no absolutely right answers to this exercise. You may have described a paragraph in a different way from our description (illustrated in Figure 3A-b) and still be perfectly correct. Similarly, you may have noted more or fewer guide words and key words. The important point is that the combination of guide words, key words, and paragraph notation should combine to expose the skeleton of the article quite clearly. Above all, remember that this procedure—rather painstaking right now—is intended to sharpen your perception so that on your own reading you will be able to mentally analyze and evaluate both with speed and confidence.

Key-Word Reading

In the last application, we asked you to pick out key words before we had even talked extensively about them as such. This was done quite deliberately. We have tried to show you that you can pick out the essential words when you are actively seeking them, especially when you are skim-reading at the same time. Now we will discuss and practice key-word reading as one more of the several techniques you can use to make paragraph analysis an effective reading tool.

Any piece of writing—whether a newspaper article, a committee report, a legal contract, or a book chapter—has two essential elements: the *subject* (what it is about) and the *predicate* (what is said about the subject).

HOW TO LIVE
WITH TENSION
AND ENJOY IT

THE stereotype of the business executive — in fact, the way many foreigners think of most Americans — is of a person under constant tension. He swallows tranquilizers by the bushel, and he drinks gallons of black coffee as he sits late at night at his desk, working himself to death. And to watch certain TV commercials, it seems evident that the entire population suffers from the jitters, raw nerves, headaches, indigestion and complete inability to sleep.

It is certainly true that many of the people who seek medical advice these days have complaints which can be attributed to excessive tension.

At the same time, working hours are much shorter than they were — coffee breaks are an established routine — vacations are longer and more frequent — and we are constantly reminded that we have more leisure time than ever before.

Why, then, do we hear so much about tension and pressure? Part of it is the age in which we live. Instantaneous communication has brought the complexities of the world into every home. Constant crises, transmitted to us in solemn voices and big black headlines, provide an atmosphere of anxiety. Because we experience only the present, the perils of today seem worse than anything that has come before. Yet, as we review the advance of the human race, we have never been more secure.

Without at the moment trying to reconcile these seemingly contradictory facts, let us recognize that people who suffer from symptoms caused by tension are faced with a very real and very disturbing condition. Excessive tension can bring about physical ailments, such as indigestion, headache, pain in almost any part of the body. And for people under constant tension, life can be a torture.

However, what is a tension producing situation for one person, is taken in stride by another. Everyone has a threshold for tension, and everyone should learn whether his threshold for tension is high or low.

WHAT'S YOUR TENSION THRESHOLD?

1. Do you have frequent headaches? ____Yes ____No
2. Do you have difficulty sleeping, even after a long day at the office? ____Yes ____No
3. Do you find yourself increasingly irritable with your family and business associates? ____Yes ____No
4. Are you having trouble getting things done in your job? ____Yes ____No
5. Do you have frequent bouts of indigestion? ____Yes ____No
6. Do you often sit rigidly "at attention" while at work? ____Yes ____No

If you answer "yes" to even one of the above questions, you may be suffering from excessive tension. We suggest you read carefully this issue of GUIDELINES, and we hope you will find it helpful.

STRESS AND TENSION—SIMILAR, BUT NOT THE SAME

The human body has been designed to resist an infinite number of changes and attacks brought about by its environment. The secret of good health lies in successful adjustment to changing stresses on the body.

Stress is the rate of wear and tear on the body. In simplest terms, whatever you do that seems strenuous or wearing is stress. Going out into the cold or the heat produces stress. There is stress on the body from disease, physical or mental effort, crossing the street or being exposed to a draft. Any emotion, any activity causes stress.

The feelings of being tired, jittery or ill are subjective symptoms of stress. It is how we react to stress that makes the difference between pleasant

Figure 3A-a

healthful living, and suffering from a variety of unpleasant symptoms.

Again, stress represents a direct physical attack on the body — and excessive tension is one such stress producing agent.

What, then, is *tension?* First of all, tension is normal and beneficial. It is part of the normal functioning body — in fact, we cannot live healthfully without it. Tension has been defined as "psychic energy that needs to be released." Tension is that inner drive which is usually considered the mark of a successful person, whether he is a top athlete, a bishop, a business leader, a general. Tension is what makes people "go."

By contrast, many psychotics such as schizophrenics, experience no tension whatsoever. They live in another world, in almost complete tranquility.

For some reason, there seems to be a popular notion that tension is bad. This isn't so. Like so many other things in life, tension is only harmful in large doses. A watchspring, for example, cannot perform its function without being under constant tension, but we all know the results of overwinding the watch. It is the same with the human body. Tension that keeps us interested and alert is good and necessary. When we move over the fine borderline where we become apprehensive and anxious and fearful, only then is it bad.

Tension, then, like seasoning in food, gives zest and effectiveness to life. Life without tension is like soup without salt. When we participate in sports or watch a football game, we all become tense.

Under circumstances such as the football game, people aren't conscious of being tense. They only realize it when the grip of tension loosens and they experience a feeling of relief.

Doubtless you can recall many situations when you have been tense and then began to unwind. Perhaps you drove the last hour of a long trip through heavy traffic, then checked into a comfortable hotel room. Gradually you realized that you no longer had to be on the alert and you felt contented and relaxed. These are the good moments of living. But imagine if instead, you just couldn't unwind, you couldn't relax even in the comfort of your room, and you laid awake reliving the perils of your trip. This is *excessive tension*.

The serious thing about excessive tension is that it can bring about very real changes in the body itself if it persists over a period of time. That is why it is essential, if you have any of the symptoms of excessive tension, to find the causes of the tension as quickly as possible.

THE SYMPTOMS OF EXCESSIVE TENSION

The physical symptoms of excessive tension include headaches — fatigue — irritability — indigestion — back pains — insomnia — muscular rigidity.

Any one of these symptoms can, of course, arise from an organic disorder or a disease. But this can be determined by a physical examination. This is why the annual health audit is so important.

We also know that many of these symptoms can arise from an emotional disorder. This is a complicated situation involving a person's entire pattern of emotional stability. It is not as likely a cause as many people seem to think. Excessive tension is more likely to be the culprit.

Our experience in examining nearly three million persons since 1914 has confirmed that the most common single symptom of excessive tension is fatigue. A feeling of exhaustion may be present during the entire day, yet the person has difficulty in sleeping at night.

Another common symptom is a feeling of chronic restlessness and inability to concentrate. I recall one executive in a large company who told me, "No matter how hard I work, I can't seem to get anything done. I hurry through the day at top speed, but I accomplish little." The layman has a phrase for this: "wheel spinning."

Then there is the so-called tension headache which people describe as a tightness and pulling and aching in the back of the neck and head. Tension is probably the commonest cause of headache among businessmen. It develops regularly late in the day, but X-ray and examination will not reveal any organic cause.

There are also many characteristic symptoms from the gastrointestinal tract — "indigestion," gas, constipation and lower abdominal cramps — which may be caused by tension.

Finally, palpitation of the heart accompanied by a sensation of tightness in the chest around the heart area can be the result of tension.

Every one of these symptoms is unpleasant, to say the least. They are also a warning that you may be headed for serious trouble.

HOW WIDESPREAD IS EXCESSIVE TENSION?

While excessive tension can disturb people in all walks of life, we think of it most commonly as an "executive disease." It is fashionable to refer to "the rat race" as the villain, and the ulcer is supposedly the Madison Avenue badge of honor.

To find out how widespread tension is among executives, therefore, we made a study of 6,000 business men. Our purpose was to determine the prevalence and degrees of tension as well as the effects of kinds of jobs upon tension. The results, which were widely publicized, were gratifying: excessive tension among executives is not nearly as prevalent as is commonly supposed.

For instance, 78 percent of the businessmen reported that they were not working too hard.

81 percent said that they liked their jobs very much.

Only 1 percent reported serious personality conflicts with their business associates.

The great majority reported good health habits as to sleep, recreation, eating, drinking and smoking.

What it boiled down to was this: only 13 percent of the executives complained of excessive tension, that they worked under constant tension.

Figure 3A-a (Cont.)

This was most encouraging and corrected an important misunderstanding about executive life. However, 13 percent of all executives in the country is still a sizable number of persons to be suffering from excessive tension. We should do our best to understand the causes of this excessive tension to reduce the number of sufferers to a much lower figure. The effect on the economy, to say nothing of the human misery among a family of a tension ridden executive, is such that we should make every effort to eradicate tension diseases.

SOME TENSION CASE HISTORIES

Several cases come immediately to mind. I recall John Jones, an extremely successful executive with a large corporation. John is what is known as a "hard running" executive. He has an inner drive that has propelled him to the top and which makes him impatient for results.

This is an example of the good effects of tension. However, when John came to us for an annual physical, he complained of painful headaches, trouble in sleeping and increasing irritability with his associates and with his family. It didn't take long to determine that John was now a victim of excessive tension. And it didn't take long either to find out the cause, once we had talked over his usual business day.

John had recently taken over a new division of his company which had a bad profit picture. Even though he worked long and hard, he couldn't seem to make a dent in all of the multiple problems involved. He began to think he was the only person "carrying the load." As his tension built up, he increased the pressure on his staff with resulting ill will and loss of cooperation.

Gnawing away at him also was a fear that his superiors were not happy with his progress. His president was a type who was sparing in his praise and John didn't know where he stood. We suggested to John that he settle this matter immediately with his superiors, even if it meant getting another job.

In a week John came in to see me and already he was beginning to be like his old self. His confrontation with his president had revealed that the company's officers were more than happy with what he was accomplishing, in fact, thought it was "miraculous." The president was so fearful, in fact, that John might leave that he insisted that John take an extra vacation immediately and promised meanwhile to give him some additional staff to help him.

This case has two lessons: 1. If you feel you're getting out of depth on your job, find out exactly where you stand. Face up to it regardless of the consequences. 2. And if you have a conscientious man like John Jones on your staff, tell him occasionally that you're pleased with his efforts.

You don't have to be a business executive to suffer from excessive tension. I remember a housewife who had always been contented with her home and social life. Now she was "tensed up" all the time and given to unpredictable outbursts of temper. Often she would wander through her house in the middle of the night completely incapable of sleep. A brief discussion revealed that she was worried about the lack of progress of her teen age son who was more interested in mechanics than in preparing for a law career as his fond mother wanted. Once she faced up to the fact that both law and industry would be better off if her son headed for mechanical engineering, her symptoms vanished.

DON'T BLAME THE "RAT RACE"

Many people who complain of excessive tension brush it off with a reference to the old "rat race" — and obtain a certain perverse pleasure in the illusion that they are working too hard.

I think I can state categorically that few people these days are really working too hard. Rarely do we hear of symptoms that can be traced directly to overwork. Only fifty years ago, people worked much longer hours and there were few cases of "tension" and "nerves." Let us recognize that people today spend only *20 percent* of their time at work. The rest of the time — *80 percent* — is spent outside the office or shop. More often than not, the causes of excessive tension are to be found in the pattern of life in the non-working hours.

Sociologists have long been commenting on the problems of leisure time. As a medical man, I can testify that leisure time and "affluence" do produce health problems. Most people are not victims of the "rat race." They have created a rat race of their own. They have not learned to deal with their environment.

Because it is easier to ride or drive than walk, most people don't get enough exercise.

Because food and drink are readily available, most people have a weight problem.

Because of built in entertainment provided by TV, too many people have become passive in their leisure time activities. They do not receive the mental stimulus that active games and lively conversation provide.

Because more and more people travel long distances between home and work, they often neglect their sleep in an effort to spend more time with their families.

In solving the causes of excessive tension, then, it is not enough to examine the job situation. You should examine your whole living pattern to find where you may have strayed.

ESTABLISHING YOUR TENSION THRESHOLD

Most people understand their physical limitations. However, many do not seem to realize that the degree of tension one can withstand is highly personal. One person can take a great deal of pressure without any ill effect. The same pressure to another would be incapacitating. If your job or your home environment creates more tension than you can tolerate, don't fight it. Instead, try to change your way of life.

At the same time, you should re-examine your health habits.

In our survey on tension among executives, for instance, this is what we found about the health habits of the 13 percent who complained of excessive tension:

Figure 3A-a (*Cont.*)

When they eat:

they eat breakfast on the fly. (Under five minutes).

they bolt their lunch. (Under 15 minutes).

they hurry through their dinner. (Under 30 minutes).

and a high percentage are on diets, nursing gastric disorders.

In their recreation:

few of those complaining of tension get some form of regular exercise.

few have extra-curricular interests (church, civic, etc.).

many have no hobby at all.

and one out of five get no recreation whatsover.

For their rest:

many average six or less hours of sleep at night.

few have weekends free for family and self.

and their vacation time is 20 percent less than the overall average.

In their smoking and drinking:

most are heavy cigarette smokers.

most have cocktails for lunch, and many drink more than two.

many have more than two cocktails before dinner.

In the drugs they take:

most of them use sleep-inducing sedatives.

most of them quiet their nerves with tranquilizers.

If the overly tense person can make a shift in his health habits, this may be all that is needed. If this is not possible, however, then psychiatric help may be indicated.

HOW TO AVOID EXCESSIVE TENSION

We have talked primarily about the persons who already are the victims of excessive stress and tension. These people were not born into the world with these symptoms or, necessarily, with a predisposition to them. Somewhere along the line they acquired habits or failed to face certain situations which brought about these symptoms. If you want to avoid acquiring these symptoms, here are a few guidelines:

If you have doubts about the ability to do your job well, take steps to find out that you are in the proper line of work — and switch if it seems indicated.

Face up to the facts of the affluent life and leisure time which most of us now enjoy. Remember that it is not what you do between 9 a.m. and 5 p.m. that is as harmful as what you do between 5 p.m. and 9 a.m.

Live within your income. Don't worry about "keeping up with the Jones's." This advice may seem out of my field as a physician. However, we know that conflicts in every day living build up tension and hence affect your physical well being.

If you have trouble getting on with people, socially or on the job, better get some professional help.

Every desk bound worker should leave his chair at least once every two hours and walk about the office for a few minutes.

Chairmen should call for occasional ten-minute intermissions during meetings, breaking up both tension and boredom.

If you are always tired, you may actually need more physical activity — or you may be bored with what you're doing. Better find out which it is.

Relaxation in small and large doses is the antidote to excessive tension. This does not mean rest — it means a change of scene, a change of activity.

The best cure for tension fatigue is exercise — and the best exercise is walking.

Finally, learn your tension threshold and live within it.

Sincerely,

Harry J. Johnson

Harry J. Johnson, M.D.
President, Life Extension Foundation

Figure 3A-a (Cont.)

Permission is given to quote from this bulletin, in whole or in part, provided that credit is given to the Life Extension Foundation.

HOW TO LIVE WITH TENSION AND ENJOY IT

(introduction) THE stereotype of the business executive — in fact, the way many foreigners think of most Americans — is of a person under constant tension. He swallows tranquilizers by the bushel, and he drinks gallons of black coffee as he sits late at night at his desk, working himself to death. And to watch certain TV commercials, it seems evident that the entire population suffers from the jitters, raw nerves, headaches, indigestion and complete inability to sleep.

It is certainly true that many of the people who seek medical advice these days have complaints which can be attributed to excessive tension.

(contrary statement) At the same time, working hours are much shorter than they were — coffee breaks are an established routine — vacations are longer and more frequent — and we are constantly reminded that we have more leisure time than ever before.

(repetition of 1 & 2) Why, then, do we hear so much about tension and pressure? Part of it is the age in which we live. Instantaneous communication has brought the complexities of the world into every home. Constant crises, transmitted to us in solemn voices and big black headlines, provide an atmosphere of anxiety. Because we experience only the present, the perils of today seem worse than anything that has come before. Yet, as we review the advance of the human race, we have never been more secure.

(assertion) Without at the moment trying to reconcile these seemingly contradictory facts, let us recognize that people who suffer from symptoms caused by tension are faced with a very real and very disturbing condition. Excessive tension can bring about physical ailments, such as indigestion, headache, pain in almost any part of the body. And for people under constant tension, life can be a torture.

However, what is a tension producing situation for one person, is taken in stride by another. Everyone has a threshold for tension, and everyone should learn whether his threshold for tension is high or low.

WHAT'S YOUR TENSION THRESHOLD?

1. Do you have frequent headaches? ____Yes ____No
2. Do you have difficulty sleeping, even after a long day at the office? ____Yes ____No
3. Do you find yourself increasingly irritable with your family and business associates? ____Yes ____No
4. Are you having trouble getting things done in your job? ____Yes ____No
5. Do you have frequent bouts of indigestion? ____Yes ____No
6. Do you often sit rigidly "at attention" while at work? ____Yes ____No

If you answer "yes" to even one of the above questions, you may be suffering from excessive tension. We suggest you read carefully this issue of GUIDELINES, and we hope you will find it helpful.

STRESS AND TENSION—SIMILAR, BUT NOT THE SAME

(assertion) The human body has been designed to resist an infinite number of changes and attacks brought about by its environment. The secret of good health lies in successful adjustment to changing stresses on the body.

(definition) Stress is the rate of wear and tear on the body. In simplest terms, whatever you do that seems strenuous or wearing is stress. Going out into the cold or the heat produces stress. There is stress on the body from disease, physical or mental effort, crossing the street or being exposed to a draft. Any emotion, any activity causes stress.

(assertion) The feelings of being tired, jittery or ill are subjective symptoms of stress. It is how we react to stress that makes the difference between pleasant

74

Figure 3A-b

healthful living, and suffering from a variety of un-pleasant symptoms.

[Again,] stress represents a direct physical attack on the body – and excessive tension is one such stress producing agent.

[What, then,] is *tension?* First of all, tension is normal and beneficial. It is part of the normal functioning body – in fact, we cannot live healthfully without it. Tension has been defined as "psychic energy that needs to be released." Tension is that inner drive which is usually considered the mark of a successful person, whether he is a top athlete, a bishop, a business leader, a general. Tension is what makes people "go."

[By contrast,] many psychotics such as schizophrenics, experience no tension whatsoever. They live in another world, in almost complete tranquility.

[For some reason,] there seems to be a [popular notion] that tension is bad. This isn't so. Like so many other things in life, tension is only harmful in large doses. A watchspring, for example, cannot perform its function without being under constant tension, but we all know the results of overwinding the watch. It is the same with the human body. Tension that keeps us interested and alert is good and necessary. When we move over the fine borderline where we become apprehensive and anxious and fearful, only then is it bad.

Tension, [then,] like seasoning in food, gives zest and effectiveness to life. Life without tension is like soup without salt. When we participate in sports or watch a football game, we all become tense.

Under circumstances such as the football game, people aren't conscious of being tense. They only realize it when the grip of tension loosens and they experience a feeling of relief.

[Doubtless you can recall] many situations when you have been tense and then began to unwind. Perhaps you drove the last hour of a long trip through heavy traffic, then checked into a comfortable hotel room. Gradually you realized that you no longer had to be on the alert and you felt contented and relaxed. These are the good moments of living. But imagine if instead, you just couldn't unwind, you couldn't relax even in the comfort of your room, and you laid awake reliving the perils of your trip. This is *excessive tension.*

The serious thing about excessive tension is that it can bring about very real changes in the body itself if it persists over a period of time. That is why it is essential, if you have any of the symptoms of excessive tension, to find the causes of the tension as quickly as possible.

THE SYMPTOMS OF EXCESSIVE TENSION

The physical symptoms of excessive tension include headaches – fatigue – irritability – indigestion – back pains – insomnia – muscular rigidity.

Any one of these symptoms can, [of course,] arise from an organic disorder or a disease. But this can be determined by a physical examination. This is why the annual health audit is so important.

We also know that many of these symptoms can arise from an emotional disorder. This is a complicated situation involving a person's entire pattern of emotional stability. It is not as likely a cause as many people seem to think. Excessive tension is more likely to be the culprit.

[Our experience] in examining nearly three million persons since 1914 has confirmed that the most common single symptom of excessive tension is fatigue. A feeling of exhaustion may be present during the entire day, yet the person has difficulty in sleeping at night.

Another common symptom is a feeling of chronic restlessness and inability to concentrate. I recall one executive in a large company who told me, "No matter how hard I work, I can't seem to get anything done. I hurry through the day at top speed, but I accomplish little." The layman has a phrase for this: "wheel spinning."

Then there is the so-called tension headache which people describe as a tightness and pulling and aching in the back of the neck and head. Tension is probably the commonest cause of headache among businessmen. It develops regularly late in the day, but X-ray and examination will not reveal any organic cause.

There are also many characteristic symptoms from the gastrointestinal tract – "indigestion," gas, constipation and lower abdominal cramps – which may be caused by tension.

Finally, palpitation of the heart accompanied by a sensation of tightness in the chest around the heart area can be the result of tension.

Every one of these symptoms is unpleasant, to say the least. They are also a warning that you may be headed for serious trouble.

HOW WIDESPREAD IS EXCESSIVE TENSION?

While excessive tension can disturb people in all walks of life, we think of it most commonly as an "executive disease." It is fashionable to refer to "the rat race" as the villain, and the ulcer is supposedly the Madison Avenue badge of honor.

To find out how widespread tension is among executives, therefore, we made a study of 6,000 business men. Our purpose was to determine the prevalence and degrees of tension as well as the effects of kinds of jobs upon tension. The results, which were widely publicized, were gratifying: excessive tension among executives is not nearly as prevalent as is commonly supposed.

For instance, 78 percent of the businessmen reported that they were not working too hard.

81 percent said that they liked their jobs very much.

Only 1 percent reported serious personality conflicts with their business associates.

The great majority reported good health habits as to sleep, recreation, eating, drinking and smoking.

What it boiled down to was this: only 13 percent of the executives complained of excessive tension, that they worked under constant tension.

Figure 3A-b (Cont.)

75

This was most encouraging and corrected an important misunderstanding about executive life. However, 13 percent of all executives in the country is still a sizable number of persons to be suffering from excessive tension. We should do our best to understand the causes of this excessive tension to reduce the number of sufferers to a much lower figure. The effect on the economy, to say nothing of the human misery among a family of a tension ridden executive, is such that we should make every effort to eradicate tension diseases.

SOME TENSION CASE HISTORIES

Several cases come immediately to mind. I recall John Jones, an extremely successful executive with a large corporation. John is what is known as a "hard running" executive. He has an inner drive that has propelled him to the top and which makes him impatient for results.

This is an example of the good effects of tension. However, when John came to us for an annual physical, he complained of painful headaches, trouble in sleeping and increasing irritability with his associates and with his family. It didn't take long to determine that John was now a victim of excessive tension. And it didn't take long either to find out the cause, once we had talked over his usual business day.

John had recently taken over a new division of his company which had a bad profit picture. Even though he worked long and hard, he couldn't seem to make a dent in all of the multiple problems involved. He began to think he was the only person "carrying the load." As his tension built up, he increased the pressure on his staff with resulting ill will and loss of cooperation.

Gnawing away at him also was a fear that his superiors were not happy with his progress. His president was a type who was sparing in his praise and John didn't know where he stood. We suggested to John that he settle this matter immediately with his superiors, even if it meant getting another job.

In a week John came in to see me and already he was beginning to be like his old self. His confrontation with his president had revealed that the company's officers were more than happy with what he was accomplishing, in fact, thought it was "miraculous." The president was so fearful, in fact, that John might leave that he insisted that John take an extra vacation immediately and promised meanwhile to give him some additional staff to help him.

This case has two lessons: 1. If you feel you're getting out of depth on your job, find out exactly where you stand. Face up to it regardless of the consequences. 2. And if you have a conscientious man like John Jones on your staff, tell him occasionally that you're pleased with his efforts.

You don't have to be a business executive to suffer from excessive tension. I remember a housewife who had always been contented with her home and social life. Now she was "tensed up" all the time and given to unpredictable outbursts of temper. Often she would wander through her house in the middle of the night completely incapable of sleep. A brief discussion revealed that she was worried about the lack of progress of her teen age son who was more interested in mechanics than in preparing for a law career as his fond mother wanted. Once she faced up to the fact that both law and industry would be better off if her son headed for mechanical engineering, her symptoms vanished.

DON'T BLAME THE "RAT RACE"

Many people who complain of excessive tension brush it off with a reference to the old "rat race" — and obtain a certain perverse pleasure in the illusion that they are working too hard.

I think I can state categorically that few people these days are really working too hard. Rarely do we hear of symptoms that can be traced directly to overwork. Only fifty years ago, people worked much longer hours and there were few cases of "tension" and "nerves." Let us recognize that people today spend only *20 percent* of their time at work. The rest of the time — *80 percent* — is spent outside the office or shop. More often than not, the causes of excessive tension are to be found in the pattern of life in the non-working hours.

Sociologists have long been commenting on the problems of leisure time. As a medical man, I can testify that leisure time and "affluence" do produce health problems. Most people are not victims of the "rat race." They have created a rat race of their own. They have not learned to deal with their environment.

Because it is easier to ride or drive than walk, most people don't get enough exercise.

Because food and drink are readily available, most people have a weight problem.

Because of built in entertainment provided by TV, too many people have become passive in their leisure time activities. They do not receive the mental stimulus that active games and lively conversation provide.

Because more and more people travel long distances between home and work, they often neglect their sleep in an effort to spend more time with their families.

In solving the causes of excessive tension, then, it is not enough to examine the job situation. You should examine your whole living pattern to find where you may have strayed.

ESTABLISHING YOUR TENSION THRESHOLD

Most people understand their physical limitations. [However] many do not seem to realize that the degree of tension one can withstand is highly personal. *assertion* One person can take a great deal of pressure without any ill effect. The same pressure to another would be *admonite* incapacitating. If your job or your home environment creates more tension than you can tolerate, don't fight it. Instead, try to change your way of life.

At the same time, you should re-examine your health habits.

[In our survey] on tension among executives, for instance, this is what we found about the health habits of the 13 percent who complained of excessive tension:

Figure 3A-b (Cont.)

When they eat:

they eat breakfast on the fly. (Under five minutes).

they bolt their lunch. (Under 15 minutes).

they hurry through their dinner. (Under 30 minutes).

and a high percentage are on diets, nursing gastric disorders.

In their recreation:

few of those complaining of tension get some form of regular exercise.

few have extra-curricular interests (church, civic, etc.).

many have no hobby at all.

and one out of five get no recreation whatsover.

For their rest:

many average six or less hours of sleep at night.

few have weekends free for family and self.

and their vacation time is 20 percent less than the overall average.

In their smoking and drinking:

most are heavy cigarette smokers.

most have cocktails for lunch, and many drink more than two.

many have more than two cocktails before dinner.

In the drugs they take:

most of them use sleep-inducing sedatives.

most of them quiet their nerves with tranquilizers.

[If] the overly tense person can make a shift in his health habits, this may be all that is needed. [If this is not possible, however,] then psychiatric help may be indicated.

HOW TO AVOID EXCESSIVE TENSION

We have talked primarily about the persons who already are the victims of excessive stress and tension. These people were not born into the world with these symptoms or, necessarily, with a predisposition to them. Somewhere along the line they acquired habits or failed to face certain situations which brought about these symptoms. If you want to avoid acquiring these symptoms, [here are] a few guidelines:

[If you have doubts] about the ability to do your job well, take steps to find out that you are in the proper line of work — and switch if it seems indicated.

Face up to the facts of the affluent life and leisure time which most of us now enjoy. Remember that it is not what you do between 9 a.m. and 5 p.m. that is as harmful as what you do between 5 p.m. and 9 a.m.

Live within your income. Don't worry about "keeping up with the Jones's." This advice may seem out of my field as a physician. However, we know that conflicts in every day living build up tension and hence affect your physical well being.

[If you have trouble] getting on with people, socially or on the job, better get some professional help.

Every desk bound worker should leave his chair at least once every two hours and walk about the office for a few minutes.

Chairmen should call for occasional ten-minute intermissions during meetings, breaking up both tension and boredom.

[If] you are always tired, you may actually need more physical activity — or you may be bored with what you're doing. Better find out which it is.

Relaxation in small and large doses is the antidote to excessive tension. This does not mean rest — it means a change of scene, a change of activity.

[The best cure] for tension fatigue is exercise — and the best exercise is walking.

[Finally,] learn your tension threshold and live within it.

Sincerely,

Harry J. Johnson

Harry J. Johnson, M.D.
President, Life Extension Foundation

Figure 3A-b (*Cont.*)

The first part, the subject, can be determined quickly, often from the title or the first few lines of the text. Whenever the writer says something important about the subject—and thereby gives it a predicate—he will repeat the subject or a development of it. When you have trained yourself to respond to the subject key word, or words, you have a head start toward an understanding of the predicate key words. And once you have understood at that point, you are ready to move on to the next use of the subject key word, which very often will be in a new paragraph or series of paragraphs.

With practice, you can train your eyes to run over a series of paragraphs, concentrating on guide words, and even more important, on subject and predicate key words. Reading, or skimming, in this fashion, you can often cover pages or chapters while a more conventional (and often less aggressive) reader will still be on the first page. Very few writers care to boil down what they have to say in telegram style, but this does not mean that all they write is of equal value. When you are alert enough to recognize key subjects and predicates, you can reduce a great deal of your reading load to the telegram style, which makes the really important information and ideas come through with their greatest force.

Eye-Movement Patterns

Looking for guide words and key words will lead to a variety of eye-movement patterns. This skill is similar to eye-movement patterns in the technique of phrase reading, but in larger blocks of meaning. As was mentioned in Skill II, the eye does not glide smoothly across the page. Instead, it shifts from one position to the next quite abruptly. Reading speed is, therefore, a result of the number of stops the eye makes, as well as the rate at which it moves.

For the next application, we are going to ask you to move your eyes very rapidly and to think just as rapidly. You are to move your eyes down the page, spotting guide words and key words and, at the same time, deciding what purpose or function each paragraph provides.

Suppose the first paragraph of an article began: "Baseball is a very popular American game." You would be saying to yourself:

> *Type of paragraph:* Definition
> *Subject key word:* Baseball
> *Predicate key words:* Popular American Game

CIRCULAR

Start

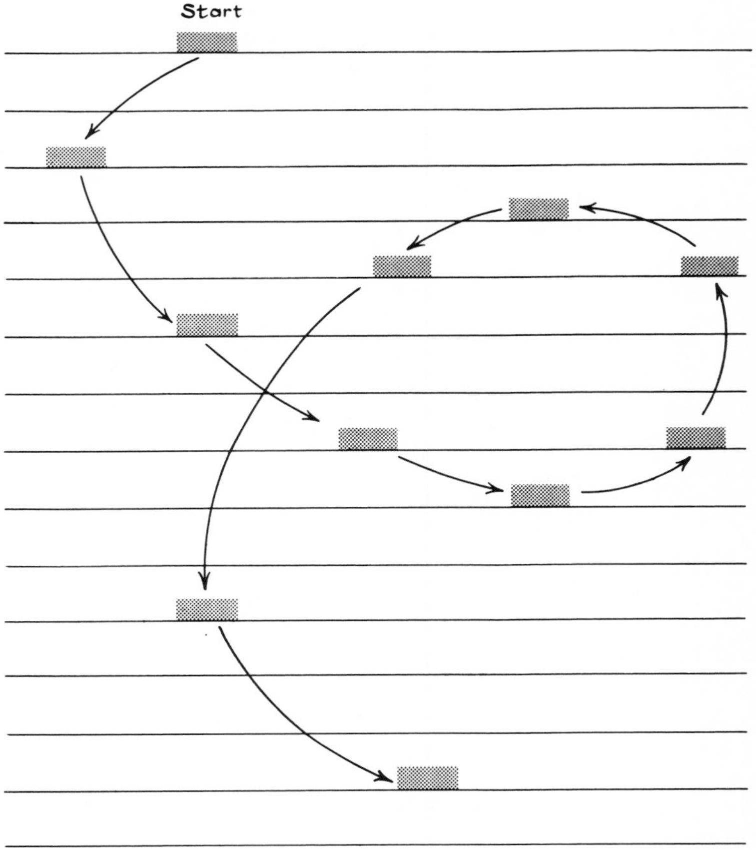

Figure 3B-b

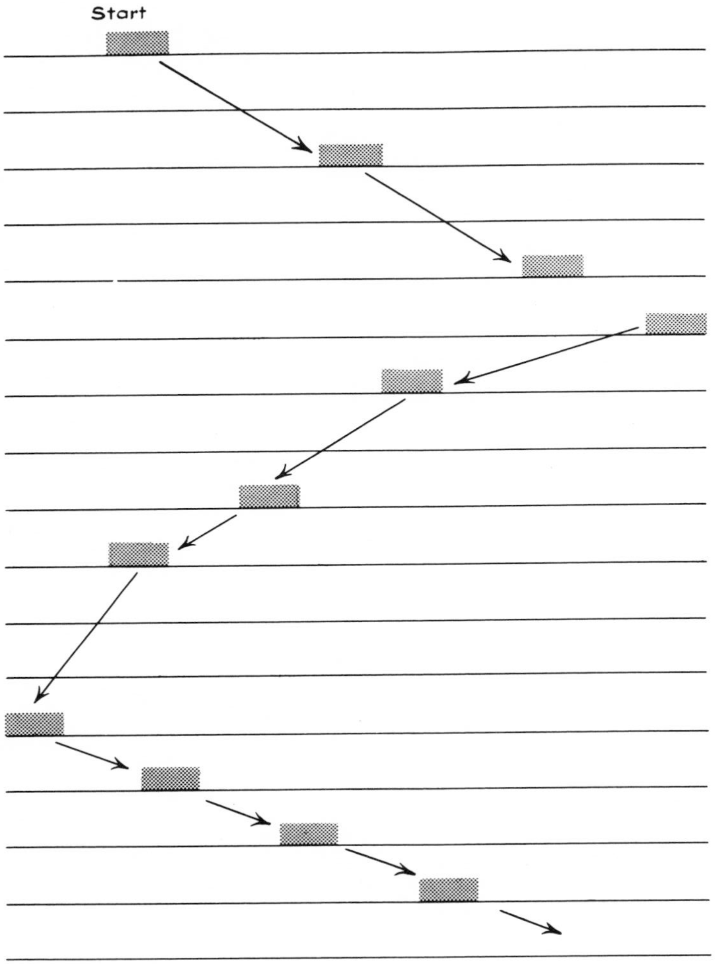

DIAGONAL

Start

Figure 3B-a

79

That much is easy enough, and no more than an average reader might do at an initial point. But from that point on, you would begin to move ahead. You would go down the page, looking for the next appearance of the key word and analyzing the kind of paragraphs in which it is used.

The next paragraph, for instance, might tell you something about the history of the game, a background paragraph. There you would look for such predicate keys as the date of the game's invention and the name of the inventor, skipping over the bulk of words that make up the conventional form of prose as we know it.

To give you a little preparation for the next sample reading, you are to practice on the eye-movement diagrams illustrated in Figures 3B-a and 3B-b. They represent two of several possible ways of moving the eyes to locate key words. Some other pattern may be just as helpful for you, as long as it does not leave too many blank areas on the page. Above all, *keep moving and keep up a regular pattern*. Once you have practiced on the diagram a few times, try a couple of pages from your own reading until you feel fairly confident that you can both rapidly spot key words and categorize paragraphs. Then return to this book for the next application.

PARAGRAPH ANALYSIS WITH KEY-WORD READING: ADVANCED APPLICATION

Skim-read the selection illustrated in Figure 3C-a, noting your start time. As you skim-read, be on the lookout for guide words and key words. Also, try to analyze the paragraphs while you are skimming. When you have finished, note your end time.

Start time: _____ minutes; _____ seconds

End time: _____ minutes; _____ seconds

SKIM-READING TIME: _____ minutes; _____ seconds

READING RATE TABLE

READING TIME:	0:30	0:40	0:50	1:00	1:10	1:20	1:30	1:40	1:50	2:00	2:30	3:00	4:00
WORDS PER MINUTE:	2300	1917	1438	1150	1045	885	766	718	638	575	460	383	288

RECORD SKIM-READING WPM SCORE: _____

In a time of mounting tensions, is there any art more worth developing than that of trying to understand what the other fellow is saying?

Are You Listening?

Condensed from "The Power of Words"

STUART CHASE

Author of "Live and Let Live," and other books

LISTENING is the other half of talking. If people stop listening, it is useless to talk—a point not always appreciated by talkers.

Americans are not good listeners. In general they talk more than they listen. Competition in our culture puts a premium on self-expression, even if the individual has nothing to express. What he lacks in knowledge he tries to make up for by talking fast or pounding the table. And many of us, while ostensibly listening, are inwardly preparing a statement to stun the company when we get the floor. Yet it really is not difficult to learn to listen—just unusual.

Listening is regarded as a passive thing, but it can be a very active process—something to challenge our intelligence. A stream of messages is coming in to be decoded; how close can we come to their real meaning? What is the speaker trying to say? . . . How does he know it? . . . What has he left out? . . . What are his motives?

Sometimes only about a quarter of an audience understands clearly what a speaker has said. To sharpen the ears of its members, the New York Adult Education Council inaugurated "listening clinics." One member reads aloud while the others around the table concentrate on what he is saying. Later they summarize what they have heard and compare notes—often to find that the accounts differ widely. Gradually the listeners improve, and often they find themselves transferring the skill to business and home affairs. As one member said:

"I became aware of a new attitude. I found myself attempting to understand and interpret the remarks of my friends and associates from *their*

80

This article first appeared in The Reader's Digest in November 1953.

Figure 3C-a

viewpoint, and not from my own as I had done previously."

Some years ago Maj. Charles T. Estes of the Federal Mediation and Conciliation Service was called in to help settle a long-term dispute between a corporation and a union. The major invented a technique for listening that has since had wide application in the labor field. He asked delegates from both union and management to read aloud the annual contract, which was in dispute. Each man in turn read a section; then all discussed it. If a dispute began to develop, the clause was put aside for later examination.

In two days the delegates really knew what was in the contract, and were competent also to explain it to their fellow managers or fellow workers. "We had conditioned them to communicate," said the major. The contract was not rewritten but was continued in force with very few changes, and renewed annually for many years. Good listening had transformed bad labor relations into good ones.

Carl R. Rogers, University of Wisconsin psychologist, suggests a game to be played at a party. Suppose a general discussion—say on the elections—becomes acrimonious. At this point Rogers asks the company to try an experiment: before Jones, who is on the edge of his chair, can reply to the statement just made by Smith, he must summarize what Smith has said in such a way that Smith accepts it. Any attempt to slant or distort is instantly corrected

by the original speaker. This means careful listening, during which emotion is likely to cool.

The result is that everyone in the circle, by listening and rephrasing, acquires a working knowledge of the other fellow's point of view, even if he does not agree with it. The players are quite likely to increase their knowledge—something that rarely happens in the usual slam-bang argument. The experiment takes courage, says Rogers, because in restating the other man's position you risk changing your own.

F. J. Roethlisberger of the Harvard Business School, in a study of training courses for supervisors, describes a significant contrast in listening. An executive calls foreman Bill to his office to tell him about a change in Bill's department. A casting will be substituted for a hand-forged job, and the executive tells Bill how to do it.

"Oh, yeah?" says Bill.

Suppose the boss assumes that "Oh, yeah?" means Bill does not see how to do the new job. It is up to the boss to tell Bill, and this he proceeds to do, clearly and logically. Nevertheless, Bill is obviously freezing up, and presently things begin to happen inside the boss. "Can it be," he asks himself, "that I have lost my power to speak clearly? No. Bill just doesn't understand plain English; he's really pretty dumb." The look which accompanies this unspoken idea makes Bill freeze up even harder. The interview ends on a note of total misunderstanding.

But, says Roethlisberger, suppose after Bill's "Oh, yeah?" the boss says, "What's your idea about how the changeover ought to be made, Bill? You've been in the department a long time. Let's have it. I'm listening."

Things now begin to happen inside Bill. The boss is not just laying it on the line; he's willing to listen. So ideas come out, slowly at first, then faster. The boss becomes really interested in Bill's approach—"Smarter man than I thought!" A spiral reaction is set up, as Bill begins to realize that he never appreciated the boss before. The interview ends on a note of close harmony.

In the first case, the boss did not listen to Bill, he *told* Bill; and though the telling was clear enough the goal moved further away. In the second case, the boss listened until he had located what was worrying Bill; then they went along together.

So far, we have been talking about sympathetic listening in face-to-face situations, to make sure we grasp the speaker's full meaning. But critical listening, too, is needed in a world full of propaganda and high-pressure advertising. Here are some techniques which help to develop critical listening to a speech or a conversation, a sales talk at your door or the testimony of a witness before a jury:

Look for motives behind the words. Is the speaker talking chiefly in accepted, appealing symbols—Home, Mother, the Founding Fathers, Our Glorious Heritage, and so on—avoiding the need for thought? Speeches are often solidly larded with symbols. The trained ear can identify them a long way off.

Is the speaker dealing in facts or inferences? You can train your ear to find this distinction in political and economic talk, and to follow the shifts from one level to the next.

The listener should also consider his own attitude toward the speaker. Is he prejudiced for or against him? Is he being fair, objective, sympathetic?

The sum of careful listening is to work actively to discover how the speaker feels about events, what his drives appear to be, what kind of person he is. The appraisal can be only a rough one, but it can be a decided help in dealing with him, in giving him a fair answer.

One other thing: I find that careful listening also helps me to keep quiet rather than sound off foolishly. The best listeners listen alertly, expecting to learn something and to help create new ideas.

Are you listening?

For information on reprints, see page 38.

𝒫ᴿᴏꜰ. Paul Weiss, of the Yale University philosophy department, has a rule for the guidance of modern man: "You can't win, but you don't have to lose right away."

—"Washington Memo" in *Minneapolis Tribune*

Now, go back over the article, just as you did before, bracketing the guide words and underlining the key words. Make a note next to each paragraph, indicating its function, and then check those paragraphs which seem most essential to an understanding of the article. See if a reading of just the bracketed and underlined words, with special attention to the checked paragraphs, actually does give you the essence of the article. If it does not, reread quite carefully to pick out key words you may have missed. Finally, without going back to the article again, write out the briefest adequate summary you can; then check your annotation against Figure 3C-b and your summary against the one that follows.

In a time of mounting tensions, is there any art more worth developing than that of trying to understand what the other fellow is saying?

Are You Listening?

Condensed from "The Power of Words"

STUART CHASE

Author of "Live and Let Live," and other books

1st Major assertion

LISTENING is the other half of talking. If people stop listening, it is useless to talk—a point not always appreciated by talkers.

elaboration

Americans are not good listeners. In general they talk more than they listen. Competition in our culture puts a premium on self-expression, even if the individual has nothing to express. What he lacks in knowledge he tries to make up for by talking fast or pounding the table. And many of us, while ostensibly listening, are inwardly preparing a statement to stun the company when we get the floor. Yet it really is not difficult to learn to listen—just unusual.

qualification

possibility

Listening is regarded as a passive thing, but it can be a very active process—something to challenge our intelligence. A stream of messages is coming in to be decoded; how close can we come to their real meaning?

What is the speaker trying to say? . . . How does he know it? . . . What has he left out? . . . What are his motives?

illustration

Sometimes only about a quarter of an audience understands clearly what a speaker has said. To sharpen the ears of its members, the New York Adult Education Council inaugurated "listening clinics." One member reads aloud while the others around the table concentrate on what he is saying. Later they summarize what they have heard and compare notes—often to find that the accounts differ widely. Gradually the listeners improve, and often they find themselves transferring the skill to business and home affairs. As one member said:

illustration

"I became aware of a new attitude. I found myself attempting to understand and interpret the remarks of my friends and associates from *their*

80

Figure 3C-b

Page 81

viewpoint, and not from my own as I had done previously."

Some years ago Maj. Charles T. Estes of the Federal Mediation and Conciliation Service was called in to help settle a long-term dispute between a corporation and a union. The major invented a technique for listening that has since had wide application in the labor field. He asked delegates from both union and management to read aloud the annual contract, which was in dispute. Each man in turn read a section; then all discussed it. If a dispute began to develop, the clause was put aside for later examination.

In two days the delegates really knew what was in the contract, and were competent also to explain it to their fellow managers or fellow workers. "We had conditioned them to communicate," said the major. The contract was not rewritten but was continued in force with very few changes, and renewed annually for many years. Good listening had transformed bad labor relations into good ones.

Carl R. Rogers, University of Wisconsin psychologist, suggests a game to be played at a party. Suppose a general discussion—say on the elections—becomes acrimonious. At this point Rogers asks the company to try an experiment before Jones, who is on the edge of his chair, can reply to the statement just made by Smith, he must summarize what Smith has said in such a way that Smith accepts it. Any attempt to slant or distort is instantly corrected by the original speaker. This means careful listening, during which emotion is likely to cool.

The result is that everyone in the circle, by listening and rephrasing, acquires a working knowledge of the other fellow's point of view, even if he does not agree with it. The players are quite likely to increase their knowledge—something that rarely happens in the usual slam-bang argument. The experiment takes courage, says Rogers, because in restating the other man's position you risk changing your own.

F. J. Roethlisberger of the Harvard Business School, in a study of training courses for supervisors, describes a significant contrast in listening. An executive calls foreman Bill to his office to tell him about a change in Bill's department. A casting will be substituted for a hand-forged job, and the executive tells Bill how to do it.

"Oh, yeah?" says Bill.

Suppose the boss assumes that "Oh, yeah?" means Bill does not see how to do the new job. It is up to the boss to tell Bill, and this he proceeds to do, clearly and logically. Nevertheless, Bill is obviously freezing up, and presently things begin to happen inside the boss. "Can it be," he asks himself, "that I have lost my power to speak clearly? No Bill just doesn't understand plain English; he's really pretty dumb." The look which accompanies this unspoken idea makes Bill freeze up even harder. The interview ends on a note of total misunderstanding.

Page 82

But, says Roethlisberger, suppose after Bill's "Oh, yeah?" the boss says, "What's your idea about how the changeover ought to be made, Bill? You've been in the department a long time. Let's have it. I'm listening."

Things now begin to happen inside Bill. The boss is not just laying it on the line; he's willing to listen. So ideas come out, slowly at first, then faster. The boss becomes really interested in Bill's approach—"Smarter man than I thought!" A spiral reaction is set up, as Bill begins to realize that he never appreciated the boss before. The interview ends on a note of close harmony.

In the first case, the boss did not listen to Bill; he told Bill; and though the telling was clear enough the goal moved further away. In the second case, the boss listened until he had located what was worrying Bill; then they went along together. So far we have been talking about sympathetic listening in face-to-face situations, to make sure we grasp the speaker's full meaning. But critical listening, too, is needed in a world full of propaganda and high-pressure advertising. Here are some techniques which help to develop critical listening to a speech or a conversation, a sales talk at your door or the testimony of a witness before a jury:

Look for motives behind the words. Is the speaker talking chiefly in accepted, appealing symbols—Home, Mother, the Founding Fathers, Our Glorious Heritage, and so on—avoiding the need for thought? Speeches are often solidly larded with symbols. The trained ear can identify them a long way off.

Is the speaker dealing in facts or inferences? You can train your ear to find this distinction in political and economic talk, and to follow the shifts from one level to the next. The listener should also consider his own attitude toward the speaker. Is he prejudiced for or against him? Is he being fair, objective, sympathetic?

The sum of careful listening is to work actively to discover how the speaker feels about events, what his drives appear to be, what kind of person he is. The appraisal can be only a rough one, but it can be a decided help in dealing with him, in giving him a fair answer.

One other thing: I find that careful listening also helps me to keep quiet rather than sound off foolishly. The best listeners listen alertly, expecting to learn something and to help create new ideas. Are you listening?

For information on reprints, see page 38.

Prof. Paul Weiss, of the Yale University philosophy department, has a rule for the guidance of modern man: "You can't win, but you don't have to lose right away."

—"Washington Memo" in Minneapolis Tribune

Figure 3C-b (Cont.)

Summary: Talking is pointless unless people listen—actively rather than passively. A summary of what a person has said is an aid to active listening. Active listening—for motives, for inferences and for one's own subjective reactions—is also important in a world as extensively propagandized as ours. To listen well, one must work to discover what the speaker is really saying.

PARAGRAPH ANALYSIS: INDEPENDENT APPLICATION

In the next selection, skim-read once more, but this time a little more slowly and without timing yourself. Instead, be absolutely sure you are defining the function of each paragraph as precisely as you can, with the aid of guide words and key words. The article is no more difficult than the last one, but you should slow down a bit to derive greater conscious control from paragraph analysis. Read the selection illustrated in Figure 3D-a now.

Although this last exercise has been marked as an "independent application," part of it has been annotated below in Figure 3D-b so that you will have some comparison for your own annotation. A summary has not been provided this time, but you should write one. Written summaries, which later can become improved mental summaries, are the surest way you have of testing yourself without the presence of a teacher or colleague. *In a summary, be brief, be precise, and be sure you can locate a key paragraph if you have to.*

You can get ahead faster

This advice will assist you in overcoming obstacles to success

"I CAME TO THIS COMPANY," said a dispirited 40-year-old engineer, "because I thought it had a future and I could advance.

"But my department's going nowhere and I'm trapped in my present position. There are already too many chiefs with too little to do. I haven't been able to wangle a transfer to another department. If I move to another company, I'm going to waste another year or two before I earn full responsibility."

In another company, a 55-year-old man whose business career had inclined upward at only a moderate angle suddenly discovered that his management had started a program of hiring recent business school graduates and moving them quickly into positions of authority.

"Now I'm reporting to kids who don't know the first thing about the business," he complained. "Maybe I'm not the greatest in the world, but I thought I'd get a little further up the ladder. But I'm stopped and there's nothing I can do. I can't afford to quit until my boys are through college. And I'm locked in by my pension besides."

A brilliant and youthful vice president of yet another company was taken to luncheon by his boss to discuss his future.

"John," the president said, "you are undoubtedly the best man this company has ever had. You could have my job some day soon. You could probably go on to the top job in almost any company. But you're not going to. Your people hate you."

These experiences typify a problem that every executive encounters, not just once but usually several times, in the course of his working life. He runs up against a roadblock which seems to threaten his career.

Sometimes the obstacle is created by the man himself or his family. Sometimes it is raised by his company or by others in it. Sometimes it results from a combination of faults and circumstances.

Whatever the cause, the experience is, at best, upsetting; at worst, shattering. Yet it is a normal experience that is usually beneficial in the end because it forces you to clarify your thinking about yourself and it may make you take long overdue action.

What to do

It is easy, however, to overlook the benefits of a roadblock when you are bemoaning your bad luck. Your mind is occupied with only one question: "What do I do now?"

The first step, says Robert F. Moore, senior partner of Richardson, Bellows, Henry & Co., management consultants, is to analyze yourself and the situation you're in. This is going to take time. You need soli-

294

Figure 3D-a

tude, pencil and a piece of paper. Ask yourself these questions:

What are my objectives? You can waste a lot of time stewing about the roadblock if you don't know what you want in your business life.

Many men, says one personnel consultant, have no goal. Some may admit this openly. Countless others conceal the fact even from themselves. In any case, when such men hit a roadblock, they are usually consciously or unconsciously relieved because they do not want to assume additional responsibilities.

For instance, several years ago when one consultant made his annual appraisal of his own staff, he concluded that one young man, though doing excellent work in his present job, was incapable of advancing further. The consultant expected the man, an eager, energetic worker, to take the news hard. But much to his surprise, the man readily agreed.

"I'd probably have been upset a while ago," he confessed. "But I've been thinking things over lately, and I realize I'm happy where I am."

Many other men do have a goal in life, but it is nebulous. Such men know only that they'd like to wind up in some well paying position in some good company in some interesting industry. They are not definite about which position, which company or which industry. Because of this, they are often badly upset by roadblocks. Their efforts to get around an obstacle may be confused and ineffective.

Such a man was a 40-year-old executive whose only aim was to make a lot of money in marketing, but whose blunt frankness had alienated several of his superiors. The man ranted to his friends about this "injustice." He made spasmodic attempts to get into other companies at the salary he thought he deserved (and which, in fact, he did).

Fortunately, nothing happened. As year followed frustrating year, he grew more mature and philosophical. Partly as a result, he became less outspoken. Then his superiors' objections began to evaporate. He was given new responsibilities and authority. Ultimately he was making the substantial salary that his personal roadblock had long denied him.

The relatively few men who know exactly where they are headed have much less difficulty with roadblocks.

The reason is obvious: To be able to set a realistic goal for yourself, you must understand your own resources and be willing to correct shortcomings. You must know what will be expected of you, not only in the position you are aiming for, but in the positions leading up to it.

One excellent salesman whose objectives were lofty but indistinct failed to consider the time he would have to spend away from home if and when he became a sales manager. Consequently, when he was given that job, he suddenly realized that he didn't want it. But having accepted publicly and enthusiastically, he hesitated to back out.

In establishing an objective, you must also reckon with the competition you will meet, face the fact that there are more candidates than positions as you move to the top. Above all, you must anticipate the problems you will encounter, and be prepared to cope with them.

Analyze roadblock

What is the nature of the roadblock? This is another question you must answer when you seem suddenly to have run against a stone wall. "Not everything that looks like a roadblock is one in fact," says a personnel consultant.

Then how can you identify a roadblock positively? Sometimes it's hard.

The outlook may seem black when you don't get a raise or as big a raise as you think you merit; when the boss consistently walks by your desk without looking at you; when you never can get in to see the boss; when your ideas fall on deaf ears.

The truth may be that there is nothing at all wrong as far as you're concerned. Perhaps the company is in a temporary profit squeeze and your raise is only delayed. Perhaps the boss is so swamped by work that he can focus only on his problems. Perhaps your ideas are not presented at the right time or have gone on to a man who is incapable of respond-

Set realistic goal

Figure 3D-a (Cont.)

ing enthusiastically to anything. Even usually reliable indicators of a roadblock may be inaccurate. For instance, the fact that an associate was promoted to a job you expected may not mean that you have reached the end of the line. The company may be holding you for a new and even bigger job you don't know about. The fact that a man from outside is given a better job than yours may mean only that you lack the specific qualifications that job requires. The fact that you are being relieved of some responsibilities may mean that you are simply being freed for other work.

On the other hand, you should accept at face value such obstacles as a permanently dwindling market for your products; a superior who is only three years older than you, his second in command; a power-hungry associate who plays politics better than you; employes who make no bones about telling your superiors that they distrust your motives.

"But even in the face of what looks like convincing evidence, quite a few of us leap to conclusions when some more or less unusual happening seems to block our forward progress," says one businessman. "I've come up against my share of obstacles, and several times, after acting impulsively (though, of course, I told myself I was thinking things through), I've discovered that the obstacles never existed. I hope I've learned that most of the things that look like road-blocks must be checked out calmly and thoroughly before they're definitely labeled as such."

But what if your roadblock is a fact? Then you must continue your questioning along these lines:

What is the present position of the company? How does it compare with competition? What is the condition of the industry? What of the future of my department, company, industry?

What is my present job? If your employer has prepared a complete job description, review that. Other-

Decision must be yours

wise make up your own description, listing objectives and responsibilities.

Who is the competition within the company? List all competitors. What are their strengths and weaknesses? How do they compare with you and what are their chances? What roadblocks have they encountered?

What has been my progress to date? Has it been marked by genuine accomplishment? What routes have you traveled? Have you come along rapidly? At the same pace as your associates? Slowly?

One company personnel manager believes that the average man moves ahead in five-year steps. If you have been moving at a faster rate, it may be that your present roadblock is a good thing: it gives you time to assimilate what you have discovered, adjust completely to your present job and get ready to move on again.

What are my training, experience, outside activities? Are you deficient in any area? Could you stand broadening?

The public relations manager of a large company some years ago decided that he had gone about as far as he could. So he went to night school for three years to get a law degree. He figured that the additional knowledge might equip him for a job as assistant to the president or chairman. It didn't work out that way, but he did wind up in a newly created position with greater scope and authority.

What are my personal qualifications? Analyzing these is one of the hardest parts of your soul-searching. Although an industrial psychologist says that most men see themselves pretty clearly, it is difficult not to overrate or underrate yourself. And the list of questions you must answer is long.

Your personal qualifications—health, vitality, principles and policies, appearance, manners.

Your personal characteristics—adaptability, perseverance, self-reliance, initiative, loyalty, sense of humor, imagination, enthusiasm, tact.

Your ability—to analyze keenly, speak effectively, write clearly, originate ideas, listen.

Take stock of self

Figure 3D-a (Cont.)

YOU CAN GET AHEAD FASTER

Your job—do you understand it, know how to execute it, enjoy it? Are you adequate in all ways? Are you on the right track?

Your working habits—punctuality, accuracy, neatness, thoroughness, follow-through.

Your motivation—does your satisfaction come from economic reward, personal recognition, service to others?

Your executive potential—how do you train others? Do you delegate authority? Are you cost and profit minded? Do you organize well? Are you a leader rather than a driver?

Your human relations—what do the people you know and with whom you work think of you? Are you friendly, cooperative, courteous? Do you inspire confidence? Are people comfortable with you? Do you value people?

Having put down the answers to these questions about yourself, your job and your company, it is possible you have so cleared the air that you can readily see the solution to the main problem:

"What do I do to get around the roadblock I've hit?"

Value of advice

If you are still uncertain, the next step is to talk to a wise counselor. (This, incidentally, is a sound idea even if you are sure of where you stand and what you should do; an outside viewpoint is always helpful.)

The counselor may be your wife, a personal friend, a business friend, a former teacher or guidance counselor. Sometimes you can talk with a superior, but unless you know that he is a man who deals with others sympathetically and objectively, this may involve some risk.

If the answer is to seek a transfer to another department, join another company or go into business for yourself, you should, like any man moving into a new field, analyze the organization or business you want to get into.

Your answer may be to stay put. Perhaps your study and consultations show that your roadblock is only temporary and that, after a period of marking time, you will start moving ahead again. On the other hand, perhaps you must face the fact that you have finally reached the limit of your abilities. You may be unhappy and restive from time to time in the future; but deep down you may feel some relief that your struggle is over and that from now on you can do what you know you can do as well as you can.

Or your answer may be to undertake a self-improvement program which will correct the personal faults and deficiencies that raised the roadblock in the first place.

Roadblocks are rarely pleasant. But if you look at them as a challenge rather than a defeat, you should be able to turn them to your advantage.

—STANLEY SCHULER

Figure 3D-a (Cont.)

You can get ahead faster

This advice will assist you in overcoming obstacles to success

1/ What obstacles ?
2/ How ?

descriptive paragraphs stating problem

"I CAME TO THIS COMPANY," said a dispirited 40-year-old engineer, "because I thought it had a future and I could advance.

["But] my department's going nowhere and I'm trapped in my present position. There are already too many chiefs with too little to do. I haven't been able to wangle a transfer to another department. If I move to another company, I'm going to waste another year or two before I earn full responsibility."

In another company, a 55-year-old man whose business career had inclined upward at only a moderate angle suddenly discovered that his management had started a program of hiring recent business school graduates and moving them quickly into positions of authority.

"Now I'm reporting to kids who don't know the first thing about the business," he complained. "Maybe I'm not the greatest in the world, but I thought I'd get a little further up the ladder. [But] I'm stopped and there's nothing I can do. I can't afford to quit until my boys are through college. And I'm locked in by my pension besides."

A brilliant and youthful vice president of yet another company was taken to luncheon by his boss to discuss his future.

"John," the president said, "you are undoubtedly the best man this company has ever had. You could have my job some day soon. You could probably go on to the top job in almost any company. But you're not going to. Your people hate you."

statement

[These experiences typify a problem] that every executive encounters, not just once but usually several times, in the course of his working life. He runs up against a roadblock which seems to threaten his career.

explanation

[Sometimes] the obstacle is created by the man himself or his family. [Sometimes] it is raised by his company or by others in it. [Sometimes] it results from a combination of faults and circumstances.

294

[Whatever the cause,] the experience is, at best, upsetting; at worst, shattering. [Yet] it is a normal experience that is usually beneficial in the end [because] it forces you to clarify your thinking about yourself and it may make you take long overdue action.

qualification elaboration

What to do

It is easy, however, to overlook the benefits of a roadblock when you are bemoaning your bad luck. Your mind is occupied with only one question: "What do I do now?"

The first step, says Robert F. Moore, senior partner of Richardson, Bellows, Henry & Co., management consultants, is to analyze yourself and the situation you're in. This is going to take time. You need soli-

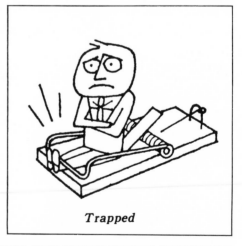

Trapped

REPRINTED FROM NATION'S BUSINESS, FEBRUARY 1963

Figure 3D-b

90

tude, pencil and a piece of paper. Ask yourself these questions:

What are my objectives? You can waste a lot of time stewing about the roadblock if you don't know what you want in your business life.

Many men, says one personnel consultant, have no goal. Some may admit this openly. Countless others conceal the fact even from themselves. In any case, when such men hit a roadblock, they are usually consciously or unconsciously relieved because they do not want to assume additional responsibilities.

For instance, several years ago when one consultant made his annual appraisal of his own staff, he concluded that one young man, though doing excellent work in his present job, was incapable of advancing further. The consultant expected the man, an eager, energetic worker, to take the news hard. But much to his surprise, the man readily agreed.

"I'd probably have been upset a while ago," he confessed. "But I've been thinking things over lately, and I realize I'm happy where I am."

Many other men do have a goal in life, but it is nebulous. Such men know only that they'd like to wind up in some well paying position in some good company in some interesting industry. They are not definite about which position, which company or which industry. Because of this, they are often badly upset by roadblocks. Their efforts to get around an obstacle may be confused and ineffective.

Such a man was a 40-year-old executive whose only aim was to make a lot of money in marketing, but whose blunt frankness had alienated several of his superiors. The man ranted to his friends about this "injustice." He made spasmodic attempts to get into other companies at the salary he thought he deserved (and which, in fact, he did).

Fortunately, nothing happened. As year followed frustrating year, he grew more mature and philosophical. Partly as a result, he became less outspoken. Then his superiors' objections began to evaporate. He was given new responsibilities and authority. Ultimately he was making the substantial salary that his personal roadblock had long denied him.

The relatively few men who know exactly where they are headed have much less difficulty with roadblocks.

The reason is obvious: To be able to set a realistic goal for yourself, you must understand your own resources and be willing to correct shortcomings. You must know what will be expected of you, not only in the position you are aiming for, but in the positions leading up to it.

One excellent salesman whose objectives were lofty but indistinct failed to consider the time he would have to spend away from home if and when he became a sales manager. Consequently, when he was given that job, he suddenly realized that he didn't want it. But having accepted publicly and enthusiastically, he hesitated to back out.

In establishing an objective, you must also reckon with the competition you will meet, face the fact that there are more candidates than positions as you move to the top. Above all, you must anticipate the problems you will encounter, and be prepared to cope with them.

Analyze roadblock

What is the nature of the roadblock? This is another question you must answer when you seem suddenly to have run against a stone wall. "Not everything that looks like a roadblock is one in fact," says a personnel consultant.

Then how can you identify a roadblock positively? Sometimes it's hard.

The outlook may seem black when you don't get a raise or as big a raise as you think you merit; when the boss consistently walks by your desk without looking at you; when you never can get in to see the boss; when your ideas fall on deaf ears.

The truth may be that there is nothing at all wrong as far as you're concerned. Perhaps the company is in a temporary profit squeeze and your raise is only delayed. Perhaps the boss is so swamped by work that he can focus only on his problems. Perhaps your ideas are not presented at the right time or have gone on to a man who is incapable of respond-

Set realistic goal

Figure 3D-b (Cont.)

91

ing enthusiastically to anything. Even usually reliable indicators of a roadblock may be inaccurate. For instance, the fact that an associate was promoted to a job you expected may not mean that you have reached the end of the line. The company may be holding you for a new and even bigger job you don't know about. The fact that a man from outside is given a better job than yours may mean only that you lack the specific qualifications that job requires. The fact that you are being relieved of some responsibilities may mean that you are simply being freed for other work.

On the other hand, you should accept at face value such obstacles as a permanently dwindling market for your products; a superior who is only three years older than you, his second in command; a power-hungry associate who plays politics better than you; employes who make no bones about telling your superiors that they distrust your motives.

"But even in the face of what looks like convincing evidence, quite a few of us leap to conclusions when some more or less unusual happening seems to block our forward progress," says one businessman. "I've come up against my share of obstacles, and several times, after acting impulsively (though, of course, I told myself I was thinking things through), I've discovered that the obstacles never existed. I hope I've learned that most of the things that look like road-blocks must be checked out calmly and thoroughly before they're definitely labeled as such."

But what if your roadblock is a fact? Then you must continue your questioning along these lines:

What is the present position of the company? How does it compare with competition? What is the condition of the industry? What of the future of my department, company, industry?

What is my present job? If your employer has prepared a complete job description, review that. Other-

Decision must be yours

wise make up your own description, listing objectives and responsibilities.

Who is the competition within the company? List all competitors. What are their strengths and weaknesses? How do they compare with you and what are their chances? What roadblocks have they encountered?

What has been my progress to date? Has it been marked by genuine accomplishment? What routes have you traveled? Have you come along rapidly? At the same pace as your associates? Slowly?

One company personnel manager believes that the average man moves ahead in five-year steps. If you have been moving at a faster rate, it may be that your present roadblock is a good thing: it gives you time to assimilate what you have discovered, adjust completely to your present job and get ready to move on again.

What are my training, experience, outside activities? Are you deficient in any area? Could you stand broadening?

The public relations manager of a large company some years ago decided that he had gone about as far as he could. So he went to night school for three years to get a law degree. He figured that the additional knowledge might equip him for a job as assistant to the president or chairman. It didn't work out that way, but he did wind up in a newly created position with greater scope and authority.

What are my personal qualifications? Analyzing these is one of the hardest parts of your soul-searching. Although an industrial psychologist says that most men see themselves pretty clearly, it is difficult not to overrate or underrate yourself. And the list of questions you must answer is long.

Your personal qualifications—health, vitality, principles and policies, appearance, manners.

Your personal characteristics—adaptability, perseverance, self-reliance, initiative, loyalty, sense of humor, imagination, enthusiasm, tact.

Your ability—to analyze keenly, speak effectively, write clearly, originate ideas, listen.

Take stock of self

Figure 3D-b (Cont.)

YOU CAN GET AHEAD FASTER

Your job—do you understand it, know how to execute it, enjoy it? Are you adequate in all ways? Are you on the right track?

Your working habits—punctuality, accuracy, neatness, thoroughness, follow-through.

Your motivation—does your satisfaction come from economic reward, personal recognition, service to others?

Your executive potential—how do you train others? Do you delegate authority? Are you cost and profit minded? Do you organize well? Are you a leader rather than a driver?

Your human relations—what do the people you know and with whom you work think of you? Are you friendly, cooperative, courteous? Do you inspire confidence? Are people comfortable with you? Do you value people?

Having put down the answers to these questions about yourself, your job and your company, it is possible you have so cleared the air that you can readily see the solution to the main problem:

"What do I do to get around the roadblock I've hit?"

Value of advice

If you are still uncertain, the next step is to talk to a wise counselor. (This, incidentally, is a sound idea even if you are sure of where you stand and what you should do; an outside viewpoint is always helpful.)

The counselor may be your wife, a personal friend, a business friend, a former teacher or guidance counselor. Sometimes you can talk with a superior, but unless you know that he is a man who deals with others sympathetically and objectively, this may involve some risk.

If the answer is to seek a transfer to another department, join another company or go into business for yourself, you should, like any man moving into a new field, analyze the organization or business you want to get into.

Your answer may be to stay put. Perhaps your study and consultations show that your roadblock is only temporary and that, after a period of marking time, you will start moving ahead again. On the other hand, perhaps you must face the fact that you have finally reached the limit of your abilities. You may be unhappy and restive from time to time in the future; but deep down you may feel some relief that your struggle is over and that from now on you can do what you know you can do as well as you can.

Or your answer may be to undertake a self-improvement program which will correct the personal faults and deficiencies that raised the roadblock in the first place.

Roadblocks are rarely pleasant. But if you look at them as a challenge rather than a defeat, you should be able to turn them to your advantage.

—STANLEY SCHULER

Figure 3D-b (Cont.)

SUMMARY

As you probably realize, this chapter—like the entire book—has had two aims. The first is to give you information about the techniques. The second is to have you practice them at a highly conscious level. But, as you practice and as you become more proficient, the techniques should become an integral part of your mental life. Perhaps key word reading and paragraph analysis require more constant and extensive practice for satisfactory results than any of our other techniques. But after some practice, you may wonder why you ever spent so much time on those books and articles which deserved only a brief amount of time.

You may wonder how to tell the difference between a skill that has been so successfully learned that it becomes unconscious and one that simply has been forgotten. In the area of paragraph analysis and key word reading, the test is very easy. If you find yourself having to go back over material a second or a third time before you understand it, and if you find it difficult to tell a friend or associate briefly and accurately what you have learned, you need more planned practice in the technique. If, on the other hand, you find certain words—key words and guide words—springing up from the page almost as if they were printed in color, and if you are aware of just how the machinery of an article or chapter or book functions, and, finally, if you find it quite easy to summarize and to relate what you have read, you have succeeded very well in this crucial aspect of reading.

Paragraph analysis is at all times an active procedure. It demands constant questioning, and it yields a much higher level of comprehension than the passive and often inattentive procedure that characterizes most reading activity. Once you have mastered paragraph analysis and have made yourself aware of paragraph functions and the essential role of guide words and key words, you are well on your way toward success with the next technique, structured reading.

SKILL REMINDER

To analyze paragraphs, do this:

1. Look for key words.
2. Be alert for guide words.
3. Summarize each paragraph briefly as you read.
4. Note functions of each paragraph to the whole selection.

STRUCTURING IDEAS

The key to comprehension and lasting RECALL

Skill

IV

What the Skill Is: The ability to pick out the different organizational parts of a reading selection and to see the relationship of one part to another.

What Structuring Does: Once you know how to organize the material into the general category, the main points, and the supporting details, and you can see the relationship among these parts, you will become aware of the *substance* of any reading material. Thus, you will be able to recognize the important facts from the less important illustrations. Perhaps more importantly, through the interrelationship, you will be able to categorize the material into a general thesis for *better retention* of what you have read.

How to Use It: Give a watchmaker the hundreds and hundreds of parts that make up a delicate watch, and, in time, he can produce a beautifully functioning little mechanism. Give the same parts to someone who has no knowledge of the craft, and you might as well get yourself a sundial. What distinguishes the two—what does craft mean? In reading, craft describes the extent to

95

which a reader can analyze the mechanism in any written selection. The watchmaker knows what a watch should look like, how it should operate. As a skilled reader, you must try to create the same sort of functioning mental image as you read. What are the parts of a reading selection, either in a sentence, paragraph, or entire book or article? How do they relate to each other? What are they supposed to do when understood together?

Some of the structural patterns chosen by an author are voluntary, while others are forced upon him by the nature of the language and culture. He may choose to create a special air of semiconsciousness or dream-state through long sentences and lack of punctuation; but, within this mood, English sentences almost invariably follow the pattern of subject, verb, and object: "I see the cemetery," rather than "The cemetery is seen by me." This sentence pattern is one we have recognized and conformed to since the age of three or four.

Paragraph patterns are less fixed in our language, yet there are some conventions which can help simplify your structuring of the author's ideas. Main ideas will usually be placed at the beginning of paragraphs—in the so-called topic sentence. Even those writers who do not put the most important idea of the paragraph in the first sentence will usually follow some predictable pattern of their own.

The most common structural pattern in expository prose is that of introduction and development. When the material is didactic (i.e., trying to persuade or instruct us to think or act in a certain way), there will usually be a conclusion or recommendation included as a fundamental part of the structure. Letters, of course, follow a traditional pattern of salutation, body, and closing—no doubt, familiar to you. Newspapers and periodicals also have their own unique structures. Material for each publication is chosen according to the interests of most of the readers and is arranged in an individual, yet consistent, pattern for reading convenience. Once a reader becomes aware of the publication's structural aspects, he can better understand its objectives and content and be prepared to render a valid criticism.

In this section, you will be concerned with finding the structural patterns by looking for the author's *general ideas,* which may stem from a great variety of details and assertions. Next, you will look for a sequence of *main points,* which, linked together, give a coherent pattern of ideas, information, or instruction to develop the general category. Finally, you will be seeking to find those *supporting details* which seem to illustrate best the main points. Thus, reading for structure will help you avoid an excessive commitment to the very first details of the first main point. Instead, you will be aggressively seeking a complex of main points and a general category that describes the whole piece. After considering all the superstructure, the details may have quite a different value from your initial impression.

APPLICATION

In the sample readings to follow you will work with structure in magazine articles, book chapters, and correspondence. For each application, you will begin with a brief *skim-reading* of the selection, reading the title, the beginning and end paragraphs, and the topic sentences. From this skim-reading, you will attempt to state the general category of the material—in other words, what, in the broadest terms, is it about? How would you classify it for filing purposes? How would you describe it in a sentence if someone asked about it?

Once you have determined the general category that fits the material, you will be ready to distinguish the main points. If you discover a large number of main points in your skim-reading, try to consolidate them into just three to five. The human mind functions best with about that many things to remember at a given level of importance. If you have a variety of topics to deal with, always try to regroup them into three to five more inclusive ones for maximum understanding and recall.

After you have singled out or regrouped the main points of the selection from your skim-reading, you will be prepared for a *thorough reading* to check your structure of the main points and to find supporting details. You may wish to examine all the details for some of the main points and not even look at the details for those main points irrelevant to your purpose, but no matter how many details you examine, you *must* hold in your mind the interaction among the main points. Without this view of the structured whole, details are liable to have little meaning or the wrong meaning.

The sample readings chosen for this chapter represent the broad range of reading expected of the average business or professional man. It is impossible, of course, for this book to supply the exact reading matter you are going to meet at the office. Application there is up to you. Probably the best pattern would be for you to begin application to your own material as soon as you have completed the first or second sample given in this chapter. After a trial run on your own material, you can return to one of the sample readings to check yourself and to perfect the skill.

STRUCTURING: BASIC APPLICATION

You are going to skim-read the selection "Two Roads to New Products" (Figure 4A) by reading only the underlined material: the entire first paragraph, the first sentences of succeeding paragraphs, and all of last two paragraphs. Then, record your time for this skim-reading and answer the questions on structure. After answering the questions and checking your answers, you are going to reread the article in its entirety and answer the accuracy questions. Now turn to Figure 4A and skim-read the underlined material, noting your start and end time.

Start time: _____ minutes; _____ seconds

End time: _____ minutes; _____ seconds

SKIM-READING TIME: _____ minutes; _____ seconds

READING RATE TABLE

READING TIME (min.; sec.):	1:00	1:15	1:30	1:45	2:00	2:20	2:40	3:00	3:30	4:00	5:00
WORDS PER MINUTE:	1000	800	666	572	500	429	375	333	286	250	200

RECORD SKIM-READING WPM SCORE: _____

Structure Statements

For each of the following structure statements, read the statement and then indicate whether you think the statement refers to the general category, a main point, or a detail in the selection. Since your decision regarding the structural significance of any one of these statements is based upon its relative contribution to overall organization, after you have answered each item, you may wish to review and possibly change your choice for some of the earlier statements.

1. The "market-oriented new-products program" represents lower costs and lower risks.
     _____a. General Category.
     _____b. Main Point.
     _____c. Detail.

2. The market-oriented program, dominated by the creative marketing expert, yields substantial rewards with low cost and predictable pay-off.

Major expenses are incurred after an assurance of success.

     ____a. General Category.

     ____b. Main Point.

     ____c. Detail.

3. The laboratory-oriented program, dominated by the scientist-inventor, *can* yield spectacular rewards, but cost is high and pay-off unpredictable. Major expenses are incurred before any assurance of success is possible.

     ____a. General Category.

     ____b. Main Point.

     ____c. Detail.

Answers: 1. c
2. a
3. b

Reread for Detail

Your skim-reading has probably enabled you to establish the general category of the selection, to single out the main points, and to recognize some details. In your own reading, you might at this point feel you knew as much about the selection as you wished to know, and you might prefer not to read it thoroughly. On the other hand, you might feel that you wished to know more about only *one* of the main points, and you might close-read only that section.

For the purpose of this exercise, let us assume that you wish to read the entire article thoroughly, focusing on the *supporting details* and noting the inferences implied by the author, though not directly stated by him. For instance, which program does the author favor? These inferences seem hidden in the author's organization—yet, by following the skill of first skim-reading for main points and general category, and then reading thoroughly for the details, you are free to notice not only what is said, but what is not said. This reading between the lines can often lead you to far greater comprehension, necessary for a complete structure of the author's ideas. Now, go back and reread the material illustrated in Figure 4A, noting your start and finish times.

Two Roads to New Products

BY DR. ROBERT J. WILLIAMS, director, marketing intelligence, Edward Dalton Co., Mead Johnson & Co.

It's not very difficult to distinguish between a Hemingway and a hack writer or between a Picasso and a house painter. Some people believe they can even distinguish between pure and applied research. The basis for all these distinctions is the contrast between an activity which is motivated by a desire for remote gains and glory and one which is motivated by a quest for more immediate personal profit.

Something of this same distinction can be applied in the area of new-product development. Some firms, for example, distinguish between "basic research," which has as its objective the creation of new substances or radically new products, and "customer applications research," which attempts to adapt existing products to the varying needs of the consumer. In some R & D programs, the major emphasis is on "research"; in others, on "development." Some programs are planned for an efficient short-term payoff, while others are meant to provide returns over a longer period. For the sake of uniformity, they use the terms "laboratory-oriented" and "market-oriented" to refer to the two contrasting types of programs.

In the laboratory-oriented new-products program the scientist-inventor is the key figure. He is a person of unusual scientific accomplishments, hired because his professional interests parallel those of his company. He is usually encouraged to pursue his own interests and to develop products which he thinks will provide his company a profit advantage. The fruits of his labors are passed on to the marketing man who must then determine a basis on which the invention can be profitably and effectively marketed.

The market-oriented new-products program, on the oriented program. In it, the marketability of a new product is virtually assured before development work is begun. Indeed, the proper stimulus for physical development of a product, in a market-oriented program, is evidence of the marketability of a particular product concept. Laboratory work, in a market-oriented program, is directed toward specific goals and is never speculative. The new products suggested by such a program very rarely involve great technological strides and so are unlikely to appear as scientific "break-throughs." They are more likely to be extensions of present technology, or modifications of existing products for greater convenience or increased effectiveness.

A laboratory-oriented research program must commit large sums of money to providing the facilities and manpower for much speculative basic research. New products which issue from this research may or *may not* be marketable—even if the research itself is well conceived and properly executed.

The margin between success and failure is incredibly slim, and no one can predict with certainty on which side of this margin the outcome of a particular research project will fall. Because we hear largely of the successes and seldom of the failures, we may lose sight of the fact that failure is the more common outcome of such research ventures. This means that the company committing itself to a laboratory-oriented new-products program must be ready, to underwrite the cost of many failures for each research effort that results in a marketable product.

The market-oriented new-products program also requires research, some of which may end in failure. In this case, however, the first investment is in *marketing*

Figure 4A

Reprinted with permission from the May 1963 issue of *Madison Avenue*.

other hand, is one in which the creative marketing expert is the dominant figure. He is hired because of his ability to identify market vacuums and consumer needs that his company can profitably fill. When he has identified a marketing opportunity, he writes the functional specifications for the new product and passes them on to the scientist. The laboratory man must then do his best to engineer a product which fits the marketing specifications.

The choice of a laboratory- or market-oriented program will have a decided effect on the type of new product which a company brings to market. Historically, the giant steps in new-product development have occurred within laboratory-oriented programs. For example, we would classify as "laboratory-oriented" the research programs which produced the electric light, penicillin and nylon.

The new products which issue from a market-oriented program are usually less dramatic, "evolutionary" changes. A marketing man may perceive the need, for example, for a filter on cigarettes, a ball applicator for a deodorant, pre-mixed cake ingredients, or a pouring spout on a soap package. None of these, obviously, qualifies as a product "breakthrough." Yet, innovations such as these have had marketing significance sufficient to bring fame and fortune to the companies that produced them.

In summary, revolutionary new products which virtually redefine a company's business and exert a profound social effect are likely to emerge only from a laboratory-oriented new-products program. The countless minor changes, which strengthen a company's leadership in a defined field by better adapting its products to the needs of its customers are most likely to issue from a market-oriented new-products program. Obviously, the two programs differ in the pay-off-period. They differ also in the cost-period. They differ also in the degree of risk involved. Lower costs and lower risks favor the market-

research, dealing mainly with concepts and ideas. Its cost and the cost of the company facilities required to support it, is modest by comparison with laboratory research.

A company that chooses to allocate a major portion of its new-products research effort to laboratory-oriented activities must accept the fact that profit flow from year to year will be quite uneven. Even the best of laboratory research programs cannot be counted on to produce a sensational new-product breakthrough every year. When a breakthrough *does* occur, however, the profit advantage, for a while, may be enormous. Thus, the profit flow from a laboratory-oriented new-products program takes the form of occasional tidal waves.

A market-oriented new-products program *can* be counted upon to generate product improvements or innovations in service on a fairly regular schedule—perhaps three or four a year. Profits from any individual development may not, however, be enormous. Thus, the profit flow would take the form of a series of regular ripples.

The pro's and con's of both types of new-product development programs may be summarized as follows:

• The laboratory-oriented program yields spectacular rewards for the rare product breakthrough. The rewards are so great that a single success can pay for many failures. But the costs of such a program are high, the pay-off irregular, and the risks great. The major costs of laboratory-oriented product development are necessarily incurred *before* the marketability of the product is assayed.

• The market-oriented program, on the other hand, yields smaller but substantial rewards for minor product improvements and adaptations to the customer's needs. The costs are relatively low and the pay-off more predictable. And major investments are incurred only after an indication of marketability has been secured. *This article was developed from a talk by Dr. Williams to an American Marketing Association conference.*

Figure 4A (*Cont.*)

Start time: _____ minutes; _____ seconds

End time: _____ minutes; _____ seconds

READING TIME: _____ minutes; _____ seconds

READING RATE TABLE

READING TIME (min.; sec.):	1:00	1:15	1:30	1:45	2:00	2:20	2:40	3:00	3:30	4:00	5:00
WORDS PER MINUTE:	1150	920	766	656	575	492	429	383	328	287	230

RECORD CLOSE-READING WPM SCORE: _____

Accuracy Statements:

Indicate whether the following statements are true or false and supply main points or details from the selection to defend your assertion.

1. The author suggests that the best road for new-produce development would be a combination of laboratory and market orientation.

   _____True; _____ False. Why? _____

   _____

2. The company that commits itself to laboratory-oriented program development must be ready to underwrite the cost of many failures for each research effort that results in a marketable product.

   _____True; _____ False. Why? _____

   _____

3. The author of the selection is biased in favor of the market-oriented approach to product development.

   _____True; _____ False. Why? _____

   _____

   Answers: 1. False. The author does not suggest any combination.
   2. True. Although we hear largely of the successes and seldom of the failures, we often do not realize that failure is the more common outcome of research effort.
   3. Could be true. The author, Williams, is Director of marketing intelligence for

Edward Dalton Company. He does stress the rate of failure, the expense before any assurance of marketability of the laboratory-oriented research. Perhaps an equally persuasive case can be built up for bias on the laboratory side.

STRUCTURING: ADVANCED APPLICATION

Skim-read the selection "Managers Must Manage" (Figure 4B). Before you start to skim-read, decide upon the meaning of the title and note the three subheadings that appear as part of the title. These will reappear as subheadings in the selection:

1. What is the manager's job?
2. The span of managerial responsibility.
3. The manager and his superior.

As you skim-read, use these subheadings as anchors in your structuring of the selection. Read the opening paragraph of each subheading, and as soon as you have been informed of the meaning of the subheading, move down to the next subheading and read the last paragraph. Be especially alert for a possible series of statements expanding on each subheading. Use the underlining of subheadings, beginning and end paragraphs, and topic sentences to help your skim-reading for main parts and general category. Go ahead and read Figure 4B, taking note of your start and finish times.

Start time: _____ minutes; _____ seconds

End time: _____ minutes; _____ seconds

SKIM-READING TIME: _____ minutes; _____ seconds

READING RATE TABLE

READING TIME (min.; sec.):	0:30	0:45	1:00	1:20	1:40	2:00	2:30	3:00	4:00	5:00
WORDS PER MINUTE:	2700	1800	1350	1012	810	675	540	450	338	270

RECORD SKIM-READING WPM SCORE: _____

Structure Statements

For each of the following structure statements, read the statement and then indicate whether you think the statement refers to the general category,

CHAPTER 12

MANAGERS MUST MANAGE

What is a manager's job?— The span of managerial responsibility—
The manager and his superior.

What Is a Manager's Job?

A manager's job should be based on a task to be performed in order to attain the company's objectives. It should always be a real job—one that makes a visible and, if possible, clearly measurable contribution to the success of the enterprise. It should have the broadest rather than the narrowest scope and authority; everything not expressly excluded should be deemed to be within the manager's authority. Finally, the manager should be directed and controlled by the objectives of performance rather than by his boss.

What managerial jobs are needed and what each of them is should always be determined by the activities that have to be performed, the contributions that have to be made to attain the company's objectives. A manager's job exists because the task facing the enterprise demands its existence—and for no other reason. It has its own necessity; it must therefore have its own authority and its own responsibility.

It should always be a job of managerial proportions. Since a manager is someone who takes responsibility for, and contributes to, the final results of the enterprise, the job must have sufficient scope. It should always embody the maximum challenge, carry the maxi-

mum responsibility and make the maximum contribution. And that contribution should be visible and measurable. The manager should be able to point at the final results of the entire business and say: "This part is my contribution."

* * *

The Span of Managerial Responsibility

In discussing how big a manager's job should be, the textbooks start out with the observation that one man can *supervise* only a very small number of people—the so-called "span of control." And this in turn leads to that deformation of management: levels upon levels, which impede co-operation and communication, stifle the development of tomorrow's managers and erode the meaning of the management job.

If the manager, however, is controlled by the objective requirements of his own job and measured by his results, there is no need for the kind of supervision that consists of telling a subordinate what to do and then making sure that he does it. There is no span of control. A superior could theoretically have any number of subordinates reporting to him. There is, indeed, a limit set by the "span of managerial responsibility" (the term was coined, I believe, by Dr. H. H. Race of General Electric): the number of people whom one superior can assist, teach and help to reach the objectives of their own jobs. This is a real limit; but it is not fixed.

The span of control, we are told, cannot exceed six or eight subordinates. The span of managerial responsibility, however, is determined by the extent to which assistance and teaching are needed. It can only be set by a study of the concrete situation. Unlike the span of control, the span of managerial responsibility broadens as we move upward in the organization. Junior managers need the most assistance; their objectives are least easy to define sharply, their performance least easy to measure concretely. Senior men, on the other hand, have supposedly learned how to do their job; and their objectives can be defined as directly contributing to the business, their performance measured by the yardsticks of business results.

The span of managerial responsibility is therefore wider than the span of control. (H. H. Race thinks that the theoretical limit is around a hundred.) And where good practice would counsel against stretching the span of control, a manager should always have responsibility for a few more men than he can really take care of.

Figure 4B

Otherwise the temptation is to supervise them, that is, to take over their jobs or, at least, to breathe down their necks.[1]

The Manager and His Superior

What then is the job of the manager's superior? What is his authority? What is his responsibility?

If only for aesthetic reasons, I am not over-fond of the term "Bottom-up Management," coined by William B. Given, Jr., of the American Brake Shoe Company.[2]

What it means, however, is important. The relationship between higher and lower manager is not just the downward relationship expressed in the term "supervision." Indeed, it is not even a two-way, up-and-down relationship. It has three dimensions: a relationship up from the lower to the higher manager; a relationship of every manager to the enterprise; and a relationship down from the higher to the lower manager. And every one of the three is essentially a responsibility—a duty rather than a right.

Every manager has the task of contributing what his superior's unit needs to attain its objectives. This is indeed his first duty. From it he derives the objectives of his own job.

He has secondly a duty toward the enterprise. He has to analyze the task of his own unit, and define the activities needed to attain its objectives. He has to establish the management jobs these activities require, and he has to help his managers to work together and to integrate their own interests with those of the enterprise. He has to put men in these jobs. He has to remove managers in his unit who fail to perform, reward those who perform well and see to it that those who perform superbly receive extraordinary return or promotion. He has to help the managers in his unit to develop to the limit of their capacities and prepare themselves for the management tasks of tomorrow.

These are heavy responsibilities. But they are not responsibilities for what somebody else—a subordinate—is doing. They are, as all responsibilities should be, responsibilities for what the manager himself is doing. They are inherent in his own job, not in those of his subordinates.

[1] This point has been made with a wealth of supporting evidence by James C. Worthy, formerly of Sears, Roebuck and now of the U. S. Department of Commerce.

[2] In his book Bottom-up Management, (New York: Harper & Brothers, 1949).

Finally, the manager has responsibilities downward, to his subordinate managers. He has first to make sure that they know and understand what is demanded of them. He has to help them set their own objectives. Then he has to help them to reach these objectives. He is therefore responsible for their getting the tools, the staff, the information they need. He has to help them with advice and counsel. He has, if need be, to teach them to do better.

If a one-word definition of this downward relationship be needed, "assistance" would come closest. Indeed, several successful companies—notably International Business Machines (IBM)—have defined the manager's job in relation to his subordinates as that of an "assistant" to them. Their jobs are theirs—by objective necessity. Their performance and results are theirs, and so is the responsibility. But it is the duty of the superior manager to help them all he can to attain their objectives. * * *

The objectives of a managerial unit should always and exclusively consist of the performance and results it has to contribute to the success of the enterprise. They should always and exclusively focus upward. But the objectives of the manager who heads the unit include what he himself has to do to help his subordinate managers attain their objectives. The vision of a manager should always be upward—toward the enterprise as a whole. But his responsibility runs downward as well—to the managers on his team. That his relationship toward them be clearly understood as duty rather than as supervision is perhaps the central requirement for organizing the manager's job effectively.

Figure 4B (Cont.)

a main point, or a detail in the selection. You may find it desirable to return to the earlier statements and change your choices if later statements alter their relative value.

1. The manager must be an "assistant" to his subordinates, just as his superior must be to him, in the task of realizing the objectives of the enterprise.
    _____a. General Category
    _____b. Main Point
    _____c. Detail

2. The textbook observation that a manager can effectively supervise only eight to ten people (the so-called "span of control") has led to an unfortunate piling up of management levels and consequently has impeded cooperation and communication.
    _____a. General Category
    _____b. Main Point
    _____c. Detail

3. A manager's job should be based on a task making a visible contribution to the success of the enterprise. His authority should be defined by the task, and his success determined by his fulfillment of the task. The manager's span of responsibility need not be limited to the so-called "span of control." The manager's relations with subordinates and superiors are channeled through their mutual responsibility for the objectives of the enterprise.
    _____a. General Category
    _____b. Main Points
    _____c. Details

4. The relationship of higher to lower management has three dimensions: the relationship up from the lower to the higher, the relationship of every manager at every level to the enterprise, and a relationship downward from the higher to the lower.
    _____a. General Category
    _____b. Main Points
    _____c. Details

5. A manager's job should always be a real job. It should have the broadest rather than the narrowest scope and authority. Finally, the manager

should be controlled by the objectives of performance rather than by his boss.

_____a. General Category

_____b. Main Points

_____c. Details

Answers: 1. b

2. c

3. a

4. b

5. b

Your skim-reading has enabled you to establish the general category of the selection, to single out the main points, and even to recognize some details. In your own reading of this selection, you might at this point prefer to go no further or you might decide to read further about only one of the main points. For the purposes of this exercise, let us assume as we did in the last exercise that you now wish to read the whole article quite carefully. You will not only deepen your awareness of the main points by noting details in this thorough reading, but you will also be able to read "between-the-lines" and be aware of what has been excluded from the selection.

Now go back and read the "Managers Must Manage" selection (Figure 4B) thoroughly, making use of your mastery of main points and the general category in order to vary your reading speed and attack.

Start time: _____ minutes; _____ seconds

End time: _____ minutes; _____ seconds

READING TIME: _____ minutes; _____ seconds

RECORD WPM SCORE FOR CLOSE-READING: _____

Indicate whether the following statements are true or false and supply main points or details from the selection to defend your choice.

1. There is a real, but not fixed, limit to the number of men for whom a manager can accept managerial responsibility.

_____True; _____False. *Why?* _____

_____.

2. A manager's job should have a narrowly defined and specific authority.

____True; ____False. *Why?* _____

_____.

3. The most effective method of keeping the objectives of the enterprise foremost in the minds of managers and their superiors and subordinates has been profit-sharing arrangements based on the fulfillment of stated goals.

____True; ____False. *Why?* _____

_____.

4. The picture of management suggested by this selection is an ideal, and this ideal is not likely to occur in reality.

____True; ____False. *Why?* _____

_____.

Answers: 1. True. The limit is the number of people the manager can assist, teach, and help. The limit varies according to the amount of assistance, teaching, and help the subordinates need.
2. False. It should have the broadest scope and authority; everything not expressly excluded should be deemed to be within the manager's authority.
3. False. There is no mention of profit sharing in the selection.
4. Could be either true or false. Your answer will probably reflect your own experiences. The author does try to support his point of view with references to General Electric, American Brake Shoe Company, and IBM.

STRUCTURING: INDEPENDENT APPLICATION

For independent application to your own reading matter, you might like to try a written structure exercise that can be very helpful to a thorough understanding of structural principles. Take a blank sheet of paper and construct a large pyramid with the general category at the top, the main points below that, and the details at the foot of the triangle.

GENERAL
CATEGORY

MAIN   MAIN   MAIN   MAIN

POINT   POINT   POINT   POINT

details   details   details   details   details   details

Now turn back to Figure 1B and attempt to find the structure of the newspaper article from *The New York Times,* "Algerians Seek to Heal Dispute." When you are structuring your own material on paper, remember that the position you give each element depends upon its *relative* value. You may wish to change some of your choices after you have reviewed all of the units in your pyramid. Therefore, it is best to skim-read the article first to determine the relative values of topic sentences in relation to the title, and then read the article thoroughly to digest supporting details and note possible implications.

You may wish to compare your own structure of the article with the sample structure illustrated in Figure 4C.

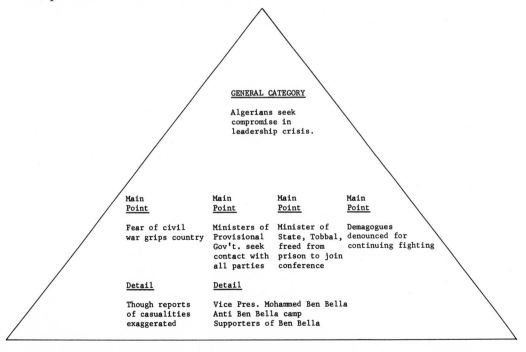

Figure 4C Sample structure of the New York Times article on "Algerians Seek to Heal Dispute":

Continue to make written structures from your own reading until you are confident that you can organize and relate essential elements *just as well in your mind.*

STRUCTURING: FURTHER INDEPENDENT APPLICATION

In the selections thus far, you had to extract the main points from a mass of illustrations, details, and even irrelevant material, and you had to notice what was said as well as what was left out. In the following application from *Fortune,* however, you will find that the magazine has done some of the work of structuring for you. The editors have supplied not only a table of contents for the issue, but also a review—or overview—of the issue, called "Fortune's Wheel." This section of the magazine presents the general category and main points of each article, so that you can decide very quickly whether or not the article falls within your range of interest. "Fortune's Wheel" also gives you the chance to get some general idea of developments in areas that would not normally be your concern.

If you were, let us say, in personnel for an electronics company, you might not be inclined to read an entire article on the ladies' garment industry or the farm problems being encountered by the European Economic Community. However, through the summaries supplied to you in "Fortune's Wheel," you have the chance to increase the breadth of your knowledge and possibly to discover something of value to your own business or profession.

We would now like you to read the Table of Contents and "Fortune's Wheel" from the May 1963 issue of *Fortune* (Figures 4D-a and 4D-b). Assuming that you are the personnel man described above, you would probably choose to read *Fortune's* own review of the first three articles. Therefore, for this exercise, record your overall reading time for the Table of Contents *and* for a thorough reading of the first three reviews in "Fortune's Wheel," rather than skim-reading them. After all, they are already condensations. You might also glance at the reviews of the other articles whose titles you noticed on the Table of Contents page. After this reading, answer the structure and accuracy statements.

Start time: _____ minutes; _____ seconds

End time: _____ minutes; _____ seconds

READING TIME: _____ minutes; _____ seconds

FORTUNE

May 1963

FORTUNE, May 1963. Vol. LXVII, No. 5
Published monthly by Time Inc.,
540 N. Michigan Ave., Chicago 11, Illinois
Subscriptions: U.S., U.S. possessions, and
Canada, one year $10; elsewhere, one
year $15. Single copies $1.25
Address all subscriptions and correspondence
concerning them to FORTUNE, 540 N. Michigan
Ave., Chicago 11, Illinois

Picture credits page 228

Figure 4D-a

111

FORTUNE'S WHEEL:

the contents of this issue in brief

Labor Unions Are Worth the Price

When George Meany says, "Strikes are part of the American way of life," he is not exulting in labor's power to disrupt, but rather expressing awareness that there are no known alternatives to collective bargaining that would not do far more damage to the American system.

Strikes actually reduced workers' time on the job by only one-sixth of 1 percent last year, but the public has somehow become convinced that the burden of strikes is growing and "intolerable." Amid the new wave of anti-unionism, labor's onetime friends, the "liberal intellectuals," are urging that government intervene more and more in labor disputes. Such regulation of labor terms repre-

sents a danger that could become more serious than the cost of strikes or of inefficiencies imposed by union contracts.

With all their faults, unions are more compatible with the market system than government wage-fixing would be. Moreover, in a period of rapid industrial change, American unionism contributes psychological, social, and political benefits to society that outweigh its economic costs.

When the Crowd Goes One Way, Litton Goes the Other

Less than a decade ago Litton Industries was one small microwave-tube company with $9-million annual sales. This year, after buying (mostly by swaps of stock) thirty-seven companies that have seventy-one U.S. and foreign plants, Litton is committed in dozens of fields and is ringing up sales of about $540 million.

An investment of $1,000 in Litton at its start would now be worth more than $85,000. Some bears say the common, about thirty times earnings, is too high,

that Litton's growth must taper off. The optimists who run the company make a good case for its heading upward for years.

Complex, intuitive Chairman Charles B. Thornton and coolly logical President Roy L. Ash guide their empire with a minimum of staff, and depend greatly on the entrepreneurial capacity of the men who head the divisions. Thornton and Ash chiefly provide the timing of acquisitions and coordinate the growth. One of their decisions, for instance, was to head now for inner, as well as outer, space—building attack submarines and the sophisticated electronic gear that goes into them. They also have expanding plans for commercial products. Moreover, they seem to have the money and personnel to carry them through.

Bringing Engineers Up to Date

"I once took my eyes off the blackboard to wipe my glasses and missed a whole semester of math." This report by a student only slightly exaggerates the demands of new cram courses in Modern Engineering now available to technical managers.

Advanced courses in management have long been provided for the engineer turned manager. But missing were courses to update such men in the basic new scientific concepts necessary for them

to continue to understand and direct specialists under them. The vacuum led U.C.L.A. to set up a six-week course, now about to start its third summer session near Los Angeles. Tuition and lodging run to almost $2,500 and the intellectual tax is severe, but participants say they profit.

Meanwhile General Electric and other companies and schools are inaugurating similar cram courses.

Figure 4D-b

"Medicare," the Cure That Could Cause a Setback

131

▶ Today 75 percent of the U.S. population is covered by private health insurance. Blue Cross alone has grown from 2,874,000 members in 1938 to 58,109,000 today.

▶ Of persons over sixty-five, about 55 percent have already provided themselves with health insurance. And this coverage may top 75 percent by 1970.

Many politicians, and others with an ax to grind, ignore the implication of these and similar little-appreciated facts. Prosperous times, enterprising private insurers, and improved relief provisions have left only a diminishing segment of the population in need of help to pay hospital and related bills. The problem of medical care for persons sixty-five and older is now acute for less than a third of that group.

In terms of legislation this calls for a program much more closely geared to the need than is any bill yet proposed. This article examines the precise dimensions of the need. And it discusses how to meet this need with a minimum of new bureaucracy and maximum use of existing nongovernmental agencies.

It's an International "Farm Mess" Now

135

The policy of protecting farmers by guaranteeing them artificially high support prices, paying them subsidies, and restricting competing imports has long been distorting the economics of Europe just as it has of the U.S. Now it has become a formidable obstacle to European unity and freer world trade.

The European Economic Community is trying to establish a common market for agriculture as well as industry. That involves reconciling the conflicting interests of member countries. The French, with half the arable land in the EEC, would like to be the breadbasket of the community; the Germans fear that their high-cost small farmers would be driven off the land.

Now agriculture threatens to stymie the forthcoming tariff negotiations under the U.S. Trade Expansion Act. Washington warns it will hold up tariff bargaining on industrial products unless it gets assurances that U.S. farm products, a third of our total exports to the EEC countries, won't be excluded by Common Market protectionist measures.

The authors probe a subject that soon may make crisis headlines.

How NSF Got Lost in Mohole

138

Eighteen years ago, when Dr. Vannevar Bush explained to the U.S. how that delicate bloom, basic science, could absorb government nourishment without being wilted by the inclement atmosphere of bureaucracy, FORTUNE gave him a sounding board. His "Science, The Endless Frontier" was printed in condensation as a supplement to the September, 1945, issue. Congress followed his recommendation and set up the National Science Foundation. After a dozen years of fine creative work sponsoring research with the advice of the scientific community, NSF came up against Project Mohole and took off on its own. The result is a mess involving one of the most promising of basic projects in Big Science.

Mohole is the project to drill three miles through the crust of the earth, underseas where it's thinnest. The scientists who conceived and started it saw this as likely to produce cores whose analysis could be fabulously revealing about the beginnings of life. They also hoped to study the globe's mantle itself, that mysterious stratum beneath the crust. And pioneering engineers saw Mohole as a stimulus to new technological developments of great value to the oil and other industries.

But NSF brushed aside scientists who originated the project, and now the Mohole Project is experiencing severe budgetary inflation and dragging delay.

Up from Gothic

142

What has the swelling tide of college students done to the looks of the American campus?

Here is a portfolio showing a baker's dozen of recent collegiate structures. Representative of the best of the buildings on which U.S. colleges are now spending a billion a year, these halls illustrate the architectural variety that is replacing traditional Gothic and Georgian.

But not all—or even most—new buildings around the country are beautiful. Students from Columbia University to the University of Texas consider innovations on their campuses eyesores, and have organized "anti-ugly" protests. An article accompanying the portfolio, "College Architecture: The Economics and Aesthetics," on page 148, discusses the reasons for changing style and the frequent ugliness. One is money. To take care of an expected 5,260,000 students by 1965 (up from 3,570,000 in 1960), college administrators say needed buildings will cost 15 or 20 percent more than funds available from all present sources.

$100 Million in "Rags"

151

"Mr. Schwartz is an easy man to hate," says an associate. But several of his rivals in the ladies' garment industry would probably be willing to be hated if it would put them where Schwartz's Jonathan Logan, Inc., has just landed: at the top of the $4-billion industry, with sales last year of $81 million.

Irascible David Schwartz himself feels an intense personal rivalry, if less than hatred, for the head of the firm he has just overtaken in the sweepstakes—imperious Maurice Saltzman of Bobbie Brooks, Inc., whose 1962 sales were $75 million. And

Schwartz is determined to beat the younger Saltzman across the $100-million line, once considered a mark no firm in the "rag" industry would ever reach.

The race for $100 million in sales calls attention to the changed ways of many garmentmakers and their customers. The latter wear more casual clothes, which change style less often. This makes possible more stable, larger-scale production. And the business itself is becoming more businesslike.

Figure 4D-b (Cont.)

READING RATE TABLE

READING TIME (min.; sec.):	0:30	0:45	1:00	1:15	1:30	1:45	2:00
WORDS PER MINUTE:	400	266	200	160	133	114	100

RECORD YOUR WPM SCORE: _____

If you spent two minutes reading the Table of Contents and the first three reviews of Fortune's Wheel, you have become *familiar* with the contents of about 10,000 words of text. You cannot claim to be reading at 5000 words per minute, but you have *other information at that rate*. For one or more of the articles, you might wish to skim-read the article itself, and then perhaps read it thoroughly. Each prior step would contribute to the efficiency of the next.

Structure and Accuracy Statements

1. Two main points supporting the claim that "Labor Unions are Worth the Price" are:

   a. _____

   _____

   _____

   b. _____

   _____

   _____

2. The summary for "When the Crowd Goes One Way, Litton Goes the Other" does not give enough information for you to determine the broad category or even the main points in relation to the title of the article. However, one significant detail is given that helps explain the title. What is it?

   _____

   _____

   _____

3. The broad category of "Bringing Engineers Up to Date" would involve a statement of the problem and its background, a statement of the solution, and some idea of its success. Give this information as concisely as you can.

_____

_____

_____

4. Describe one other article whose title and review caught your interest. Indicate its broad category or simply list a main point or significant detail.

_____

_____

_____

> *Answers*: 1-a. Unions are more compatible with the market system than government wage-fixing would be.
> 1-b. American unionism contributes psychological, social, and political benefits to society.
> 2. Litton is heading for inner space as well as outer space, building attack submarines and the sophisticated gear that goes into them.
> 3. Management courses have been available for engineers-turned-manager; but until UCLA set up its six week course, there were no courses to keep manager-engineers up-to-date to work with newly trained specialists under them. Participants say they profit from the program, and GE, among others, is starting similar courses.
> 4. Check back with the summary to determine your accuracy.

By making use of the structural assist built into *Fortune,* you are able to discover immediately articles that will be of interest to you; in addition, you are able to categorize the entire contents of the magazine, so that if something related to one of the articles comes up, you will be able to turn to the appropriate article for information. Some marginal notation in "Fortune's Wheel" will direct your later review of the publication.

Now that you have found the structure of an entire magazine, you will proceed to seek out the structure from part of a longer article in *Consumer*

Reports. However, for the purpose of this exercise, and in consideration of the length of the entire article, only the first part of the article, "We Are Living in an Epidemic," (1750 words) will be used. The full text for Parts II, III, and IV of the article has been omitted.

Begin your skim-reading for main points and the general category by reading the title and the table of contents, noting particularly the sub-headings for Part I, since that is the part you are going to structure. Then continue your skim-reading of the topic sentences. Note that as soon as you have been able to decide just what the subheading means, you can shift to the next subheading and the succeeding topic sentences. (Use the under-lining to help you skim-read this article.) Remember that your skim-reading is only fact-gathering to grasp the main points of what is stated and to recognize their relation to the general category. Skim-read Part I, section by section, timing yourself on each section, and as soon as you have finished it state the main point covered by each section. When you have stated the main points for all the sections, write the broad category which encompasses the general thesis of this part.

As in past exercises, you are to write down your start and finish times as you skim-read each section. However, you are not to convert your skim-reading into a words-per-minute score until after you have completed your skim-reading of the fourth section.

READ "THE AUTOPSY EVIDENCE" (Figure 4E-a)

Start time: _____ minutes; _____ seconds

End time: _____ minutes; _____ seconds

SKIM-READING TIME: _____ minutes; _____ seconds

State the main point of this section.

_____

_____

READ "THE DEATH RATE EVIDENCE" (Figure 4E-b)

Start time: _____ minutes; _____ seconds

End time: _____ minutes; _____ seconds

SKIM-READING TIME: _____ minutes; _____ seconds

The survey on this and the next 15 pages, in CU's judgment, constitutes a significant contribution to understanding of one of the most controversial health issues of the day. The material presented here, specially edited for this issue of the REPORTS, will appear in fuller form in "The Consumers Union Report on Smoking and the Public Interest," a major new CU book now on the press. The book, of which the section following represents about one-fifth, will be published during June, 1963. See back cover for details.

SMOKING
AND LUNG CANCER

By RUTH AND EDWARD BRECHER *working with the Editors*

of CONSUMER REPORTS, *CU's Medical Adviser, and other authorities*

A broad-scale, point-by-point review of the whole range of evidence implicating cigarettes in what has now become an international health problem. In four Parts:

I. WE ARE LIVING IN AN EPIDEMIC
  The autopsy evidence
  The death rate evidence
  Combining the evidence
  The inescapable conclusion

II. THE STATISTICAL EVIDENCE
  Occupation exposure studies
  Correlation studies
  Retrospective studies
  The Seventh Day Adventist study
  The negative evidence
  Prospective studies

III. THE EXPERIMENTAL EVIDENCE
  Statistics and plausibility
  The inherent nature of cancer
  Carcinogens and co-carcinogens
  Mucus, cilia, irritation
  Smoke and the lungs of mice
  "Mice are not men"

IV. SUMMING UP
  "Cause"—the great red herring
  The experts speak out
  Smoking is not the only "cause"
  Lung cancer is not inevitable

I. WE ARE LIVING IN AN EPIDEMIC

The autopsy evidence

IN October 1920. a young University of Minnesota pathologist, Dr. Moses Barron, performed an autopsy on a 46-year-old male patient known in the medical records as L.H., and determined that he had died of lung cancer (primary carcinoma of the lung). This seemed curious, for another University of Minnesota pathologist had performed an autopsy two months before on a 42-year-old male patient, and had also found lung cancer. And then still another death from lung cancer was found later in the same month of October.

Dr. Barron had always supposed that cancer of the lung was an exceedingly rare disease. Sometimes a whole year went by without a single case among University of Minnesota autopsies. Three cases in three months aroused Dr. Barron's interest. During the months that followed his interest grew, for additional cases turned up at a rapid rate. Startled, now, Dr. Barron went back over the university's autopsy records and unearthed some facts

Figure 4E

117

SMOKING AND LUNG CANCER
continued

which he reported to the Minnesota State Medical Society meetings on August 25, 1921.

During the 20-year period from 1899 through 1918, Dr. Barron's study revealed, only four cases of lung cancer had been identified at autopsy by University of Minnesota pathologists. There had been only one case in 1919. Yet during the single year from July 1, 1920 through June 30, 1921, eight lung cancer cases had turned up. Was this, perhaps, the onset of an epidemic?

Pathologists generally present their statistics in a standard form: number of autopsies, number of cases of one kind, percentage of these cases to all autopsies. Thus a rate of 0.1% means one case in a thousand autopsies, while 1.0% means one case in a hundred. Cast in this form, Dr. Barron's figures revealed the following remarkable increase in lung cancer deaths:

1899 through 1918	0.1%	(4 deaths in 3399 autopsies)
1919 to July 1921	0.9%	(9 deaths in 1003 autopsies)

The conclusion seemed inescapable, and Dr. Barron cautiously drew it in 1921. "This disease," he wrote, "is apparently increasing in frequency, especially during the past few years." And he was right. For the period 1949 through 1952 the University of Minnesota rate reached 3.2% (264 lung cancer deaths in 8332 autopsies).

In various other parts of the world, autopsy records were telling substantially the same story. A rise was quite generally apparent, earlier in some places, later in others, often at about the same time as Dr. Barron's findings. Here, for example, are lung cancer rates drawn at five-year intervals from the autopsy records of the Charité Hospital in Berlin:

1908	0.3%	1918	0.6%
1913	0.4%	1923	1.5%

And here are the figures, for five-year periods, from Zurich, Switzerland:

1906-1910	0.1%	1916-1920	0.7%
1911-1915	0.5%	1921-1925	2.1%

All of the autopsy records, it is true, did not fit precisely this pattern. At the Royal Infirmary in Manchester, England, for example, the increase which Dr. Barron had noted in 1921 was visible much earlier. In Reykjavik, Iceland, lung cancer rates at autopsy remained low as late as 1948. But by and large the trend was irregularly upward beginning about 1920.

An autopsy series of particular value comes from Presbyterian Hospital in New York City, where Dr. David M. Spain reviewed the autopsy findings for the 45-year period from 1912 through 1956. The diagnosis of lung cancer depends primarily on the microscopic examination of cells taken from the lungs; Presbyterian Hospital had maintained microphotographs of cancer cells for its earlier autopsies and had actually preserved the cells themselves in microscope slides for the later autopsies, so that Dr. Spain was able to review the entire series personally and

confirm or correct the diagnoses. His figures showed the following increase in lung cancer deaths:

1912-1921	0.6%	(6 deaths in 992 autopsies)
1922-1931	1.3%	(21 deaths in 1649 autopsies)
1932-1941	2.8%	(83 deaths in 2950 autopsies)
1942-1946	3.4%	(49 deaths in 1449 autopsies)
1947-1956	3.7%	(120 deaths in 3250 autopsies)

What was happening at Presbyterian Hospital was also happening at the University of Michigan, where 14,000 autopsies were performed from 1895 through 1954. As at Presbyterian Hospital, materials from the earlier University of Michigan autopsies were preserved and reviewed from time to time to confirm the lung cancer diagnoses and to make sure that cases diagnosable as lung cancer by modern standards had not been missed during the earlier years. The figures show a remarkably steady rise in lung cancer incidence for each thousand autopsies in the series:

CASES OF LUNG CANCER			
1st thousand	0.2%	8th thousand	2.2
2nd thousand	0.8	9th thousand	2.4
3rd thousand	1.0	10th thousand	2.6
4th thousand	1.4	11th thousand	3.1
5th thousand	1.8	12th thousand	3.9
6th thousand	2.1	13th thousand	3.4
7th thousand	2.2	14th thousand	4.2

The rate thus rose from 0.2% to 4.2% during the sixty-year period from 1895 through 1954—more than a twenty-fold increase. (Comparable figures for University of Michigan autopsies since 1954 are not available.)

The death rate evidence

The autopsy figures presented above are all subject to a major shortcoming. They include for the most part only patients who died in hospitals and whose relatives consented to an autopsy. Evidence concerning so highly selected a group cannot be uncritically applied to the population as a whole. Suppose, for example, that during the early years of a series most lung cancer patients died at home; and that as time passed a larger and larger proportion died in hospitals and came to autopsy. This trend of events might have produced an *apparent* increase in lung cancer of the kind described above without any *actual* increase in the disease. To rule out this and other possibilities of this kind, the causes of deaths in a total population rather than an autopsied population must be considered. For this purpose death certificates offer the broadest possible evidence.

The death certificate data fully confirm the data from autopsies.

In the United States, for example, only 371 deaths were attributed to lung cancer in 1914. This number rose to 36,420 in 1960. FIGURE 1 shows the increase in graph form year by year from 1930 on.

This epidemic, moreover, has not been limited to the United States. Indeed, the rise among men in Scotland, England, Wales, Finland, and some other countries has been even steeper.

Combining the evidence

Just as the autopsy evidence may be doubted on the

Figure 4E (Cont.)

SMOKING AND LUNG CANCER
continued

ground that the sample of deaths coming to autopsy is a selected and untypical sample, so it is possible to doubt the death certificate evidence on the ground that physicians who fill out the certificates are not always sure of what *really* caused the death—and, in some cases, they may be merely guessing. Neither kind of evidence by itself proves that there was an actual increase in lung cancer deaths.

But when the autopsy evidence is combined with the death certificate evidence, the proof emerges very clearly. The figures based on autopsies performed by skilled pathologists at the world's great medical centers cannot be dismissed as mere guesswork; and the lung cancer death rates covering substantially all of the deaths in a dozen different countries cannot be dismissed as due to biased sampling. The criticisms of each body of evidence are answered by the fact that the other body of evidence tells the same story.

This theme of combining the evidence will reappear throughout this discussion. Only rarely can a single study, observation, or experiment stand by itself. Each of the studies we will report is subject to qualifications and limitations. But the points not covered in one study are soon covered by another study. Thus a wall of evidence is gradually erected.

During the early years of the lung cancer epidemic it was sometimes argued that the apparent increase in the disease might result from improved methods of diagnosis among physicians filling out death certificates, and from a greater alertness to lung cancer among pathologists performing autopsies.

No doubt a part of the apparent increase is due to such factors, but many separate lines of evidence indicate that most of the apparent increase is in fact a true increase.

First, the simple bulk of the increase makes improved diagnosis an inadequate explanation. Physicians and university pathologists prior to the 1920's might conceivably have missed one-half of the lung cancer deaths, though that is most unlikely. But it is utterly inconceivable that they should have missed nine lung cancer deaths out of every 10 or 19 out of every 20.

Second, improvements in diagnosis also occurred with respect to such forms of cancer as stomach cancer. Yet no comparable rise in reported stomach cancer rates generally, or in cancer at other internal sites, has occurred.

Third, lung cancer is as easy to diagnose among women as among men. The proportion of the increase due to improved diagnosis must therefore make its appearance in the women's rate as well as the men's rate. Even if the entire increase in lung cancer among women shown in FIGURE 2 were attributed to improved diagnosis—a most dubious assumption—the far more rapid increase among men would remain unexplained.

Fourth, the attempt to explain away the increase as merely the result of improved diagnosis comes to grief on the rock of the well established fact that, to this very day, cancer of the lung remains a rare disease among certain groups.

Among Seventh Day Adventists, for example, the disease is almost unknown, and the few cases which do occur are primarily in recent converts. Lung cancer is as easy to diagnose in Seventh Day Adventists as in Baptists, Methodists, Catholics, Jews, or atheists. If the lung cancer increase were merely the result of improved diagnosis, the Seventh Day Adventist rate would be expected to rise with the other rates.

Finally, there is the strange but unchallenged fact that lung cancer remains today a rare disease among men and women who do not smoke and who never have smoked. It is also relatively uncommon among men who smoke cigars or pipes or both, but not cigarettes. Improved diagnosis, to the extent that it has affected the statistics through the years, would have produced a rise among non-smokers, pipe smokers, and cigar smokers as well as among cigarette smokers. The excess rise among cigarette smokers cannot be explained by improved diagnosis.

The inescapable conclusion

The conclusion is inescapable, and even spokesmen for the cigarette industry today rarely seek to escape it: We are living in the midst of a major lung cancer epidemic. This epidemic hit men first and hardest, but has affected women as well. It is occurring not only in the United States but in a number of other countries. It cannot be explained away by such factors as improved diagnosis. And, there's reason to believe that the worst is yet to come.

The American Public Health Association has called attention to this black future in a single dramatic statistic.

Figure 4E (Cont.)

State the main points of the section.

_____

_____

READ "COMBINING THE EVIDENCE" (Figure 4E-c)

Start time: _____ minutes; _____ seconds

End time: _____ minutes; _____ seconds

SKIM-READING TIME: _____ minutes; _____ seconds

State the main point of this section:

_____

_____

READ "THE INESCAPABLE CONCLUSION" (Figure 4E-d)

Start time: _____ minutes; _____ seconds

End time: _____ minutes; _____ seconds

SKIM-READING TIME: _____ minutes; _____ seconds

State the main point of this section:

_____

_____.

State the general category that encompasses the main points drawn from the four sections you skim-read. _____

_____.

Answers: 1. Autopsy records indicate that lung cancer deaths have increased steadily from 1920 on.
2. The death certificate data fully confirm the data from the autopsies.
3. The criticisms of each body of evidence are answered by the fact that the other body of evidence tells the same story.

4. We are living in the midst of a major lung cancer epidemic.

5. Autopsy records and death certificates, each confirming the other, indicate that we are in the midst of a major lung cancer epidemic.

Total reading times for all 4 sections: _____ minutes; _____ seconds.

READING RATE TABLE

READING TIME:	0:45	1:00	1:15	1:30	1:45	2:00	2:20	2:40	3:00	3:30	4:00
WORDS PER MINUTE:	2333	1750	1400	1166	1000	875	750	656	583	500	437

RECORD YOUR TOTAL SKIM-READING WPM SCORE: _____

By using a combination of skim-reading and structuring, you have distilled the essentials from this article. Unless you have some special interest in the whole argument given here, you would not normally go back to read the article thoroughly. Your reading for structure has given you the essence. If you do wish to read the article thoroughly, this skim-reading for main points will make the close reading much easier and will also help insure your recall of what you have read.

STRUCTURING: CORRESPONDENCE APPLICATION

Your ability to structure in correspondence is necessary not only for *your* thorough understanding of what should be done with the correspondence, but also for the understanding of the subsequent individuals with whom you communicate. Hence, the skill becomes the means by which you can read for important information and then relay your thoughts or decision effectively to someone else. Without this organization and clear relationship of the less important act to the operation of the whole, there results confusion, chaos, and incorrect decisions.

Test your ability at quickly structuring a piece of correspondence by skim-reading the letter illustrated in Figure 4F, using the underlined sections as a guide. As you skim-read, try to extract mentally the general category and the main points and then check your structure by answering the following questions.

On the basis of your skim-reading alone, indicate whether the statement refers to a general category, a main point, or a detail in the letter:

PEABODY AND SONS
Investment Consultants

June 26, 1963

Mr. Harvey Grey
552 Park Avenue
New York, New York

Dear Mr. Grey:

In answer to your query of last week regarding the Graham Rental Company Inc., let me assure you that in my view this company is firmly established as a successful concern.

Starting as a two-man operation just ten years ago, renting only sickroom and convalescent supplies, this company, in its first five years of existance, increased its staff to twenty-five and expanded into the field of home supply and appliance rental. Total sales the first year were only $8,000 with 700 rentals, but in its fifth year the company was grossing over $75,000 and renting over 100 items per day.

In its next five years the company continued to expand, increasing gross sales by almost 200%, and at the same time reducing overhead costs to raise the net return from 5% to 7½%. In this period the company began to diversify its investments, converting two small apartment buildings in Manhattan to low-rental nursing homes for the aged.

At present, Graham Rental is planning to move into the auto and truck rental fields, on a monthly contractual basis that provides for unlimited mileage. This move appears to have good prospects, since it will provide the only car rental in the city that favors long distance, short-term driving.

On the basis of past performance and future prospects, I feel that this company gives every indication of being a sound investment.

Yours very truly

Jay Peabody III

Figure 4F

1. The company started as a two-man operation.
     _____a. General Category.
     _____b. Main Point.
     _____c. Detail.

2. In light of the Graham Rental Company's successful history and future prospects, it would probably be a good investment.
     _____a. General Category.
     _____b. Main Point.
     _____c. Detail.

3. "In its next five years the company continued to expand . . . ."
     _____a. General Category.
     _____b. Main Point.
     _____c. Detail.

4. The company is about to expand into the auto and truck rental fields.
     _____a. General Category.
     _____b. Main Point.
     _____c. Detail.

Answers: 1. c—lines 4–6
2. a—lines 19–20
3. b—line 10
4. b—line 15

Now read the letter thoroughly. Keeping the organization and pattern of the letter firmly in mind, relate each detail to the main point which it develops.

Answer the following questions to check the accuracy of your detailed reading:

5. Total sales increased from $8,000 in the first year to $75,000 in the fifth.
     True_____; False_____.

6. In its next five years, the company began to move into the auto and truck rental business.
     True_____; False_____.

7. The significant feature of the company's auto and truck rental plan is the provision for unlimited mileage.
     True_____; False_____.

8. Favorable analysis of the company is based in each main point on both expansion and diversification.

True____; False____.

Answers: 5. True
6. False
7. True
8. True

Once you learn to recognize the structural pattern in your reading, you are able to understand what needs to be done. If the material is well-organized, this can be done without great difficulty. But if the material is poorly organized, you may have to impose a structure upon it.

STRUCTURE MODEL #1

THE ORGANIZATIONAL TABLE

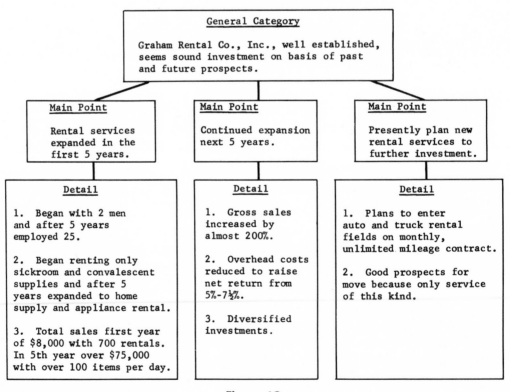

Figure 4G

STRUCTURE MODEL #2

THE INDENTED OUTLINE

I. Graham Rental Co., Inc., well established seems sound investment.

    A. First 5 years - expansion

        1. Began with 2 men and after 5 years employed 25.
        2. Began renting only sickroom and convalescent supplies and after
            5 years expanded to home supply and appliance rental.
        3. Total sales first year of $8,000 with 700 rentals. In 5th year
            over $75,000 with over 100 items per day.

    B. Second 5 years - continued expansion

        1. Gross sales increased by almost 200%.
        2. Overhead costs reduced to raise net return from 5%-7½%.
        3. Diversified investments.

    C. Present plans - further expansion and new rental services

        1. Plans to enter auto and truck rental fields on monthly, unlimited
            mileage contract.

        2. Good prospects for move because only service of this kind.

Figure 4H

In order to organize material as you read or write, you can use several types of structural aids. The two most helpful kinds of structure models are the organizational table and the indented outline. Both models are developed in Figures 4G and 4H from the letter you have just read.

SUMMARY

You must structure in order to be understood and to understand what you read. Without the ability to recognize main ideas, to relate them, and to see their significance when presented as a whole, there is no comprehension. In reality, then, you have been structuring written material most of your life. Yet, for you—for most people—the technique has probably been practiced unconsciously and inconsistently. When you are interested in the material and have a good background in the subject matter, you should have relatively little trouble in recognizing what is important and what is not, and in relating ideas to each other. But then, there are the many times when you are not particularly interested in what you are reading, or when the subject matter is new to you, or the material has not been especially well presented by the author, or the complexity of the reading is a little greater than what you are used to. When some or all of these conditions exist, understanding may take far longer than it has to and be far less complete than it might be, unless you can make structuring a deliberate and conscious process.

Once you have assimilated the technique of structuring, you have at your command one of the most powerful of all reading tools. We have given you sample readings to test you and have urged that you try written structuring of your own reading for practice in depth. Yet, the desired outcome is that you become so confident of your ability to recognize significant facts, main points, and concepts, that structuring will be an almost entirely mental procedure. When you find yourself automatically using skim-reading for the overall organization and content, then close reading for the supporting details, with constant questioning about the relationship from one part to another, you are probably well on your way to the mastery of the structuring technique, necessary not only for comprehension but also for lasting recall.

SKILL REMINDER

To structure, do this:

1. Skim-read for general category and main points.
2. Close-read for supporting details and implications.
3. Keep in mind the relationship of each part to the whole.
4. Notice common structural patterns.

CONCENTRATION

How to put your mind to work and KEEP it working

Skill

V

What the Skill Is: The ability to overcome distractions by making full use of your resources to maintain interest in your reading material.

What Concentration Does: Helps you to read with greater interest, greater command of the facts, increased speed, and more complete retention of relevant information.

How to Use It: In order to concentrate, the worst possible act is to *try* to concentrate. You will bring fullest attention to your reading, not when you are attempting to force yourself to keep your mind on it, but when you are actively engaged with the material. In other words, your objective is to create a dialogue between yourself and the printed page. Four major resources which will enable you to develop this dialogue are:

QUESTIONING
ANTICIPATING
VISUALIZING
SUMMARIZING

▶ QUESTIONING: The skill of concentrating begins as soon as you pick up the reading

127

material. Before you open the book, ask yourself questions based on the title, what you know of the author, and on your own purpose in reading the material. Suppose you were reading a book called *The Future of Automation in Middle Management Areas.* The simplest, the easiest, the most significant question to ask yourself is: "How will automation affect middle management?" As you read the book, you will keep your first, basic question in mind as an active aid to concentration. If you are unable to answer your own question at the end of the book, you will know quite definitely that you have not gotten much out of it in response to your initial interest.

▶ ANTICIPATING: Questioning leads directly to the skill of anticipating. As you are raising questions, look ahead, try to figure out what the author will say in the next sentence, the next paragraph, and even the next page. If you are right in your projection, well and good. If you are wrong, it may indicate a weakness in the author's argument, or you may find that your own understanding of a preceding point was inadequate. In either case, anticipating actively involves your mind with the author and his material.

▶ VISUALIZING: While the first two concentration skills involve your mind with the material, the third skill, visualizing, concerns your imagination. Use your senses to help create an image of the reading selection. This is often easy in exciting novels, mysteries, or an Ian Fleming book. If your subject matter has to do with mergers or proxy fights and you find your mind wandering, try to visualize the personalities involved, try to see in your imagination how lives will be changed by the operation of corporate finance. Or more simply, try to relate what you are reading to your own life—no matter how tenuous the connection may seem at first. As you practice this basic concentration technique, you may very well find yourself turning up related bits of information that might not have occurred to you at all in a passive reading.

In very abstract material, you may find it helpful to diagram, either in your mind or on paper. Charts and graphs are often supplied in books because people find it easier to see than to conceive abstract quantities. There is no reason at all, then, why you cannot supplement your reading with your own charts, graphs, and diagrams.

▶ SUMMARIZING: Paradoxically, visualizing which is extended too far beyond your present reading may possibly lead to so many pictures and relations that you will once again find your mind beginning to wander from the material. Therefore, it is necessary to reinforce the visualizing skill with summarizing in order to provide a check on your concentration. The combination of these skills will lead not only to a fuller concentration but a better retention.

You cannot possibly remember with equal clarity all that you have read. Therefore, it is extremely important that what you seek to remember warrants remembering. One of the best ways to assure this is to summarize the key points of a chapter or book or letter as soon as you have finished reading. Of course, summaries can actually be written out, but the more you train yourself to formulate and retain summaries in your mind, the easier you will find it to summarize in the first place. Never squeeze unnecessary material into a summary. A summary, mental or written, should always be restricted to the most important facts, concepts, or opinions and should demonstrate the relation between these ideas.

▶ DISTRACTIONS: A conscious use of these four resources will be a great aid in overcoming the chief enemy of concentration—distractions. Distractions fall into two classes: external and internal. External distractions can be dealt with, to a certain extent, directly. You can carpet the floor to reduce noise; you can tell the person at the water cooler that he is a loudmouth; perhaps you might even wish to close the door and disconnect the telephone. If these things do bother you, make whatever reasonable efforts you can to minimize them. But always keep this in mind: for most people a perfectly lighted, completely quiet, and superbly comfortable environment is in itself an almost insuperable distraction. Try not to blame your surroundings when the real distraction is lack of interest due to internal distractions.

Internal distractions are more insidious. They are usually associations or thoughts not immediately related to the material you are reading. Instead of letting them divert you, get in the habit of writing them down. Keep a notebook for those special flashes of insight and random thoughts. Jotting them down serves two purposes: it gets the irrelevance out of your mind, and it preserves the thought for some future time when it may do some good. Then, attack the problem actively with the four resources we have just covered.

CONCENTRATION: BASIC APPLICATION

Begin to question and anticipate by skim-reading the following article from *Financial World* (Figure 5A). Read only the underlined material for key sentences to get your concentration going before you begin your later thorough reading. After your skim-reading, you will be asked to anticipate

GROWTH IN UNLIKELY PLACES

Financial success isn't always achieved in research laboratories. Sometimes "glamour" can be found in products as prosaic as underwear, class rings, keys, shoes and sewing patterns.

PART I

TO AN INVESTOR the word "growth" usually conjures up associations with companies in the vanguard of technology. IBM, Xerox, du Pont, Control Data are some names that probably first come to mind. But there are a number of firms achieving rapid expansion in areas that might seem completely devoid of glamour.

Interesting Examples

Nothing could be more prosaic, for example, than men's underwear. And yet B.V.D. Company has parlayed this apparently mundane business into impressive growth—over the past five years its share earnings have grown at a 31% compounded annual rate. Part of the impetus behind this upsurge has come from a broadening of product lines through acquisitions. Since '62 the company has added men's and boys' outerwear and knit sportswear, neck ties, women's lingerie and a line of foundation garments and swimwear. With operating results up sharply again in the first quarter of fiscal '65, B.V.D. last month initiated cash dividends.

Making keys is another dull occupation, but not for Cole National. It sells key duplicating machines and blanks to every important chain store. A larger portion of revenues comes from operating 425 leased departments, with Sears and Montgomery Ward the main outlets. These units provide a variety of specialized services ranging from sharpening knives and scissors and repairing shoes and handbags to engraving and grinding optical prescriptions. Most recently the company acquired a line of door and car locks, locksmith supplies and door-controling devices. President Joseph E. Cole estimates earnings will reach about $1.75 a share in the year ending October

31, almost double the 94¢ netted back in fiscal '59.

Marrud, Inc., another leased department operator, is faring much better than most of its discount house landlords. The company's leased units sell drugs, cosmetics, candies, stationery, schools supplies and jewelry at a number of leading discount chains. Earlier this year Marrud formed a new subsidiary to produce and package cosmetics and toiletries under private labels for itself and others. President J. E. Margolis expects the company to show profits of around $1.40 a share for the year ended July 31, a big jump from the 83¢ reported in fiscal '63, and looks for another sizable gain in the new fiscal year.

PART II

Famous Artist Schools is earning outstanding marks in yet another unlikely growth field—correspondence courses. Its home study curriculum includes courses in art (including commercial art, illustration, cartooning and painting) and writing (fiction, advertising and business writing). Earlier this year a course in photography was added, and other new programs are in preparation. In the first nine months of fiscal '64 the company netted 78¢

Figure 5A © 1964, *Financial World*, by the Guenther Publishing Corporation.

130

a share, almost equalling the 85¢ earned in all of fiscal '63.

International Flavors & Fragrances also is enjoying the sweet smell of success. It is a leading producer of items used by other manufacturers to improve or impart flavor and fragrance of a wide array of consumer products. Cosmetics ranks as the most important outlet, followed by soaps and detergents. Profits this year are heading for the neighborhood of $1.15 a share, up from 97¢ in '63, despite heavier expansion costs.

Josten's, Inc., has carved a lucrative niche for itself. The company provides class rings, yearbooks, diplomas, announcements and awards to high schools and colleges. It also makes banknotes and executive greeting cards and does some commercial printing and bookbinding. Sales rose to a peak $37 million in the year ended June 30 from $31 million in fiscal '63 and $16 million in fiscal '59. Profits showed even wider gains, bounding to 82¢ a share from 65¢ in the previous fiscal year.

Simplicity Pattern's design for growth is relatively uncomplicated: painstaking attention to the field of paper patterns for women's and children's clothing. The company has risen to top position in this special-ized market helped by aggressive promotion through such publications as "Simplicity" magazine, "Modern Teacher" for home economics teachers and "Simplicity Sewing Book." It's also stepping up foreign operations, which now contribute around 15% of total sales. First-half earnings climbed to $1.01 a share from 80¢ a year before, indicating another significant gain for the full year.

PART III

Swingline's strong growth trend stems from its successful marketing of still another commonplace item—stapling machines and staples. The company is broadening this basic line through such recent developments as heavy-duty staple guns for home repairmen. But a more important move was a recent merger with 59%-owned Wilson Jones, which makes a diversified line of commercial stationery and record-keeping materials. Following the consolidation, these products account for more than half of over-all volume. Earnings in the year ending August 31 are expected to hit about $2.70 a share, up from $2.41 in fiscal '63.

In the lacklustre shoe business, Wolverine Shoe has dashed from 28th place in '58 to seventh slot in terms of sales, thanks to phenomenal public acceptance of its Hush-Puppies footwear. Featuring brushed pigskin uppers and soles made of a special kind of lightweight crepe, the new shoes combine comfort, lightness, durability and easy maintenance. Hush-Puppies were introduced in 1958 for men only, but now are available in styles for all members of the family, including soon-to-be marketed infant's models. Wolverine also is developing other products made of brushed pigskin, such as handbags and headgear. Earnings this year could go as high as $2.25 a share (vs. $1.67 in '63 and 27¢ in '58) and management believes it has only just begun to penetrate its potential market.

Operating in such off-beat areas, some of these unusual growth issues have tended to be overlooked and are available at reasonable price multiples. Marrud, for example, is selling at around ten times estimated earnings, while Cole National is priced at about 11 times projected '64 profits. B.V.D., Swingline and Wolverine Shoe meanwhile sell at only slightly higher multiples. While none of the group is of investment quality, they do offer promising opportunities for investors willing to assume the risks involved in venturing into unlikely places for growth.

Figure 5A (Cont.)

131

accurate and non-accurate descriptions, as well as questions which you will
want to answer in your subsequent thorough reading.

Start time: _____ minutes; _____ seconds

End time: _____ minutes; _____ seconds

SKIM-READING TIME: _____ minutes; _____ seconds

READING RATE TABLE

READING TIME (min.; sec.):	0:15	0:30	0:45	1:30	2:00	3:00	4:00
WORDS PER MINUTE:	4400	2200	1467	733	550	367	275

RECORD YOUR SKIM-READING WPM SCORE: _____

On the basis of your skim-reading of the selection, check which of the
four items below you anticipate will probably be covered in the selection,
and which will not. For each item that you think will be covered, write in
a question that you wish to have answered by your close reading of the
section:

1. Comparisons of the issues in whole industries or of different companies
   in the same field.
   _____ Probably will be covered.
   _____ Probably will not be covered.

   Your question: Which _____

   _____?

2. Comparisons between the potentials of the different stocks mentioned.
   _____ Covered
   _____ Not covered

   Your question: Which _____

   _____?

3. History of recent growth and summary of future prospects of each issue
   listed.
   _____ Covered
   _____ Not covered

   Your question: What _____

   _____?

4. Long-term prediction of competitive position of companies listed.

_____ Covered

_____ Not covered

Your question: When _____

_____?

> *Answers:* 1. Not to be covered. Each of the topic sentences refers to one company only.
> 2. Not to be covered. Same reason as above.
> 3. To be covered. By process of elimination, there is nothing else for the paragraphs to be about.
> 4. Not to be covered. Last paragraph states they are not recommended as long-term investments anyway.

Close-Reading Exercise for Concentration

You probably noticed from your skim-reading that there are three parts to this article. Now read Part I closely, recording your close-reading time only. As you read, look for answers to the questions which you asked. When you have read Part I, record your reading time and then select the most concise summary that most nearly agrees with your own impression of this part.

PART I

Start time: _____ minutes; _____ seconds

End time: _____ minutes; _____ seconds

CLOSE-READING TIME: _____ minutes; _____ seconds

(*Note:* For this exercise, your Words-Per-Minute Score will be based on your total close-reading time for Parts I, II, and III. After you have completed all three parts, add the time for each part to obtain your Total Words Per Minute.)

Choose the best summary for Part I of Fig. 5A from the following three statements:

_____a. Companies with good growth potential, but in off-beat fields, are better buys than the "glamor" stocks. A few of these unfamiliar issues are B.V.D., Cole National, and Marrud, Inc.

_____b. Impressive growth can be found sometimes in little-heralded fields. A few promising "off-beat" issues are B.V.D., which has just initiated cash dividends; Cole National, whose earnings this year will double those of 1959; and Marrud, Inc., whose profits jumped from last year's 83¢ a share to $1.40.

_____c. The B.V.D. Company, maker of men's underwear, has broadened product lines through acquisitions. Share earnings have grown by 31 per cent. Cole National sells key-making equipment and operates leased departments in national chain stores. Estimated earnings will reach $1.75 a share for the current fiscal year. Marrud, Inc. is also a leased department operator, selling drugs and cosmetics. It recently formed a subsidiary to package cosmetics under its private label. Profits should reach $1.40 a share for the current year.

PART II

Read thoroughly Part II of Fig. 5A, once again recording your close reading time, and then choosing a summary:

Start time: _____ minutes; _____ seconds

End time: _____ minutes; _____ seconds

CLOSE-READING TIME: _____ minutes; _____ seconds

Choose the best summary for Part II of Fig. 5A from the following three statements:

_____a. Famous Artists Schools, International Flavors & Fragrances, Jostens, Inc., and Simplicity Patterns are all good buys. Famous Artists Schools, which has recently added a course in photography to its art and writing curricula, earned 85¢ a share in 1963. International Flavors & Fragrances, which supplies scents to be used in consumer products, expects profits of $1.15 a share despite heavy expansion costs. Jostens, Inc. makes personalized favors, jewelry, and printed materials for schools, as well as doing commercial printing. Sales rose to an all-time high of $37 million in the last year. Simplicity Patterns makes paper patterns for women's and children's clothing. As part of its promotion program, Simplicity publishes three magazines featuring its patterns and instructions. Foreign operations contribute 15 per cent of the sales.

_____b. Four more of these "off-beat" investments include Famous Artists Schools, a correspondence school; International Flavors & Fragrances, a manufacturer of flavoring materials; Josten's, Inc., printers and suppliers of school specialty items, and Simplicity Patterns, maker of paper sewing patterns.

_____c. Four more relatively unnoticed issues with good growth possibilities: Famous Artists Schools, which netted 78¢ a share in the first 9 months of the year 1964, almost equalling earnings for the entire fiscal year of 1963; International Flavors & Fragrances has expanded heavily, but still showed a profit gain from 97¢ to $1.15 a share over the last year; Josten's, Inc. shows sales up $6 million over a year ago, $21 million over five years ago, and profits up from 65¢ a share last year to 82¢ in 1964. Simplicity Patterns has been expanding foreign sales, and shows first-half earnings this year up to $1.01 a share from 80¢ a year ago.

PART III

Read thoroughly Part III of the article illustrated in Fig. 5A, once again recording your close-reading time and then choosing the most appropriate summary:

Start time: _____ minutes; _____ seconds

End time: _____ minutes; _____ seconds

CLOSE-READING TIME: _____ minutes; _____ seconds

Choose the best summary of Part III of the article from the following three statements:

_____a. Swingline, another good growth possibility, expects earnings of $2.70 a share this year, up 30¢ from last year. Wolverine Shoe anticipates earnings of as high as $2.25 a share, vs. $1.67 last year and 27¢ six years ago. These stocks are often overlooked and, so, are priced reasonably. They are not of investment quality, but offer promising growth for investors willing to absorb the risk.

_____b. The final pair of issues mentioned: Swingline, manufacturer of stapling machines and staples, and Wolverine Shoe, who introduced the Hush-Puppies line of footwear—neither of these stocks is recommended as a long-term investment, but rather as good growth opportunity.

_____c. Swingline, which manufactures stapling machines and staples, has branched out into heavy-duty equipment for home repairmen and also, through merger, into commercial stationery and record-keeping materials. Earnings should go as high as $2.70 a share for the current fiscal year. Wolverine Shoes has moved from 28th to 7th place in the industry in sales since the introduction of its Hush-Puppies line. Plans are made to market other products of brushed pigskin, and management feels that it has only just begun to penetrate the potential market.

Answers: 1. b
2. c
3. a

TOTAL READING TIME AND SUMMARY

TOTAL CLOSE-READING TIME for all 3 sections: _____ minutes; _____ seconds.

READING RATE TABLE

TOTAL CLOSE-READING TIME:	0:30	1:00	1:15	1:30	1:45	2:00	3:00	4:00
WORDS PER MINUTE:	2200	1100	880	732	628	550	366	275

RECORD YOUR CLOSE-READING WPM SCORE: _____

Write your own summary of the entire article:

_____

_____

_____

_____

_____

_____

_____

Reading for Purpose with Variable Rate

Now for a change of pace we will ask you to read a popular-technical article from *Barron's* (Figure 5B) and add another step in concentration, that of *purpose* and *variable rate*. As you skim-read the article, anticipate the range of content and turn the topic sentences into demanding questions. Be aware of your purpose and take advantage of familiar concepts or materials which can be read more quickly than unfamiliar material. By reading at your best speed for whatever amount of comprehension you need from the material, you will achieve a correspondingly greater degree of concentration than if you simply read the material at a constant speed.

In improving concentration, the skill of skim-reading, therefore, serves three purposes: (1) the reader becomes aware of general content and organization; (2) the reader begins to create a dialogue with the author, through questioning and anticipating; and (3) the reader appraises his own familiarity with the material and decides upon his variable rate.

Keeping the above points in mind, go ahead and read "Hail Columbium" from *Barron's* (Figure 5B), noting your start and end times.

Start time: _____ minutes; _____ seconds

End time: _____ minutes; _____ seconds

SKIM-READING TIME: _____ minutes; _____ seconds

READING RATE TABLE

READING TIME (min.; sec.):	0:15	0:30	1:00	2:00
WORDS PER MINUTE:	4000	2000	1000	500

RECORD YOUR SKIM-READING WPM SCORE: _____

On the basis of your skim-reading alone, indicate whether or not each of the following points will be covered more fully in the article. If you think a point will be covered more fully, ask a demanding question which you think should be answered in your close reading of the article.

1. New uses and applications for Columbium.

_____ Probably will be covered.

_____ Probably will not be covered.

Your question: Who _____?

HAIL COLUMBIUM

Another "Glamor" Metal Is Growing Increasingly Useful

By Joseph V. Sherman

LAST year, the Linde Co. division of Union Carbide Corp. was awarded a Navy contract for more than a third of a million dollars for research and development work on capacitors made of columbium metal. The project will investigate the possible substitution of columbium for another "glamor" metal — tantalum — which currently is used in a wide variety of capacitors for many critical electronic applications. Columbium would have a number of advantages over tantalum: the far greater abundance of ores could mean both better supply and potentially lower cost; its density is only half that of tantalum, a fact which would result in an important saving in weight; and columbium possesses special nuclear and other properties which would give it added virtues in certain jobs.

High-Strength Steels

Today, columbium is enjoying a growing use not only as a basic metal for applications in the electronics, atomic energy and aerospace fields, but also as an alloying element in the production of high-strength and stainless steels. Columbium, incidentally, has another name, niobium, after Niobe, the daughter of Tantalus in Greek mythology. The name reflects the fact that the two elements, niobium and tantalum, generally are found together in the same ores and are very similar in their characteristics.

Regardless of what it is called, producers of the metal are highly optimistic about its future. Metallurgists who have been studying it for many years assert that columbium has a "promising profile" of properties, which qualify it for many new uses. It can withstand extreme heat and is highly resistant to attack by strong chemicals. Of all the refractory metals, it is one of the lightest in weight and easiest to fabricate.

Long considered a "rare" metal, columbium is much more abundant in nature than formerly realized. In fact, more columbium exists in the earth than lead, for example. Large columbium ore bodies have been found in Canada and South America, as well as in Africa.

According to the Bureau of Mines, U.S. production of columbium metal, first reported at 10 tons in 1957, increased to 60 tons by 1959, and to 126 tons in 1961. While a preliminary report indicates that output declined to "possibly only 100 tons" in 1962, this figure is for the pure metal alone; it does not include the much larger quantities of the element used in the form of ferrocolumbium in the steel industry. Consumption of ferrocolumbium has been rising rapidly and reached an estimated 1,300 tons in 1962.

Imports Up Sharply

Since no domestic ore is produced, statistics on imports provide the best indication of the upward trend in columbium usage. Last year, imports of columbium concentrate rose to an estimated 2,350 tons — 57% above 1961. The principal sources were Nigeria, Canada, and Norway.

While all major producers of columbium metal foresee a big expansion of markets in the future, they differ in the emphasis placed on specific outlets — a good indication of the broad potential for the metal.

Kawecki Chemical Co., for example, observes that the principal markets for columbium historically have been in the atomic energy program. The basic interest in the metal relects its resistance to attack by molten alkali metals, such as lithium, potassium, and cesium, which are used as working fluids in nuclear reactors. Kawecki expects interest in this application to become "quite large" as the Nuclear Space Propulsion Program develops.

Last year, Kawecki enlarged its production facilities for the metal to meet "the anticipated increase in demand for columbium metal powder and mill products, and columbium alloys, especially superconductor alloys."

Du Pont officials spell out some of the unique properties of columbium which make it extremely valuable for space programs: "Spurring production of this ductile refractory metal is the multiplicity of aerospace designs which demand materials which not only retain strength at high temperatures, but which are formable with conventional equipment at room temperature. It was not until columbium was produced in mill shapes and could be investigated by aerospace designers that it proved the exception to the generally held belief that the refractory metals were difficult, if not impossible, to work with conventional equipment at normal temperatures, and became brittle if allowed to recrystallize, and could not be welded."

They add that in addition to its relatively light weight for a refractory metal, columbium retains sufficient strength at high temperatures to withstand the rigors of launching, space flight and atmospheric re-entry. Moreover, Du Pont believes that outside the aerospace field, columbium and its alloys show promise for such down-to-earth applications as liquid metal heat exchanger

May 20, 1963 *BARRON'S*

Figure 5B Reprinted by courtesy of *Barron's National Business and Financial Weekly.*

tubing, nuclear fuel element cladding, aviation gas turbine hardware, and as additives to increase the ductility of other refractory metals and some of the reactive metals.

Meanwhile, interest is growing in columbium-zirconium alloys for superconductor devices such as large field electromagnets and solenoids. While a number of alloys become superconductors as their temperature is lowered to within a few degrees of absolute zero, most are brittle and difficult to draw into small-diameter wire. The newer alloys, however, are strong and ductile and permit greater flexibility in the design and construction of useful devices. During the first quarter of 1963, small-diameter wire (0.010-inch) became available in commercial quantities from several firms.

Despite the mounting interest and consumption of columbium, Fansteel Metallurgical Corp., a major producer of columbium and alloy mill products, says: "Most current uses of columbium and its alloys are of a developmental nature. We can look forward to a rising use in space missions and supporting research activities. There will be an increasing need in superconducting magnetic and switching applications. Important markets can be expected to develop in corrosion-resistant chemical equipment and in capacitors. In some applications, columbium's susceptibility to oxidation has held up its acceptance. Protective coatings have partially solved the problem but much more work is needed."

Tenfold Rise

For its part, Stauffer Chemical Co. foresees expanding markets for columbium in the aerospace and nuclear fields but believes that perhaps the most promising market, from the standpoint of increasing volume, is the use of columbium additives to steel and to nickel alloys. The company cites one estimate that by 1965 the addition of ferrocolumbium and columbium master alloys to carbon steel and to super-alloys may reach 25 million pounds of contained columbium metal a year. This would represent a tenfold increase over present consumption.

Besides the producers of columbium metal and alloys, a number of other companies have been doing research and development work on products containing the versatile material. Recently, for example, there has been a surge of interest in the field of superconductivity and cryogenics, in which columbium-based materials play an important role. Perhaps the best indication of the high potential of this business is the fact that the list of firms developing new columbium products includes such industrial giants as Bell Telephone, General Electric Co., North American Aviation, Radio Corp. of America, and Westinghouse Electric Corp.

Figure 5B (Cont.)

2. Detailed descriptions of smelting and milling processes.

_____ Probably will be covered.

_____ Probably will not be covered.

Your question: _____?

3. Examples of research on superconductors.

_____ Probably will be covered.

_____ Probably will not be covered.

Your question: _____?

4. Indications of the financial future of Columbium.

_____ Probably will be covered.

_____ Probably will not be covered.

Your question: _____?

5. Considerable discussion of other refractory metals.
   _____ Probably will be covered.
   _____ Probably will not be covered.

Your question: _____?

> *Answers:* 1. Will be covered; see especially paragraph beginning, "While all major producers . . ."
> 2. Not covered. Why not? What other source might have the proper information?
> 3. Covered, but only slightly. Super-conductors are mentioned in the last paragraph and the paragraph fourth from the end.
> 4. To be covered. Key words in the article are "expanding" and "rising" market, "Increasing volume," etc.—all indicating a good future.
> 5. Not to be covered. The article concentrates fully on Columbium; other metals are mentioned, but only tangentially.

Now, review the questions you have written above. Are there any more that you think should be answered, or that you want answered? Jot them down here, briefly: _____

_____

_____

Summarizing While Reading

Now that you have skim-read the article, you are to read the same article thoroughly in a close-reading and summarize the key elements. Your aim should be to develop skill in summarizing each part of a selection *while reading* so that the overall summary will be arrived at through your earlier summaries, rather than through a complete review and reconstruction of all of the details you have read. This cumulative summarizing of information and ideas into blocks of meaning as you read is particularly helpful in sustaining concentration throughout lengthy, difficult, or dull material. Look for answers to your questions. Try to visualize the facets of the material as presented—statistics, characteristics of the metal, etc.

After your close-reading, record your reading time and select the best summary, filling in as you see fit. Now go back and reread the article illustrated in Figure 5B.

Start time: _____ minutes; _____ seconds

End time: _____ minutes; _____ seconds

CLOSE-READING TIME: _____ minutes; _____ seconds

READING RATE TABLE

READING TIME (min.; sec.):	0:30	1:00	1:15	1:30	1:45	2:00	3:00	4:00
WORDS PER MINUTE:	2200	1100	880	732	628	550	366	275

RECORD CLOSE-READING WPM SCORE: _____

Now summarize the whole article by choosing the best beginning from the three possibilities given below and complete the summary. This overall summary should be an accumulation of those points you summarized while reading, but it should not be too detailed. Do not hesitate to use your own symbols and abbreviations—if you are sure you will understand them when you return to them. Notes of this type are good permanent reminders; they can be kept in a working notebook for especially relevant material or can be scribbled in the margins of journals or books you intend to keep and refer to later.

1. Research and development in the use of Columbium, a relatively light and ductile refractory metal, indicate _____

   _____

2. Columbium production is expanding. This can be attributed to _____

   _____

   _____

3. The financial future of Columbium is bright. Use is expanding in industries and applications such as _____

   _____

> ● Some reference should be made to present and developmental use of the metal, with a possible focus on the finance. The article's focus is clearly on the *future* of the metal.

As a follow-up on your application of questioning and answering, which of the questions you formed during and after the skim-reading have been answered? Perhaps more important, *which have not?* Why not—did you aim wrong, expecting the wrong things? Or was the author hedging, indicating a scope the article did not achieve? Jot down references to your earlier questions below, and whether they were answered, and why or why not:

_____

_____

_____

● This is an important step, but one for which a prescribed answer cannot be prepared. If you can spot failures in the article's coverage you are pretty well prepared to judge what it *has* covered.

CONCENTRATION: FURTHER APPLICATION

If some of these steps for applying concentration skills seem to take more time than you would ever want to take on reading such an article, don't despair. The ability to concentrate on your reading material, especially on material which is boring to you, is essential for your overall improvement in reading. Hence, it is necessary to conscientiously and carefully apply the skills step-by-step in the beginning. Assess your own ability at this point and decide whether you should proceed with the further application, or whether you can skip directly to the advanced application of the skill.

The article for this application—Figure 5C—is taken from *Sales Management*. Skim-read the article, and you will again answer anticipating questions. The title is a question which should prompt more questions on your part. If you feel that your skim-reading of the last article was too full, skim this more rapidly, reading only the title and the topic sentences.

Start time: _____ minutes; _____ seconds

End time: _____ minutes; _____ seconds

SKIM-READING TIME: _____ minutes; _____ seconds

READING RATE TABLE

READING TIME (min.; sec.):	0:30	1:00	1:15	1:30	1:45	2:00	3:00	4:00
WORDS PER MINUTE:	2300	1150	885	767	639	575	383	288

RECORD SKIM-READING WPM SCORE: _____

Are SALESMEN more professional than PLUMBERS?

By Mary Louise McGowan

Selling a profession? Let's quit kidding ourselves, says this author. What it actually is is dynamic communication and it must be sold that way—to the experienced salesmen as well as the youngsters on their way up.

What the world of sales—and sales training—needs is the stimulus of an honest controversy. Not because controversy, viewed in itself, is particularly valuable, but because without some form of mental and vocal violence we're all going to choke to death on the pompous platitudes we've mouthed into ancient and eternal truths.

Nor should it be difficult to stir up controversy among ourselves. There are at least as many theories of salesmanship as there are salesmen—to say nothing of training directors, customers, managers, and mothers. It's a field where everybody's an expert—everybody, after all, at some time or other, went to school. And there is no surer way to become an expert as any college senior can readily demonstrate.

But if we are, in fact, to reach this college senior—if we are to convince him that a sales career is worth investigation and preparation—then we've got to stop writing and talking drivel. We've got to start talking sense.

I personally do not subscribe to the unspoken philosophy that salesmen are a bunch of retarded idiots. And, obviously, I don't for a minute believe that all those responsible for sales training are charlatans. But you must admit that all of us—on both sides of the selling scene—are deluged with seemingly endless amounts of sheer garbage, spawned in the not so fertile minds of a whole new generation of voodoo practitioners—the kind with an attaché case full of eight magic formulas, 12 super secrets, and nine thousand and nine Golden Keys to Success in Selling—usually set to music.

And we are still confronted—despite notable gains in recent years—with industry's own personal Neanderthal man. He represents that segment of the business community whose philosophy is characterized by an absolute aversion to anything that smacks, however remotely, of sales dynamics. He favors, of course, "the old time religion" of aggressive selling, complete with suede shoes, loud jacket and louder mouth. But he does so with neither an understanding of, nor the appreciation for, the unique and complex factors involved in the one-to-one relationship that is the selling situation.

Today's Concern: Tomorrow

Tomorrow is the prime concern of the sales supervisor—his prime concern today. Is it enough to try, however sincerely, to merge and mold into an acceptable mean two untenable extremes? Isn't that what we've been trying to do for at least a generation? Make a silk purse out of a sow's ear? And we haven't succeeded! . . . despite those billions of dollars of marketed goods that we bandy about as a sign of progress!

Ask your sons and daughters. Ask the intense young college students on your local university campus. Ask them about the dynamic, challenging, rewarding profession of selling. But try it.

Selling a profession? Let's quit kidding ourselves! Selling is about as much of a profession as plumbing—and there are plenty of bright young men that consider the latter profession cleaner. Selling isn't a profession. It never was. And that notwithstanding the golden memories of a certain breed of retired sales manager who is prone to refer to the Bible as the great sales manual and to quote the prophet Micah as an epitaph to the salesmen of yesteryear.

Selling is more of an art than a science. It deals more with people

Figure 5C

143

than with things. It traffics in ideas, not absolutes. It is, when all is said and done, nothing more and nothing less than dynamic communication. As such it never was, and never can be, a profession in the strict sense of the word, nor will it ever be a trade. It is itself unique. It must be explained that way. It must be sold that way.

That does not mean to imply that selling is not a professional career. It is, or rather it should be. But it does not become one by the simple expediency of striking what one considers to be a pose of irreproachable dignity. It does not become one by sprucing up the image with a solid blue suit and a silver blue tie. It does not become one by saying to ourselves and to each other, 20 to 100 times a day: "I am a professional salesman."

The Price of Professionality

We're going to have to earn the right to call selling a professional career. We're going to have to define the components of the sale, the terms of knowledge and skill, and we're going to have to demand the mastery of both before we ourselves call a man a salesman. We must set up standards of behavior, develop codes of ethics, establish minimum educational requirements. In a word, we must pay the price of professionality or resign ourselves, with some modicum of intellectual honesty, and accept the fact that we hold none too savory jobs.

Sales management and companies alike could, however, make a significant contribution towards the establishment of selling as a profitable, productive career. They could, for example, bring pressure to bear on the business divisions of our colleges and universities. They could urge the development of sales courses in depth, perhaps initially as a minor field to a marketing major. They could act, indi-

vidually, in their own locale, in their own community.

Training directors could, individually and through their professional societies, draw up basic course materials in conjunction with the faculties of these same universities, preparing a curriculum that would reflect the high level of intelligent performance that we in industry intend to demand of our sales force.

Specifically, the professional salesman should, I think, have a mastery of the principles of motivational psychology, the techniques of individual interviewing and the science of group communications (including conference leadership and the preparation and use of audio-visual aids). More and more, the salesman of tomorrow will be called upon to make group presentations to executive committees. He must become a consummate public speaker. He must have obtained understanding of, and appreciation for, the humanities. He must be thoroughly grounded in the social as well as the business sciences. And he must be able to write coherent, concise, effective English.

But our responsibility for the development of selling as a profession does not stop with a delegation of it to the university campus. We must simultaneously demand in business a higher caliber sales trainee. We must demand more careful, realistic screening by personnel executives. We must give them more definite, more specific lists of qualities and requirements for selling assignments. And we must insist upon professional salaries for professional personnel.

Would we rather talk about professional stature, than live in accordance with it? It's not something we can win in a contest or find in a grab bag of tricks! It has to be lived, not once in a while but all the time. With the intelligence and integrity we want associated with the American salesman. As we are, our image will be.

Sales Management MAY 3, 1963

Figure 5C (Cont.)

144

On the basis of your skim-reading only, indicate whether or not each of the following points will be covered more fully in the article. Again, add your own questions.

1. Standards of professionalism in selling.
   _____ Probably will be covered.
   _____ Probably will not be covered.

   Your question: _____

   _____?

2. Professionalism in plumbing.
   _____ Probably will be covered.
   _____ Probably will not be covered.

   Your question: _____

   _____?

3. The need for a better type of salesman and more imaginative, selective recruiting.
   _____ Probably will be covered.
   _____ Probably will not be covered.

   Your question: _____

   _____?

4. A real controversy about the "standards of the profession."
   _____ Probably will be covered.
   _____ Probably will not be covered.

   Your question: _____

   _____?

5. A new plan for training salesmen.
   _____ Probably will be covered.
   _____ Probably will not be covered.

   Your question: _____

   _____?

> *Answers:* 1. To be covered. The whole section entitled "The Price of Professionality" discusses the topic.

2. Hardly. If you were misled by the title and not corrected by the skim-reading, you should skim a bit more thoroughly.
3. To be covered. The author makes specific recommendations for the ideal salesman.
4. To be covered. She calls for an honest controversy. Does she provide the basis?
5. No. This is the clarion call to arms; but no real direction is indicated.

Close-Reading Exercise

In your review and further questioning, do you find that you already know the answers to the questions, either from your skim-reading or from your previous knowledge? Or are you totally uninterested? If either is true, perhaps this is the point to stop—if you think that the article is going to add nothing to your knowledge that you need or might benefit by, skip it.

However, there may be something new and interesting—at least, so the author seems to promise. If you want to, then, read the selection *closely*. As you noticed in your skim-reading, this article is larger than previous ones. It is also divided into three parts, so read it part by part, summarizing as you go along.

PART I

Start time: _____ minutes; _____ seconds

End time: _____ minutes; _____ seconds

CLOSE-READING TIME: _____ minutes; _____ seconds

(*Note:* Wait until you have completed a close reading of Parts I, II, and III before converting your time to a close-reading WPM score.)

Choose the better beginning for a summary and complete the idea (summarize to consolidate information):

1. Salesmen are not "a bunch of retarded idiots," although some are close; however, _____

_____

_____

2. Controversy is necessary to _____

_____

_____

● Probably "2" is the better start; this section is a call to arms; the author is stating her thesis: that the theory of selling needs examination.

Review the questions you raised at the beginning, then close-read Part II.

Part II

Start time: _____ minutes; _____ seconds

End time: _____ minutes; _____ seconds

CLOSE-READING TIME: _____ minutes; _____ seconds

Choose a beginning summary and complete one of the following:

1. Selling is not a profession, but _____

_____

_____

2. We must look forward to the future; therefore, _____

_____

_____

● "1" is probably best; not a profession; certainly not a science; perhaps an art; we must strive for professionalism.

Review mentally the questions you formed. Are there any yet unanswered? Will you find the answer here? Close-read now Part III.

Part III

Start time: _____ minutes; _____ seconds

End time: _____ minutes; _____ seconds

CLOSE-READING TIME: _____ minutes; _____ seconds

Choose a beginning summary and complete one of the following:

1. We must earn the right to call selling a profession by _____

_____

_____

2. The professional salesman should _____

_____

_____

● There are *two sides* to her recommendations: *first* that the salesman should improve—learn psychology, communications, public speaking, humanities, social sciences, and writing. *Second,* the personnel people must screen applicants more realistically (or idealistically), then perhaps selling will be a professional calling.

SUMMARIZE THE WHOLE

Review your section summaries (mental review may be enough). This should prepare you to state in brief the substance of the whole article.

Brief overall summary for entire selection:

_____

_____

_____

● Selling should move from an inexact and sometimes less than admired art to a level of professionalism, by improving standards both in training and hiring.

TOTAL CLOSE-READING TIMES FOR PARTS I, II, AND II: _____ minutes; _____ seconds.

READING RATE TABLE

CLOSE-READING TIME (min.; sec.):	0:30	1:00	1:15	1:30	1:45	2:00	3:00	4:00
WORDS PER MINUTE:	2300	1150	885	767	639	575	383	288

RECORD YOUR CLOSE-READING WPM SCORE: _____

CONCENTRATION: ADVANCED APPLICATION

In previous applications you have been skim-reading magazine articles to determine, first, what is included in the material ("What questions could I *expect* to have answered in this selection?") and, second, to focus your particular interest on the material, the kind of specific questions that you

The

Management

Makers

THE IDEAS, PEOPLE, AND INSTITUTIONS

THAT MAKE AND MAR MANAGEMENT

by Auren Uris

THE MACMILLAN COMPANY · NEW YORK

A DIVISION OF THE CROWELL-COLLIER PUBLISHING COMPANY

Figure 5D-a © by Auren Uris 1962, reprinted with permission of The Macmillan Company.

wish to have answered by the material ("What of the content do I *wish* to know?").

In the case of a book, you can often gather the general content and formulate the kind of questions you wish to have answered merely by reading the table of contents and introduction. When the book has relatively little information in the table of contents and the introduction, you may find it necessary to skim-read the first and last chapters before determining the possible questions appropriate for that book. However, the following selection for advanced application to a book contains considerable information. Through a conscious use of questioning, anticipating, visualizing, and summarizing of these portions, you will find yourself in active concentration without having to force yourself to concentrate, and you will be more aware of the contents than if you had read the whole book in an unsystematic fashion.

Read the *title page* below (Figure 5D-a) and seek to formulate questions based only on the title page. The questions you form before going on to read the content of the book should be the questions that you have tried to answer yourself, but have been unable to answer from the title page alone. For a change in tactics, below are some questions which could be asked—see if you can answer them after your reading of the title page.

1. What are *makers?* _____

_____

2. Who is Uris? _____

_____

> *Answers:* 1. You may have to defer answering your questions at some points because of lack of information. The important thing is that the title *be* questioned, rather than passively accepted. Answers will turn up in the table of contents.
> 2. You may not know who he is, although you may have read one of his previous books.

The *table of contents* (Figure 5D-b) is a distillation of the entire book, so you will need to read it quite carefully. Therefore, it is best to employ the skim-reading approach—noting first the five parts into which the book has been divided—and then to go back to examine the chapter titles under each part.

Contents

Contents

Figure 5D-b

151

The part titles have been turned into questions below. Based on your reading of Figure 5D-b, indicate which of the questions in the book can be answered in part from the table of contents. *All* of these questions will presumably be answered by the table of contents.

1. Who makes management? _____

   _____.

2. How are management ideas made? _____

   _____.

3. How are managers made? _____

   _____.

4. In what way is management itself a product? _____

   _____.

5. What pushes management forward? _____

   _____.

> *Answers:* 1. Table of contents only gives a chapter title, which in itself tells nothing.
> 2. The book will discuss brain-storming, organizational controversies, decision-making, and a new concept of leadership.
> 3. Development in the company: IBM, the university program.
> 4. For the Research Institute of America, the management magazines, and for the American Management Association, management is a product.
> 5. The table of contents does not tell us the answer, but the book will.

Skim-read the *introduction* (Figure 5D-c) by reading only the subtitles and beginning sentences. You will note that the first unlabelled section contains the objective of the book; the second section contains the general attack of the book; the next five sections parallel the table of contents; and the last section contains some advice for the reader.

Having skim-read the whole introduction, you should now read carefully only those sections of the introduction about which you desire further

Introduction

The objective of this book is to help the practicing manager improve the mastery of his profession. Of course, the same may be said of many other books. But the approach developed here, it is hoped, is particularly fruitful.

The aim is not to supply specific formulas or panaceas for solving management problems but to put the executive in a position to "make his own management." How can he do this? By gaining a behind-the-scenes view of management, seeing how management is made and unmade by the people and institutions that act as *management makers*. The benefits of this approach are that the executive can—

1. Better appraise the management tools presently available. For example, you may more knowingly evaluate a decision-making method, or a leadership concept.

2. Refine and modify available management tools so that they better suit the problems at hand. For example, you may tailor the organizational structure of your department or company to fit needs rather than to coincide with abstract theory as to what's "right."

3. Devise his own management tools—principles, procedures, guidelines. For example, if you're considering development of your people, you can develop policies and procedures that derive from your particular goals, rather than other people's formulas.

This, then, is a how-to-do book in the most sophisticated sense. It aims to make the manager his own best management expert. In possession of the information and insights to be found in an analysis of

management in the making, the manager may pick and choose his way more surely through the intellectual murk of management lore. He can see clearly the inconsistencies—and in some cases the sheer nonsense—that exist in the field, cheek by jowl with the useful verities.

A MAJOR SOURCE OF UNDERSTANDING

Since both the weakness and the strength of management derive from the forces that produce it, it is to the process of *management making* itself that we turn for insights and understanding.

As we progress in any area, it's natural for methods, goals, and values to obsolesce. For this reason, at the present stage of management growth, we are handicapped. Many of our ideas have lost not only their credibility, which is bad enough, but their applicability, which can be catastrophic.

How does the working executive, concerned both with the rationale of his activities (because he is a serious-minded practitioner) and with results (because his job, his culture, and usually his personality make him a pragmatist) retain a firm footing?

The answer lies in an exploration that aims to distinguish the firm ground from the bog, the hard rock of the real from the *papier maché* of the phoney. We make our exploration in key areas, the main parts of this book: an investigation of some fundamental management *ideas*; an examination of some *institutions and methods* by which individual managers are "professionalized"; and a study of some organizations that manufacture *management as a product*.

PART ONE: WHO MAKES MANAGEMENT?

Chapter 1 makes the point that management is not uniform, monolithic. On the contrary, it is a highly variegated entity. The reason is to be found in the multiple origins of management—a circumstance curiously overlooked, which in itself sheds considerable light in dark places.

The answer to the question, "*Where does management come from?*" shows how each of the many tributaries of the management stream has both its very real benefits and its very real faults. For the

Figure 5D-c

first time, perhaps, you may learn why experts are not always expert, and why "principles of management" may sound fine in the abstract but prove to be nonsense in reality.

PART TWO: THE MAKING OF MANAGEMENT IDEAS

In Chapter 2, the phenomenon of brainstorming is put under the microscope, because its rise and fall in popularity are extremely revealing of basic managerial thinking. This case history of a concept reveals the danger of faddism, and may help you salvage something of value from management's vast junkheap of discarded ideas.

In Chapter 3 we examine a troublesome issue that has long roiled management waters: the see-saw conflict centering on company organization. Are organization charts worth the paper they're printed on? The executive who says "No" may be as wrong as the one who says "Yes." Seeing how certain "principles" of organization are built up and whittled down provides another insight into management making that may help restore the subject of organization to useful perspective.

The next two chapters, 4 and 5, deal with subject areas that reveal further weaknesses and strengths in management making: *executive decision* and *executive leadership*. Here again we see how muddle-headed thinking creates false ideas that enmesh managers in "principles" that are worthless and practices that exacerbate the very problems they are intended to assuage.

Having seen how management ideas are made and mangled, we now can benefit from a close-up view of some of the institutions that actually make managers.

PART THREE: THE MAKING OF MANAGERS

Chapters 6 and 7 examine the company's role in training and developing managers. What kind of job is being done? Company training centers loose an endless stream of "graduates" into the field. Are these "developed" executives better performers as a result of their experience? Or are they simply more acceptable because they have been through the mill—meaningless as the experience itself may have been? Answers to these and other leading questions are suggested

by a detailed description of some of the country's more ambitious company training programs.

Chapter 8 deals with the role of the university in executive development. Good job or bad? And how about the university professor turned industrial trainer? Is it safe to assume that just because an individual wears a mortarboard, he isn't talking through his hat? To illustrate the kind of thinking that goes into academic attempts at management making, the chapter describes at some length one of the best-known university programs, that of Columbia's Arden House.

PART FOUR: MANAGEMENT AS A PRODUCT

Chapters 9, 10, and 11 describe organizations to whom management is a product to be turned out for general consumption. What's the nature of this type of operation? Can there be real value to "commercialized" management making? Some of the answers emerge in Chapter 9's behind-the-scenes description of how one organization, the Research Institute of America, does it.

Chapter 10 takes up the phenomenon of the management magazines. *Fortune, Harvard Business Review, Factory Management and Maintenance*—what, if anything, do publications like these have to offer? In Chapter 10 you may find what many executives have wanted but haven't before had available: an over-all, comparative view of leading periodicals in the management field.

Chapter 11 offers for your enlightenment a study of the organization that stands in the forefront of the management training and information field. What's the story behind the American Management Association and the people who guide it? The answer provides a clearer view of what has been described as the "management supermarket."

PART FIVE: WHAT PUSHES MANAGEMENT FORWARD?

Our voyage concludes with an analysis of the forces that encourage—but may also impede—management growth (Chapter 12). You may be able to anticipate some factors, but others are almost certain to surprise you. At any rate, this final chapter may help refine

Figure 5D-c (Cont.)

your personal view of the "motor" that propels management on its sometimes reef-strewn course.

SOME WORDS FOR THE READER

At one or more points you are likely to find yourself in disagreement, perhaps violent, with certain of the conclusions or opinions expressed by the author. Fine. Your opposed view verifies a basic theme here espoused, that the realities of a management situation—including the unique experience and outlook of the individual—alter cases. But even if you're not satisfied with the answers, I hope you will agree that the questions raised are those which today's executive must ask in order to cut through the fog surrounding much of his professional activity. The hope and intention, of course, is not to gild the past but to brighten the future. Only when we understand the true nature of management—*who* makes it, *how*, and *why*—will we be able to clear the way for accelerated professional progress.

Fortunately or unfortunately, this book is the result of where I've been, what I've been, and what I am. My roots are in the practical rather than the academic or scientific world. I once owned and operated a small business, and I have worked as a member of management in a large corporation. This experience, together with my field work at the Research Institute of America as a member of the management research staff, has obviously influenced my approach.

Many authors seem to like to cover their tracks and present the reader with their work as though it had been produced in a vacuum by the wave of a magic wand. I don't attempt to maintain this pretense. The efforts that have gone into the making of this book are quite evident. The questionnaires, interviews, and correspondence upon which much of it is based are mentioned as they become appropriate. Other groundwork—endless phone calls, discussions, and arguments, hours spent pawing away at a tangle of ideas to separate fact from fiction—may be evident from the toolmarks.

Figure 5D-c (Cont.)

information. When you finish reading a section, summarize it and compare your summary with that in this book.

1. The objective of this book is _____

_____.

2. A Major Source of Understanding _____

_____.

3. Who Makes Management? _____

_____.

4. The Making of Management Ideas _____

_____.

5. The Making of Managers _____

_____.

6. Management as a Product _____

_____.

7. What pushes management forward? _____

_____.

8. Some words for the reader _____

_____.

Answers: 1. To help the practicing manager improve the mastery of his profession through an awareness of how management-makers operate.

2. Can be found in the processes by which managers are made.

3. Management has multiple origins, but still we are not given a clue as to what they are. A skim-reading of the chapter itself would be necessary in order to discover the origins: experts, management journals, universities, the executive, the scientist, company training programs, specialized organizations, management consultants, and business and professional groups.

4. The faddism of "brainstorming," the use of organization charts, and executive decision-making are illustrations of how management ideas are made and mangled.

5. This section considers whether company training programs or university programs are effective. There is an examination of the content of such programs.

6. This introductory section does not tell you much more than you could have inferred from the table of contents. It raises questions about "commercial management making" (or, at least, promises that a chapter will raise them) and about the Management Magazines and the AMA.

7. You may be able to anticipate from the whole book some of the factors, but the author expects to give you some surprises in this chapter. The aim of the chapter is to assist you to refine your own view of what pushes management forward.

8. Uris encourages disagreement with his answers, so long as you consider the questions. He describes his own experience in business and management and gives some idea of his method of gathering materials for his book.

SUMMARY

The ability to overcome distractions through questioning, anticipating, visualizing, and summarizing is the key to improvement in all areas of reading. When you discover that you "read" a page or chapter by letting your eyes wander over the print but have no idea of what you have read because your mind has been elsewhere, it is time to actively and consciously apply these concentration skills to whatever you are reading, beginning with written exercises. You should soon be able to concentrate intensively with much less written work, with improvement in speed, comprehension, and retention—but without having to *try* to concentrate.

SKILL REMINDER

To concentrate, do this:

1. Ask demanding questions of the author before and during reading.
2. Anticipate what the author is going to say.
3. Visualize or diagram what he is saying.
4. Summarize concisely what he has to say.

CRITICAL READING

For the most complete CONTROL of your material

What the Skill Is: The ability to meaningfully compare or relate the material to other readings and to your own experiences in order to evaluate the material in terms of its tone of voice, assumptions, inferences, and logic.

What Critical Reading Does: Critical reading helps you to treat written material with greater objectivity and discernment, increases your interest, and enables you to measure its usefulness by constant cross-examination of the material and by reference to information you already possess.

How to Use It: A flexible or increased reading rate seems the final objective to many business and professional men. This is especially true for those who are surrounded by piles of unread material. Others seek highly accurate comprehension and thorough recall. When a person lacks the ability to read with reasonable speed and accuracy, advanced work on critical reading would probably be misplaced energy. But given a flexible reading rate and sound comprehension—skills that have been thoroughly covered in the earlier portions of this book

Skill

VI

—the development of a critical reading technique is the next desirable objective.

We do not expect you to be easily misled. Yet, in much of the reading you do you will find—if you are on the lookout for it—that the author is not wholly objective, or else that his notion of objectivity is somewhat different from your own. As a rule, you will respond, even to factual writing, in an intuitive fashion. Therefore, you can often judge written material for the wrong reasons and be left with the inadequate comment that: "I like it/ do not like it." Or, "I agree/ do not agree."

Suppose you begin a book by the noted author Jones, and by page ten you know that you and Jones are never going to get along. There is a strong temptation to say, "Jones is a fool," and to put the book aside without ever looking at it again. Yet, a close, critical evaluation may show you that what you are actually saying is that Jones has an irritating tone of voice or that his book is not well-organized—factors that may conceal the real value of what he has to say.

In another variation of the same problem, you may be reading a very persuasive book or article, feel yourself being convinced by it, and yet— almost below the conscious level—suspect that you are being convinced against your better judgment, just because the author is shrewd at argument.

In both cases, the need is for a reading skill to deal with essentials that may be obscured by non-essentials. And even when an author writes well and to the point, it is still a great benefit if you can see beyond the written word to the sort of thinking that has produced the report, article, or book in question.

By the time they are in their mid-twenties, the majority of people—writers and readers alike—have a few deeply held convictions or a great many conventional beliefs. The convictions on the one hand and the conventional beliefs on the other may be just and useful, or they may not be. In any event, it is your job as a truly skilled reader to recognize them and how they affect the written word.

Your goal as a critic, as well as a receiver of information, is not to become a Solomon. No matter how hard you try, you will have a point of view, biases, and special interests. Yet, as a critical reader, you can employ all of your reading skills to recognize unstated assumptions, inferences, and logic (or lack of logic) when they appear.

You have now read through several techniques designed to give you a flexible reading rate and the best possible understanding through a running analysis and a structured approach to reading. Now, to give a better foundation to your reactions, we want you to reduce the material by answering the following questions:

> 1. What is the author's tone?
> 2. What is his point of view?
> 3. What are his main arguments?

As the first application in critical reading, you will be given two articles on the same general topic. Skim-read and then close-read the first selection, then answer the questions about it. After doing the same thing with the second article, we will ask you to note *similarities* and *differences* between them. The second and third applications will follow the same pattern. The final application, however, will be your reading of a single article and comparison with information you already have stored in your mind.

CRITICAL READING: BASIC APPLICATION

On the basis of a skim- and a close-reading of the article "How to Resign and Die and Things Like That" by Nicholas Samstag (Figure 6A), answer the following questions.

1. The tone of Samstag's article is
    _____a. Sarcastic.
    _____b. Quite serious.
    _____c. A combination of humor and seriousness.

2. Samstag's article states that
    _____a. Firing a man can sometimes be good for him.
    _____b. Firing a man can be done with compassion.
    _____c. The best way to fire a man is to let him get very angry.

3. Choose the best summary of the Samstag article:
    _____a. In breaking off any relationship, preparations should be made with such care that the sufferer accepts the situation and sees in his errors a corrective for successful future conduct.
    _____b. The feelings of the person who has to do the firing are just as important as the feelings of the person who is being fired.
    _____c. It would be treating a man as a thing to fire him with no consideration whatsoever, yet, if he will not accept the situation reasonably, it is probably best to let him get angry.

How to Resign and Die and Things Like That

How do you fire a man—or resign from a job? How do you tell a client you don't want to handle his business any more? How do you break an engagement (to play golf or get married)? How do you die?

There are two reasons why any human relationship should be terminated gingerly—even tenderly, if possible. One reason is the other fellow; the second reason is you. Obviously, you don't want to make an enemy or bruise feelings—but, more than that, you don't want to brutalize yourself. Someone has said that slavery is as bad for the master as for the slave. Maybe it's worse. Treating people as if they were things (there's a word for it, "reify") turns the mucous membrane of compassion into a callus. Repeated often enough, the callus spreads over all other regions of sensitivity—and you end up a beast.

In firing a man it is too customary to persuade him that the failure is his fault—and his alone. He was given every chance, wasn't he? Didn't you spend patient hours with him, trying to make it work? Maybe he isn't suited to contact work or copywriting or even advertising. Get yourself off the hook; get the company off the hook; get him nodding at his own inadequacies and— And what? And he jumps out of the window.

Compassion takes many forms. There is a great deal of kindness, for instance, in the statement that the least you can do for a man when you have to fire him is to let him get good and sore at you. Buoyed up by adrenaline, he'll stalk out cursing you and your forebears, sure that he was unappreciated and, in this mood, get another job much more easily than if he drags himself out doing a *mea culpa*.

A small agency I know has surrendered several accounts all in the same tone of voice—furious. In a sort of benevolent dissembling the agency head feigns rage over a non-existent betrayal.

"I hear you invited Papert, Koenig in to talk to you," he announces apoplectically. "The hell with it. If that's all the confidence you've got in us—" etc. Same technique as above—let everybody involved get good and sore. Afterwards, you can laugh at it together—if you want to resume your relationship.

As for how to break an engagement and how to die, information on these subjects will be mailed in plain wrappers (pink and black respectively) to those requesting it.

Figure 6A   161

Reprinted with permission from the May 1963 issue of *Madison Avenue*.

Answers: 1. c
2. b
3. c or b

Correct your answers and then go on to skim- and close-read the second selection "When You Fire Him" by Clarence Randall (Figure 6B). Having completed this reading, answer the following questions.

1. The tone of Randall's article is:
_____a. Idealistic.
_____b. Humane and realistic.
_____c. Embittered.

2. Randall's article states that:
_____a. The welfare of the institution as a whole should dictate when to fire a man.
_____b. A man should never be fired if it seems he will not recover from the blow.
_____c. Embezzlement is not sufficient reason to fire a long-term employee.

3. Choose the best summary for the Randall article:
_____a. When a man is fired, his family is fired as well. To save the agony of facing them with the bad news, the family should be present at the final interview.
_____b. Firing an employee is never an easy task. It is a matter that requires fine judgment and humanity. However, the real task is to hire selectively enough so that the problem will not often arise.
_____c. Since men react very differently to being fired, the conscientious executive should first determine whether the man will be redeemed by his firing or will be driven into uselessness for the rest of his life.

Answers: 1. b
2. a
3. b

Critical Evaluation

1. The tone of the two articles is quite different. Which do you feel is more appropriate to the article and why?

When You Fire Him

by Clarence Randall

In this article, CLARENCE RANDALL, formerly the president of Inland Steel, confronts one of the most sensitive situations in business, the necessity of discharging an employee who has been too long on the payroll. When does a company move too fast in such crises, when too slowly?

MANAGEMENT is rapidly being overtaken by methodology. Practices and programs which we of the senior generation had to master in the school of experience can now be learned from textbooks. And this is good.

There are still problems, however, which every executive must face at some time in his career where he will be strictly on his own, with no background of theory to guide him. There are still crises so personal, so intimately involved in the whole welfare of the corporation that no outside analyst, brilliant though he may be, can safely offer a solution. A man must fight his own way through, relying on nothing but his instinct for the right, his courage, and his own intelligence. Of all such experiences, there is none more poignant, none that calls for greater staunchness of character than that required in the discharge of an employee who has been on the payroll for a long time.

Whether the employee whose service clearly must be terminated be an attractive misfit or the senior vice president, the man who bears the ultimate responsibility for making the decision has a lonely task. There are none to help him. The better qualified he is as an executive, in terms of sensitivity to human values, the greater will be his anguish when at long last he decides that the firing simply must be done. The night before he will have no sleep. And when his own career ends, and he enters into retirement, he will say to his wife, "Well, at any rate, I shall never have to do that again."

Our forebears were not so squeamish. They fired men right and left, for good reason or out of animosity or for no reason at all, thus, by their callousness, setting in motion the forces that have hastened our own increasing social maturity. Through their shortcomings we have been brought to see that human values must be weighed against the dollar values before the drastic step of severance is taken.

When a man is fired, it is not only he who is discharged, but his family as well. In a good company the employee's wife and children are known to many of the other workers or officials — not as numbers on the files of the personnel office, but as human beings. Their welfare is properly a matter of concern for management. Possibly the wife has a lingering illness which is making a heavy drain on the family budget, and her treatments must be continued or her recovery will be endangered. Perhaps the oldest daughter is just about to enter college, or the final payment is due on the home of which they are all so proud. Every such consideration must be brought into play in the mind of the responsible officer and evaluated against the welfare of the institution as a whole, before he makes his decision.

Weighed, also, must be the question of what the impact of the discharge will be upon the man him-

Figure 6B   58

self, what will be the consequences in terms of his usefulness to society during the remaining years of his life.

We have all known men who have boasted that their success began from the day they were fired, and who insisted that they were grateful to the man who discharged them. And it is certain that this totally unexpected event can bring an individual up short in a salutary way. It can so shake him out of complacency, so challenge his whole way of life that the turnabout which his friends have so long hoped for begins at that point.

On the other hand, there have been men who, upon being fired, have walked straight out of the boss's office and committed suicide. They were so overcome with shame that they could not bring themselves to face their families and friends. More common are the experiences of those who never again secure steady employment. For years they drift from job to job, gradually turning to alcohol as they seek escape from frustration and chagrin.

Thus, the conscientious executive may find himself at grips with a problem that is almost too big for him. Some men move swiftly and impulsively and suffer later for their errors; others temporize, putting off what they know they ought to do, hoping vainly for a miracle. It is never easy.

The catalogue of the reasons why employees are discharged is long. There is the man who refuses to carry out instructions. He thinks he knows better than the boss. Occasionally he may be right. But an order must be obeyed or there is no management. He must either comply or leave.

There is the man who is never on time. He punches the clock late every day or invariably is the last to return from lunch. Because he is a team member, his conduct reduces the efficiency of others, and if he ignores repeated warnings, he must be removed.

Then there is the man who so constantly annoys everyone around him that group morale is seriously affected. His language is too coarse for decency, his barbed remarks hurt, he "bears false witness against his neighbors," he lacks respect for the women on the staff, or is an inveterate practical joker. Here again, a reprimand is the first step, but if the abuse is chronic, it must be stopped.

More subtle to detect, and more baffling to deal with, are the psychological problems — the alcoholic, for example. The problem of alcoholism may take the form of drunkenness on the job, which is dangerous, or it may consist in the constant dulling of the senses from quiet, solitary slugs. Parallel in effect are the deeply disturbing emotional experiences — the secretary whose engagement of long standing has been broken, or the husband whose wife has just deserted him and the children. Here the responsible officer may need

both medical and psychiatric advice, but in the end he alone must make the decision as to when the limit of tolerance has been reached.

ABOVE these are the crises in discharge which come once or twice in a man's business career and which test him to the very limit.

These fall into two main categories: the first, a serious breach of trust, and the second, incurable incompetence. Worst of all, the agony is usually compounded by the fact that the employee involved has for years been the close associate of the executive. Strangely enough, our behavior is not the same in both these circumstances. We tend to move swiftly and in anger for dishonesty, and to procrastinate for proven lack of ability.

My views will be thought unorthodox, but I believe that our prevailing practice should be reversed. I think that we should move more slowly than we do when confronted by dishonor, and more rapidly with respect to incompetence.

Breach of trust may take many forms, ranging all the way from the falsification of records to crass venality, but let us take the embezzlement of funds as an example. What do we do at such a time? Nothing more simple! The man who robs the till is fired immediately upon discovery of the theft. Within the hour he is gone; thereafter he will be seen only in the courtroom.

Our reaction is exactly the same as that which causes a man to strike a snake with a stick. No thought whatever is given to the man's future, or to whether it is part of our obligation to society to help rehabilitate him and restore him to useful living. Who else will do it? We cast him from us at the one time in his life when he most needs our help. He had capacity or he would not have held that job at all, and now those abilities will be forever wasted, for without our backing he cannot possibly have a decent second chance, no matter how penitent he may be.

Yet, in situations where breach of trust is involved, the actual injury to the corporation is seldom significant in terms of its overall operations. If it is, management itself is usually vulnerable for having so long permitted an unwholesome situation to continue without investigation. Ordinarily, too, the money loss is covered by insurance. Seldom is the forward progress of the company even noticeably endangered. Morally the circumstances are spectacular, but economically they may be negligible, and we should display more balanced judgment. In terms of company policy, human considerations should be the controlling ones, unless we honestly believe that the welfare of the institution itself is seriously threatened.

Figure 6B (Cont.)   59

Discharge for incompetence, however, is an altogether different matter. There the ultimate success of the venture may already be at stake. When, through the glacial pressure of seniority, or nepotism, or any similar cause, a man of insufficient capacity comes to a position of substantial responsibility, forward progress is blocked. His mediocrity settles down over his range of authority like a thick fog. Perhaps he is bold, but solely because he lacks the sensitivity to foresee the consequences of his actions; perhaps he is wise, but weak; perhaps he is kindly, but dull. Whatever the reason, his incapacity must not be permitted to block the progress of the company. The man must be removed.

Once the situation is fully recognized, there should be no delay whatever. Immediate surgery shows the greatest mercy for all concerned. By hypothesis, there is no reasonable prospect of improvement, and the welfare of the individual has to yield to that of the institution as a whole.

Nor is the potential damage to the man as great as in a case where dishonor is involved. Since no moral stigma is attached to his leaving, there is always a reasonable chance that he can re-establish himself in some other calling.

The corporation must, of course, deal generously with him, particularly if his service has been long and conscientious, which is nearly always true in the really tough cases. A good formula is to set up for him a pension equal to the median between what is due him as of the time of the discharge and what would have been due him had he gone all the way through to retirement. That is little enough burden for the corporation to bear as a penalty for its own neglect in permitting the intolerable situation to develop.

The supreme crisis occurs, of course, when it is the chief executive himself whose mediocrity and indecisiveness so blanket the affairs of the company that initiative and creative effort are thwarted at every level. The situation can then be saved only by the board of directors, and that calls for industrial courage of the highest order. Most of the directors are there because he nominated them. If it is an inside board, composed only of company officers, the case is completely hopeless. Their own jobs are at stake if they should organize a palace revolution and lose. But even if the majority are from the outside, their interest in the company is so nominal that only a man of exceptional fortitude will face up to his old friend and tell him that he must resign. Usually nothing is done, and the company gradually withers away.

There is only one answer. We must so improve our methods of selection and training that mediocrity will be detected before it is permitted to ripen into authority.

Figure 6B (Cont.)

2. What assumptions are shared by both Samstag and Randall?

3. Review your mental structure of the two articles. Do you detect structural defects in either one of them?

4. Using each article as a comment on the other, which would you say represents a more readily acceptable solution to the majority of executives?

_____

_____

_____

Answers: 1. The tone of voice in Randall's article seems more acceptable. It is uniformly serious, and the subject matter is certainly serious. Samstag is alternately serious and facetious. He has probably used this tone to catch the reader's interest and put him in a receptive frame of mind. This is a standard writing device, but it is dangerous to the extent that the reader may be amused and never take the issues seriously.

2. Both Samstag and Randall share the belief that the business community cannot be indifferent to the problems of the individual human personality, even though that is not the main concern of business. Because this assumption is not universally accepted, it is important that you recognize it. Note especially Randall's paragraph beginning: "Our forebears were not so squeamish."

3. Samstag's article may be less effective, but structurally it is quite coherent. Randall's, on the other hand, shows an important structural defect. In the last paragraph—the resolution of his article—he includes a sentence that begins: "We must so improve our methods of selection . . . ," thereby introducing a vast subject he has not mentioned previously, and which he cannot begin to cover in a few lines.

4. Samstag's article is unquestionably easier to accept because it involves far less responsibility for the executive concerned. Note that Samstag deals with the situa-

tion in which the decision to fire has already been made. Randall, despite his title, brings up the agonizing question of whether or not the situation really justifies the extreme solution of firing a man. In addition, consider that his real answer, better methods of selection, is not made specific, so that an executive would find it much more difficult to implement Randall's proposal.

REMEMBER: In any work with critical evaluation, you are dealing with relatives. No letter-perfect answers exist. However, if your answers differ markedly from ours, examine both your reasoning and the text to be sure they can be justified.

CRITICAL READING: FURTHER APPLICATION I

Here is another pair of articles. Each one is an introduction to a book published by Avon. The books are clearly intended to be contrasted with one another, and the introductions offer several initial points of contrast. You are to skim-read and then close-read the first selection (Figure 6C), answer the questions on it, and then repeat the procedure for the second selection before going on to the similarities and differences.

1. According to Goldwater, conservatives are

    _____a. United in their belief that liberty is more important than security.

    _____b. Opposed to liberal programs and to forward action.

    _____c. Reviving.

2. Choose the best beginning for a summary from those below and complete it in a few words.

    a. Americans are unmanageable, but, with proper conservative

    guidance, they can _____.

    b. The conservative revival is misnamed since _____

    _____; furthermore, _____

    _____.

INTRODUCTION
By Senator Barry Goldwater

Americans are an unmanageable lot.

Just when it appears that they have been propagandized enough, or scared enough, or subsidized enough to turn over their basic responsibilities to those who claim to know what is best for them—they rebel.

It's enough to turn a government planner's hair gray.

In my ten years as a United States Senator, I have been privileged to talk personally to hundreds of thousands of Americans in every part of our nation. I have watched their rebellion take shape and grow into the Conservative Revival we hear so much about today.

Actually, it is not entirely accurate to call it a "revival," because that term implies regaining something which has been lost. We must remember that most Americans have been essentially conservative since the founding of our country. What is happening today is that millions of them are becoming aware of the dangers which threaten our free institutions and they are beginning to speak out for what they have always believed.

Conservatism offers thought-provoking reading for these newly-aroused conservatives, as well as for all other Americans who are concerned about our nation in this critical decade. For some readers, the points of view this book present will be new and striking. For others, the book will help explain and support positions long espoused. For those whose beliefs are in opposition to those of conservatives, it will offer a standard against which to measure those beliefs.

This book has been written for laymen, by a layman. Dean Smith, who has had experience as a reporter and editor, uses both backgrounds in presenting the viewpoints of selected conservative spokesmen from pre-Constitution days to the present. Among those spokesmen are scholars and practical politicians, Presidents and businessmen, philosophers and reporters on the national scene.

It is interesting to note that, despite the many differences of

ix

opinion among conservatives through the years, these spokesmen have been in agreement on basic principles. They all value liberty over security, for example. They believe that power should be diffused. They believe that the marketplace regulates our economy more efficiently than could any government bureau. And they believe that Americans can attain the greatest possible spiritual and material benefits only in a society which guarantees individual freedom of choice.

Today the benefits of these giants of conservatism are being challenged.

I cannot agree with those who tell us that America is now so big and complex that individuals must surrender their rights and responsibilities to an all-powerful central government. I cannot agree that the Constitution is old-fashioned, or that its grants of powers to the states and the people are no longer valid. In short, I cannot believe that we Americans will ever be willing to surrender the management of our lives to a central officialdom which purports to know more about what is good for us than we do.

Conservatives, as this book points out, cannot be content with simple opposition to liberal programs which lead to the monolithic welfare state. We must take a positive approach, developing and advocating programs based on Constitutional principles and dependent for their motive power on individual and community initiative.

The problems which face us today are many and complex, and they have been made more numerous and more complex by repeated tampering with the natural laws which have governed the lives of men for thousands of years. But these problems can be solved, and will be solved, when we at last determine to abandon frenzied social experimentation and return to the tested governmental principles which made our nation the greatest the world has ever known.

When can we expect our nation's government to be guided once again by conservative principles?

We can expect that day when the millions of Americans of conservative inclination are motivated enough to discover conservatism, to learn more about it, and to go to work on its behalf.

I believe *Conservatism* may help provide that motivation.

Figure 6C Permission to reprint Introduction by Barry Goldwater and Avon Books Division, The Hearst Corporation, New

c. If conservatives steadfastly oppose the liberals, they can succeed

in _____.

> *Answers:* 1. a
> 2. b. The conservative revival is misnamed
> since America has always been a basically
> conservative nation; furthermore, the
> complex problems of today will be best
> dealt with when we return to the tested
> principles which made this country great.

Check your answers and go on to the second article (Figure 6D).

1. Humphrey's introduction defines "the liberal" as
   _____a. Daring and courageous.
   _____b. Idealistic and utopian.
   _____c. Experimental and striving for improvement.

2. Choose the best beginning for a summary from those below and complete it in a few words.

   a. Liberals feel that change is desirable for its own sake and

   should be a _____.

   b. The inevitable radicalism of "self-satisfied" liberals must be

   controlled by _____.

   c. This is an essentially liberal nation because _____

   _____.

> *Answers:* 1. c. The first answer is correct because
> Humphrey has made exactly that point,
> but, basically, he sees the liberal as a
> person willing to try new ideas.
> 2. c. . . . change is an essential part of
> America, and the liberal is willing to
> work with it instead of against it. Furthermore, our programs of social welfare
> and foreign aid over a period of many
> years is proof of our basically liberal
> temper.

INTRODUCTION
By Senator Hubert H. Humphrey

Liberals fully recognize that *change* is inevitable in the patterns of society and in the challenges which confront man.

The liberal cannot accept the status quo. He seeks to guide the constant tides of change, rather than ride them aimlessly toward unknown ends.

The liberal strives for improvement, and believes that representative government in a free nation should be a positive influence and force to improve society's conditions and opportunities.

The liberal dares to try the difficult and even "the impossible." He is willing to experiment. He respects dissent. He knows that his ideas, opinions and policies are frequently in need of criticism and re-examination.

Milton Viorst's candid and provocative study of liberalism in America offers that criticism.

There is much in this book with which I disagree, but I welcome its publication.

Other liberals may also disagree with certain ideas and points of view put forth in this book. But they would do well to remember the words of President Franklin D. Roosevelt on being asked why liberals so often are divided and conservatives united:

"There are many ways of going forward," he said. "But there is only one way of standing still."

The flood of books, magazine articles and foot-stamping rallies let loose by conservatives in recent years has been marked by a distinct mood of self-satisfaction.

Dedicated conservatives have little room for self-criticism. They tend to view all social and human problems with black-and-white clarity. They offer easy answers to the immensely difficult challenges the Nation and the world face. They offer simple solutions for the complex problems of the individual and society-at-large.

LIBERALISM offers no easy answers or simple solutions. It *does* challenge liberals to seek new and more effective methods to strengthen freedom and spur man's progress.

Today, liberalism may get less attention in newspapers and magazines than does conservatism. Its advocates may be less noisy and less prolific as orators and writers.

But the basic principles of liberalism have become—as Mr. Viorst illustrates—a vital part of America's character, mood and society.

For a Nation committed to programs guaranteeing equal economic and social opportunities to *all* its citizens is a liberal Nation. A country committed to helping underdeveloped nations to progress and freedom is a liberal country.

There may be a "conservative tide" running in America today. But, at best, that tide can only ebb against the solid—and still growing—wall of achievement and progress which liberal policies and programs have built during the nearly 200 years history of the United States of America.

Senator Hubert H. Humphrey

Figure 6D Permission to reprint Introduction by Hubert H. Humphrey and Avon Books Division, The Hearst Corporation, New York, 1963.

Similarities and Differences

The following grid is designed to help you order the points of similarity and difference between the two articles. Perhaps you will see more; perhaps in the questions that follow you will disagree with the interpretation put upon one or another statement. That is perfectly acceptable *if* you can support your contention with evidence from the text.

1. What characteristics does each author attribute to conservatives on the one hand and liberals on the other?

CHARACTERISTICS

Conservatives   *Liberals*

AUTHOR: Goldwater

AUTHOR: Humphrey

● Goldwater implies that the liberal is a propagandizer and one who claims to "know what is best" for the American people; that liberal programs "lead to the monolithic welfare state"; that liberals claim that "the Constitution is old-fashioned"; and that "its grants of powers to the states and the people are no longer valid"—although he attributes none of these traits directly. The conservative, however, values liberty over security; believes that power should be diffused, and that "the marketplace regulates our economy more effectively than could any government bureau."

● Humphrey, on the other hand, feels that the liberal "cannot accept the status quo," "seeks to guide . . . change," "dares to try the difficult," "is willing to experiment," yet "respects dissent" and welcomes criticism. The conservative, however, is "marked by a distinct mood of self-satisfaction," views "all social and human problems with black-and-white clarity," offers "easy answers" and "simple solutions."

2. What similarities do you find between the two points of view? What beliefs do the two obviously hold in common? Is there good evidence in the text?

_____

_____

_____.

Are any of the similarities primarily rhetorical (of the "Sin is bad" variety)?

_____

_____

_____.

● Consider Goldwater's paragraph beginning: "The problems which face us today are . . .," with Humphrey's beginning: "Dedicated conservatives have . . ." In these paragraphs the two authors state their analyses of the conditions and needs in America today. Both agree that the problems are complex, and they agree that the conservative position advocates a return to "basic principles" (Goldwater) or "simple solutions" (Humphrey). Other similarities of a similar type can be singled out, usually colored by the political allegiance of the author.

● There are primarily rhetorical agreements as well. These include the generally accepted opinion that America is a great nation, and the object of government should be the guarantee of certain benefits to the nation's citizens—although the two men differ in their definition of benefits: "greatest possible spiritual and material benefits" (Goldwater) and "equal economic and social opportunities" (Humphrey).

Critical Evaluation

3. Finally, with which statements and positions do you agree? Why? Are your choices consistent? Get them down—this last step is the real purpose of the preceding analysis.

_____

_____

_____

_____ .

The answers to these questions will be as varied as the number of readers. What you should look for in checking yourself is logic in your answers. Can you detect strengths and weaknesses in both arguments, putting aside your own political allegiance?

CRITICAL READING: FURTHER APPLICATION II

The following two articles describe quite different programs of advanced education for middle and upper level executives. Such programs are becoming more common and are supported by a single, basic premise which should be readily inferred. But the secondary assumptions of the two programs— assumptions about the proper aims of advanced education for management —are far from alike.

Read the first article (Figure 6E) and answer the comprehension and summary questions that follow before tackling the second.

ANSWER THE FOLLOWING QUESTIONS ABOUT FIGURE 6E

1. The institute was

_____a. Originated by the University of Pennsylvania and sold to Bell.

_____b. Requested by Bell and developed by the University.

_____c. Developed by Bell and carried on by the University.

2. Choose the best beginning for a summary from those below and complete it in a few words.

e. digby baltzell

Bell Telephone's Experiment in Education*

Many leaders in American business have been frankly worried about the supply of broadly educated executives for top management positions. Talented and conscientious young men who are now climbing the large corporation ladders too often exhibit the "trained incapacity," of the narrow expert, and for understandable reasons: many of them are recruited from business and engineering schools rather than liberal-arts colleges. Moreover, the pressure of their jobs narrows rather than expands their interests in the world about them.

W. D. Gillen, president of the Bell Telephone Company of Pennsylvania and a trustee of the University of Pennsylvania, determined several years ago to find some way of broadening the educational background and expanding the point of view of Bell's most promising young men. In 1952, he discussed with the representatives of the University of Pennsylvania a new kind of education for executive leadership; together they decided that in contrast to the usual executive *training* program, young executives needed a really firm grounding in the humanities or liberal arts. A well-trained man knows *how* to answer questions, they reasoned; an educated man knows *what* questions are worth asking. At the policy level, Bell wanted more of the latter.

* From *Harper's* magazine (March, 1955). By permission of Dr. E. Digby Baltzell.

The first group of Bell executives arrived the following September and, as a member of the faculty assigned to keep close tabs on the experiment, I got to know them and their problems well. There were seventeen of them, a carefully chosen lot from various sections of the country. But they were all from the middle levels of management. Eleven were between thirty-five and forty years of age, three were in their early thirties, and one was forty-eight; their average length of service with the Bell System was thirteen years; all were married and all, save one, were fathers; fifteen were college graduates, nine had B.S. degrees and six had B.A.'s.

Each of them was granted a ten months' leave of absence with full salary from his regular job in order to devote his full time to the Institute. The first nine months of the program included 550 hours of lectures, discussions and seminars. The final four weeks of the program were set aside for a reading period during which the men were entirely on their own.

To jar the businessmen-students out of the job atmosphere from which they had come, the courses were deliberately arranged so as to proceed from unfamiliar ideas and material to those closer to their own lives and experiences. In the early months of the program the men received a highly concentrated dose of systematic logic, the study of Oriental history and art, and the reading of such works as the *Bhagavad-Gita*, *Monkey* and *The Tale of Genji*—a far cry from the American suburban groove and business routine. By December many of the students were depressed; the "Bagdad Geisha," they felt, was a waste of time.

On the other hand, as the end of the program approached, the men were prepared to bring a wide-ranging intellectual experience to bear on problems much closer to home. In the final and most popular course, American Civilization, they spent twelve weeks discussing such problems as: the making of the Constitution; the Haymarket Riot and the industrialization of America; *Sister Carrie* and the revolution in American sex

174

Figure 6E   Reprinted with permission of the author, E. Digby Baltzell, from the March 1955 issue of *Harper's Magazine*.

mores; *Main Street* and the disillusionment of the 1920's; and *The Lonely Crowd* and American character structure. The course was organized on the theory that one approached Carol Kennicott's struggles with Main Street from a broader point of view for having known something about Prince Genji in eleventh-century Japan.

For ten months the seventeen Bell men were kept busy. In addition to the regular classwork, they read constantly (more than the average graduate student); they went on formally planned trips to art galleries, museums and historical sights in Washington, New York and Philadelphia; a block of seats was reserved for them at the Philadelphia Orchestra concerts; and they visited and studied in some of the distinguished examples of residential and institutional architecture in the city.

In Utopia, perhaps, men will be "trained" in their teens and "educated" in their thirties.

"This is my one big opportunity," one of the men said to me after he had been in the course for several months, "and I mean to make the most of it." This sense of cramming into a short ten months what might have been for many men several years of education raised several questions. Were these men interested primarily in doing a good job in the Institute because it might mean later promotions in the Bell System for them? Having been exposed to an experience that would presumably change their attitudes toward their jobs and their leisure, was there a chance that they would never again be satisfied with the struggle up the corporate ladder? These were questions that those of us on the faculty asked ourselves, and some of the answers became apparent during the course of the year. Others will remain unanswered for some time.

As the course was drawing to its close, each of its members was asked to fill out an anonymous questionnaire in which he was to give his opinion of the course and the effect it had on him. A number of revealing, if not surprising, changes in attitude came to light. Reading habits, for one thing, had changed.

"I'm taking more advantage of library facilities, reading two newspapers, and reviewing several good news magazines," one man said. Another reported, "I approach newspapers and periodicals with much more curiosity and speculation than before; politics make more sense; the art section in *Time* is not only readable but interesting; I read the book-review section in the *New York Times*; questions concerning McCarthyism are thought through with some real attention to ultimate questions."

The men all went back to their jobs in July. Almost six months later, during Christmas week, I talked with seven of them and had had long letters from three others. Although the effects of such an educational program as this one cannot be measured with any precision, some interesting effects that it has had on the men are already apparent.

In the first place, it must be remembered that they were chosen because of their demonstrated abilities and strong drives toward success in the Bell System. They are, they report, glad to be "in harness" again, and on the whole they have found the transition back to their jobs much easier than getting used to the program of the Institute. One theme runs through their comments on the effects of the program: they have considerably more confidence in themselves, which, in turn, has "created an even stronger desire for more and broader responsibility in the business."

What Americans proudly call know-how has produced many things: great corporations, great bombs and a great many automobiles and refrigerators. In the Institute of Humanistic Studies for Executives, however, Bell's high managers are seeking to remedy a weakness in American democracy which Tocqueville discerned over one hundred years ago. "It would seem as if the rulers of our time," he said, "sought only to use men in order to make things great; I wish they would try a little more to make great men; that they set less value on the work, and more value upon the workman."

a. Bell Telephone Company realized that its younger managers were exhibiting a "trained incapacity"; therefore, the company requested a program to include the following courses: _____

_____.

b. President Gillen of Bell and representatives of the University of Pennsylvania devised a training Institute. Its objectives were

_____

_____; and its method and operation were _____

_____.

c. Education of specialists is in such a state of narrow expertism that President Gillen decided to do his part toward preparing his executives in "how to answer" the very complex questions proposed by their jobs and by our society. Therefore, he and the University of Pennsylvania stressed _____

_____.

> *Answers:* 1. b. What is significant about the Institute
> is that it originated in the felt need of a
> major corporation, rather than in the
> University.
> 2. b. This is the best beginning, since it sets
> you up for a fairly inclusive summary.
> Your notes should include the Institute's
> objectives: broadening educational back-
> ground, expanding point of view, incul-
> cating an ability to "ask the right ques-
> tions." You should also mention the In-
> stitute's method: lectures, extensive read-
> ing, concerts, museums, and an approach
> that began from broad, far-ranging cate-
> gories to those closer to the executives'
> experience.

The following selection (Figure 6F) describes another executive-level education course. In order to make your summary at the end more precise, stress paragraph analysis and a running summary as you read.

Bringing Engineers Up to Date

by George A. W. Boehm

Nicholas Solovioff

The best engineers working for U.S. business are apt to be the ones most in need of retraining. General Electric and U.C.L.A. have a new scientific cram course that does the job in six hectic weeks.

The onrush of science and technology has created a perplexing employment problem, not only for steelworkers and longshoremen, but for engineers. The problem is likely to be largest, ironically, for the *best* engineers: for the man who has not stuck to some narrow specialty over the years, but has risen into management, and been given responsibility for, say, a diverse engineering group or a development laboratory. His problem now, stated simply, is that he finds it increasingly hard to understand what the young men under him are talking about.

He will probably be utterly baffled by any chemists, physicists, mathematicians, or biologists in his group. He may even have trouble with the young engineers. The school he himself went to was probably strong on how-to-do-it courses, but today a good engineering college gives the students stiff doses of basic science, including quantum physics, relativity theory, advanced thermodynamics, and matrix algebra. The schools also offer courses in feedback control, computers, nuclear engineering, inertial guidance, rocket propulsion, plasma physics, solid-state electronics—subjects that hardly existed when the forty-five-year-old manager was in school.

How can he manage men with whom he can scarcely communicate? How can he judge the capabilities of men to be hired and advanced, or evaluate proposed development programs, when his own education is so hopelessly out of date? What, in fact, can be done with him?

If he were an engineering specialist, his problem would be minimal, especially if he worked for one of the large, technologically oriented companies, like Bell Telephone Laboratories or I.B.M. Virtually all such companies sponsor training programs for many of their engineers, often paying the tuition and releasing them from work so that they can study. Their re-education is coming to be viewed more as a duty than a fringe benefit. The young engineer not long out of college is encouraged to pursue a master's or a doctor's degree. The older men who are specialists take courses in their own fields offered by schools, technical societies, or their own companies.

But none of these programs are of much use to the engineering manager. It is obvious that he needs a special kind of educational help. He probably lacks the scientific background he would need to take individual courses in quantum mechanics, for example, or statistical inference. But he also lacks the time it would take to re-educate himself from the bottom up. What he needs is something in between. It doesn't exist within the framework of conventional education, but it does exist, now, under the sponsorship of some businessmen and educators with a special interest in the problem.

Six weeks to sophistication

The new program consists of a six-week cram course in the fundamentals of science and technology. The aim is to make the student conversant with the concepts important in modern engineering. While he does not become an expert in any particular field, he gains at least enough insight to comprehend and evaluate research and development work he may be called upon to direct.

The idea for this course originated in 1959 at a meeting of the American Society for Engineering Education, in St. Louis. Stanley M. Little, director of industrial relations for Boeing's Aerospace Division, observed during a committee meeting that there were already plenty of courses to educate engineers in management; what was lacking, he argued, was a course to bolster the managers' understanding of modern science and engineering. J. Morley English, an engineering professor at U.C.L.A., seized upon Little's suggestion and began organizing just such a course. He first considered a broad review of science and technology that would have taken at least nine weeks, and perhaps as many as thirteen. But after discussing his plans with a number of industrial executives, he concluded that few companies would consent to release key people for that long. He settled for an intensive six-week course, entitled "Modern Engineering."

The first session was held during June and July of 1961 at the posh Ojai Valley Inn and Country Club, seventy-five miles northwest of Los Angeles. Among the thirty-five students who attended were a dozen military officers; the rest came mainly from the area's aerospace and electronics industries and included one company president (M. O. Kappler of System Development Corp., Santa Monica) and two vice presidents. Most of the lectures were given by U.C.L.A. professors, but English added to his faculty outstanding scientists and engineers from local industry and from other universities.

The course was repeated a year later at Ojai, and it will be given again this summer at Santa Ynez Inn in Pacific Palisades, just twenty minutes from the U.C.L.A. campus. The success of the course has helped the university attract an impressive list of guest speakers, including Nobel laureate chemist Harold C. Urey; physicist Edward Teller; Richard E. Bellman, a leading mathematician associated with Rand Corp.; and neurophysiologist Warren S. McCulloch of M.I.T. Despite the high costs—U.C.L.A. charges $1,500 for tuition and $20 a day to house the student—there has been no difficulty in enrolling thirty or thirty-five each time. That is about as many as English thinks should be taught in one class.

G.E. buys a course

Meanwhile, his Modern Engineering course has had an interesting and significant offshoot. Francis K. McCune, General Electric's engineering vice president, sent two of his engineering managers to attend the first Ojai session. They returned full of enthusiasm for the course, and McCune decided to offer something like it just for G.E. men. This proposition was turned over to the company's Engineering Administrative Consulting Service (a staff group that does technical consulting and trouble-shooting within the company). It arranged for English to offer the course at G.E.'s management-training center in Crotonville, New York. U.C.L.A. got a lump sum of $50,000 to cover all its costs.

English descended on Crotonville a year ago, bringing with him much the same staff of lecturers that had taught at Ojai, but supplementing them with professors from M.I.T., Dartmouth, Polytechnic Institute of Brooklyn, and other eastern schools. G.E. assembled a student body of twenty-four of its engineering managers. Almost all were between thirty-five and forty-five, had been with the company more than ten years, and within the last five years had been promoted to managerial positions in which they were directing technical staffs of twenty to more than a hundred people.

G.E. had bought the Modern Engineering course on a one-shot basis, with the understanding that the company itself would take over any subsequent sessions. The participants were generally so enthusiastic about the first trial that Charles C. Leader, manager of the Engineering Administrative Consulting Service, decided to give the course again last fall, this time at the stately old Gideon

Putnam Hotel in Saratoga Springs, New York. From his staff Leader named Dolph G. Ebeling "dean" of Modern Engineering. Ebeling, forty-two, a lanky, energetic New Yorker, is a graduate of Rensselaer Polytechnic Institute who has done some teaching from time to time since joining G.E. in 1946. An extraordinary breadth of experience in metallurgy (in which he holds a Ph.D.), turbine generators, chemistry, research, and atomic energy had given Ebeling clear ideas about what engineers should know in order to communicate with scientists and mathematicians—and with one another.

Ebeling began at once to make revisions that would bring the course into closer alignment with G.E.'s specific needs. Many of the participants at Crotonville had complained that U.C.L.A. put too much emphasis on economics, systems engineering, and the philosophy of engineering design—subjects that G.E.'s veteran engineers felt they already knew well enough. In place of these, Ebeling substituted extra lectures in basic science, mathematics, and engineering fundamentals. He then partially rearranged the order in which various subjects would be taken up. His concept of the course, essentially in agreement with English's, requires the students to absorb two parallel streams of knowledge: in one stream are pure and applied mathematics; in the other are physics, chemistry, engineering, and a little biology. While he was still planning the course, in midsummer, Ebeling was joined by Loyal V. Bewley, who had just retired as dean of engineering at Lehigh University and come to G.E. Together they solved with astonishing success the problem of timing the course so that the topics in the physical sciences would come in logical order and would be preceded by the necessary mathematics.

At Saratoga Springs, G.E.'s version of Modern Engineering consisted of some hundred ninety-minute lectures spread over six weeks. Major topics followed this order:
- First week: review of calculus (which all the students once knew), differential equations, vector analysis, introduction to atomic and nuclear theory.
- Second week: complex variables (numbers containing the square root of minus one), matrix algebra, relativity theory, electromagnetic theory, fission and fusion power.
- Third week: probability, statistics, the concept of entropy (originated in thermodynamics to describe disorder among particles but now applied also to the flow of information), wave mechanics, statistical mechanics.
- Fourth week: mathematical theory of decisions, tensor analysis, solid-state physics, optics, and cybernetics as it applies to biology.
- Fifth week: flow of heat and materials, metallurgy, stress and vibration analysis, chemistry of polymers (long-chain molecules typical of plastics, films, and fibers), power from fuel cells.
- Sixth week: feedback control, information theory and communication, computer design and application.

Don't wipe your glasses

G.E. is a company that has always been strong on employee education, and all the men at Saratoga Springs had been through some of its training programs—e.g., courses in management—but none had ever been exposed to a grind like Modern Engineering. The schedule called for three or four lectures a day (two on Saturday) plus frequent after-dinner talks by notable scientists and engineers. Although no homework was required or examinations given, each man got a ponderous stack of textbooks, and some studied almost every evening until midnight. Every lecture was a grueling experience in itself. Most of the teachers maintained a pace that left no time for relaxation. One

Figure 6F (Cont.)

student remarked, exaggerating only slightly, "I once took my eyes off the blackboard to wipe my glasses and missed a whole semester of math."

The word is getting around G.E. that absorbing the content of Modern Engineering calls for some special techniques of studying. After the first week or so most of the students realize that it is important not to get bogged down in details; they don't take copious notes in class or spend hours wrestling with some knotty textbook problem. Several have felt a need for some diversion, such as bowling, during the six weeks. But it is clear that the course must be approached as a full-time job. A few men who have tried to take the course while running their offices by long-distance telephone have missed a great deal.

A third session of G.E.'s Modern Engineering is beginning at Crotonville as this article goes to press. Ebeling has again made some minor modifications in the curriculum, chiefly by adding a few lectures on industrial design, processing, and marketing strategy, and a weekly workshop on the application of computers to problems that come up in the mainstream of the course. But, basically, the course continues to stress the fundamentals of science and engineering – particularly such great unifying ideas as relativity theory, fluid dynamics, and quantum mechanics.

Ebeling has also been busy expanding his faculty. He can hardly count on all his teachers to be on call every time he needs them, and so he must line up able alternates. It is no easy job to get the right kind of men. Not every brilliant lecturer can effectively teach a large body of knowledge to a group of mature and experienced engineers in just a few hours. The students have objected vigorously to a few teachers who displayed their own virtuosity by working out complex problems on the blackboard at breakneck speed. On the other hand, they have applauded clear and patient expositors, notably, Robert S. Elliott of U.C.L.A.; University of California physicist Harvey White, famous for his television lectures on *Continental Classroom;* and polymer chemist Herman F. Mark of Brooklyn Polytech. After hearing Elliott give a lucid explanation of relativity theory, one of the G.E. engineers exclaimed, gratefully, "I feel like I grew up with Einstein."

No lack of students

G.E. now plans to continue giving its Modern Engineering course twice a year, spring and fall. With about thirty men in every class, the company will never run out of candidates. It has some 750 men in high-level engineering management, and even allowing for those who are close to retirement and a few others who simply don't want to take the course—its intellectual challenge seems to inspire deep anxieties in some men— the turnover is great enough to keep the classrooms full indefinitely.

The course represents a considerable investment for the company. The students' salaries range from $15,000 to $30,000 a year; living expenses are $30 per day; administrative costs are $60,000 a year, including instructors' fees, books, and traveling expenses; and there are the salaries of Ebeling, a secretary, and assistant dean A. Noel Reagan (who is a graduate of the Saratoga Springs session). All together, Leader estimates, the course costs about $6,000 per student— a total of roughly $350,000 a year.

This expense would be hard to justify objectively to a literal-minded accountant, but the engineering managers who have taken Modern Engineering are convinced that G.E. is getting its money's worth. Harold E. Stocking, of the dishwasher and Disposall department, says that before he took the course he had been having trouble recruiting bright young engineering-school graduates; he wanted them, he remarked recently, but hardly knew how to go about interviewing them. Charles H. Holley of the turbine-generator department observed that Modern Engineering was worth taking simply as a sort of "language course," i.e., it introduced him to the new concepts and technical jargon that are necessary to discuss some problems with scientists and engineers in the company, or to plow through technical journals in diverse fields. Other graduates say that Modern Engineering renewed their confidence in their ability to learn, and several have followed it up by taking formal courses in such subjects as modern probability theory.

While most of the students have been satisfied with the subject matter of the course, Ebeling himself is not. Aware that he has a scant six weeks to expose his students to a sizable proportion of all scientific knowledge, he is still striving to make his peculiar educational process even more efficient. He will actually never be through; Modern Engineering will have to be modified continually to keep pace with modern engineering.

The bandwagon

Not surprisingly, G.E. has been bombarded with inquiries from other companies that would like to start similar courses. It seems unlikely that any but a very few highly technological industrial giants could afford to sponsor Modern Engineering on their own. A company with only a few engineering managers might find the cost per student exorbitant. And so some companies have looked to the engineering schools for help.

Thus far, none of these schools (except, of course, U.C.L.A.) have organized anything comparable to Modern Engineering, but several are becoming aware of the growing demand for this kind of course. Michigan State, for example, has been exploring much the same ground in ten weekend seminars extending from September through June. The 1961–62 series was given for twenty engineering managers of Lear Siegler, Inc.'s aerospace-instrument division. This year thirty engineering managers, mostly from industries in the Detroit area (including two from G.E.), are taking the course. Brooklyn Polytech is contemplating a four-week survey course for executives without any previous engineering training; the course might also be offered to certain legislators—e.g., Congressmen who must grapple with the technical aspects of atomic energy, advanced weapon systems, water-resource control, and air pollution.

Few schools, however, can now put on an effective, high-quality, far-ranging cram course of the kind U.C.L.A. and G.E. have developed. Ebeling and English, after all, have been able to enlist lecturers from all parts of the country; most engineering schools would be hard put to furnish a superlatively good teacher from their own faculties for each topic.

Gordon S. Brown, dean of engineering at M.I.T., believes that the best schools should start now to develop new institutes specifically geared to retraining engineers in industry. Many schools today are reluctant to throw the experienced engineer into classes with undergraduates and young graduate students—and with good reason. The older man is usually so rusty in his mathematics and other problem-solving techniques that he has a hard time keeping up with the class; on the other hand, he may be far ahead of it in areas calling for the kind of judgment he has developed through experience.

What Brown would like to see is an institute so flexible that it could upgrade all levels of engineering skill, both in breadth and in depth, and for the varying periods of time that industry is willing to release men for study. He envisions a broad spectrum of courses, including brief refreshers during the summer, full-year programs, and eight- to ten-week surveys not unlike Modern Engineering. In time, Brown says, companies will accept the fact that a policy of educational sabbaticals is one of the wisest investments that they can make. END

Figure 6F (Cont.)

ANSWER THE FOLLOWING QUESTIONS ABOUT FIGURE 6F

1. The Modern Engineering course was begun because

_____a. High-level engineering managers found themselves unable to understand the younger engineers they were directing.

_____b. Advances in science and technology had left the practicing engineers high and dry.

_____c. Managers had come to assume the direction of research in unfamiliar fields, and were unable to understand the jargon used by their researchers.

2. Choose the best beginning for a summary from those given below and complete it in a few words.

a. Engineers who have assumed management responsibilities for a diverse engineering group or development laboratory must _____

_____.

b. Because G.E. managers have to be familiar with advances in science and technology if they are to do an effective job, the company _____

_____.

c. Upper level management engineers complained that they were losing confidence in their ability to learn, so G.E. _____

_____.

Answers: 1. a.

2. b. Since we have given the broad objective of the course in the summary beginning, it is up to you to supply the most essential facts about the course: its length, subjects covered, depth to which participants were supposed to learn each subject. Keep in mind the importance of communication between the managers and their subordinates as one of the defining aspects of the whole program.

Similarities and Differences

1. List some of the *similarities* between the two programs as stated in the articles.

a. _____

b. _____

c. _____

2. Apparently both programs are based on a single, major assumption.

What is it? _____

_____

_____.

3. Upon further analysis, you should see that the objectives, and the resultant courses, are nearly opposite. To clarify the differences, try listing them in grid form.

Men Involved + Company's Objectives = Result

Bell

G.E.

Answers: 1. Both programs are for men well beyond college age; both are for men on management levels; both are intensive; and both require full-time participation.
2. The major assumption in both cases is that further education is necessary if management personnel are to do the best possible job.
3. The Bell men were younger specialists and *future* executives. The G.E. men were already in upper management positions, but specifically responsible in engineering fields. The Bell men needed training in what questions to ask—in

other words, broad, decision-making roles; while the G.E. men were being caught up on developments already going on. As a result, the Bell course is a broad, humanistic survey, while that given by G.E. concentrates on a review and intensive training in the more specialized field of mathematics and the sciences.

Critical Evaluation

4. Which program do you think is more likely to fulfill its objectives? Why?

_____

_____

_____.

5. Are there other facts you would like to have before coming to a decision? What are they?

_____

_____

_____.

● Remember in both these questions that you are judging the programs *through the articles.* With that proviso in mind, your answer might very well be that the G.E. program probably will be able to fulfill its objectives more uniformly because the objectives, according to *Fortune,* have been much more clearly defined than those of the Bell program. On the other hand, and as a critical reader and thinker, you may argue from the first article that the G.E. program is really encouraging the kind of trained incapacity that Bell has attempted to minimize by a broader approach. However—and this might be the wisest decision of all—you might try to find further information about the exact rank that the two sets of executives held or might be destined to hold. You also might try to find out if Bell has made studies comparing the progress of men who took the course and those who did not. Finally, you might consult your own experience and that of colleagues to find out just what areas seem most in need of further education.

CRITICAL READING: ADVANCED APPLICATION

In this application, critical reading will be applied to a single selection. Your evaluation will be based first on a comparison of the selection with your own experience and, second, on the article's internal consistency.

Here you are to apply as many of the reading techniques as you possibly can. Using paragraph analysis and a structured approach to the article, try to decide as soon as possible what the author's assumptions are, what his tone of voice implies, and whether he has tried to be objective in the case he makes. If you find specific areas of agreement or disagreement, try to isolate them and, in your mind, specify what it is that causes your response.

For this selection, the answers will be given immediately after the questions.

Skim-Read for Structure

Quickly skim-read the selection (Figure 6G) noting its basic organization and those paragraphs which will probably give you the essentials of the article most concisely.

> ● *What you should have noticed:* There is an introductory section with three key statements set off typographically. The remainder of the article is divided under the following subheadings: "The Great Illusion," "Ideas Not Enough," "Need for Discipline," "Parkinson's Flaw," "Conclusion," and "Adding Flexibility." (There are three statements set off by black dots in this last section.)

Next, close-read the first two sections (the unlabeled introductory section and "The Great Illusion" of Figure 6G); and then answer the following questions.

1. Have you already formed a tentative attitude toward the selection?
    _____a. Probably will agree.
    _____b. Probably will disagree.

    Because _____.

Creativity

Is Not Enough

By Theodore Levitt

"Creativity" is not the miraculous road to business growth and affluence that is so abundantly claimed these days. And for the line manager, particularly, it may be more of a millstone than a milestone.

Those who extol the liberating virtues of corporate creativity over the somnambulistic vices of corporate conformity may actually be giving advice that in the end will reduce the creative animation of business. This is because they tend to:

. . . confuse the getting of ideas with their implementation, that is, confuse creativity in the abstract with practical innovation;

. . . not understand the operating executive's day-to-day problems;

. . . underestimate the intricate complexity of business organizations.

The Great Illusion

The trouble with much of the advice business is getting today about the need to be more vigorously creative is, essentially, that its advocates have generally failed to distinguish between the relatively easy process of being creative in the abstract and the infinitely more difficult process of being innovationist in the concrete. Indeed, they misdefine "creativity" itself. Too often for them "creativity" means having great, original ideas. Their emphasis is almost all on the thoughts themselves. Moreover, the ideas are often judged more by their novelty than by their potential usefulness, either to consumers or to

the company. In this article I shall show that in most cases having a new idea can be "creative" in the abstract but destructive in actual operation, and that often instead of helping a company it will even hinder it.

Ideas Not Enough

Many people who are full of ideas simply do not understand how an organization must operate to get things done, especially dramatically new things. All too often there is the peculiar underlying assumption that creativity automatically leads to actual innovation. In the crippled logic of this line of thinking, "ideation" (or "creativity," if you emphasize the idea-producing aspect of that term) and "innovation" are treated as synonyms. This kind of thinking is a particular disease of advocates of "brainstorming," who often treat their approach as some sort of ultimate business liberator.[1] "Ideation" and "innovation" are not synonyms. The former deals with the generation of ideas; the latter, with their implementation. It is the absence of a constant awareness of this distinction that is responsible for some of the corporate standpatism we see today. (Lest there be any confusion, it is not essential that innovation need be successfully implemented to qualify as innovation. The object of the innovation is success, but to require in advance that there be no doubt of its success would disable its chance of ever getting tried.)

The fact that you can put a dozen inexperienced people into a room and conduct a brainstorming session that produces exciting new

AUTHOR'S NOTE: I wish to acknowledge the helpful suggestions, substantive and otherwise, of Professor Raymond A. Bauer and to absolve him of all possible implication of either agreement or disagreement with the ideas or even the facts of this article.

[1] See, for instance, Alex F. Osborn, *Applied Imagination: Principles and Procedures of Creative Thinking* (New York, Charles Scribner's Sons, 1953).

ideas shows how little relative importance ideas themselves actually have. Almost anybody with the intelligence of the average businessman can produce them, given a halfway decent environment and stimulus. The scarce people are those who have the know-how, energy, daring, and staying power to implement ideas.

Whatever the goals of a business may be, it must make money. To do that it must get things done. But having ideas is seldom equivalent to getting things done in the business or organizational sense. Ideas do not implement themselves — neither in business nor in art, science, philosophy, politics, love, war. People implement ideas.

Need for Discipline

Writers on the subject of creativity and innovation invariably emphasize the essential primacy of the creative impulse itself. Almost as an afterthought they talk about the necessity of teaching people to sell their ideas and of stimulating executives to listen to the ideas of subordinates and peers. Then they often go on casually to make some "do-gooder" statement about the importance of creating a permissive organizational climate for creative people. They rarely try to look at the executive's job and suggest how the creative genius might alter his behavior to suit the boss's requirements. It is always the boss who is being told to mend his ways. The reason for their one-sided siding with the creative man is that they are often hostile, just as he is, to the idea of "the organization" itself. They actively dislike organizations, but they seldom know exactly why.

I think I know the reason. It is that organization and creativity do not seem to go together, while organization and conformity do. Advocacy of a "permissive environment" for creativity in an organization is often a veiled attack on the idea of the organization itself. This quickly becomes clear when one recognizes this inescapable fact: one of the collateral purposes of an organization *is* to be inhospitable to a great and constant flow of ideas and creativity.

Whether we are talking about the United States Steel Corporation or the United Steel Workers of America, the U.S. Army or the Salvation Army, the United States or the U.S.S.R., the purpose of organization is to achieve the kind and degree of order and conformity necessary to do a particular job. The organization exists to restrict and channel the range of individual actions and behavior into a predictable and knowable routine. Without organization there would be chaos and decay. Organization exists in order to create that amount and kind of inflexibility that are necessary to get the most pressingly intended job done efficiently and on time.

Creativity and innovation disturb that order. Hence, organization tends to be inhospitable to creativity and innovation, though without creativity and innovation it would eventually perish. That is why small, one-man shops are so often more animated and "innovationary" than large ones. They have virtually no organization (precisely because they are one-man shops) and often are run by self-willed autocrats who act on impulse.

Organizations are created to achieve order. They have policies, procedures, and formal or powerfully informal (unspoken) rules. The job for which the organization exists could not possibly get done without these rules, procedures, and policies. And these produce the so-called conformity that is so blithely deprecated by the critics of the organization and life inside it.

Parkinson's Flaw

It is not surprising that C. Northcote Parkinson and his *Parkinson's Laws* enjoy such an admiring following among teachers, writers, consultants, and professional social critics. Most of these people have carefully chosen as their own professions work that keeps them as far as modern society lets anyone get from the rigorous taskmaster of the organization. Most of them more or less lead a sort of one-man, self-employed existence in which there are few make-or-break post-mortems of their activities. They live pretty much in autonomous isolation. Many of them, I suspect, have avoided life in the organization because they are incapable of submitting to its rigid discipline. Parkinson has provided them a way in which they can laugh at the majority, who *do* submit to the organization, and feel superior rather than oppressed, as minorities usually do.

It is also not surprising (indeed it is quite expected) that Parkinson himself should be anything but an organization man — that he is a teacher of history, a painter, and, of all things, a historian on warfare in the Eastern Seas. This

Figure 6G (Cont.)

185

is about as far as you can get from the modern landbound organization. Parkinson's writings have in recent years brought him into such continuing contact with business that he has now decided to go into business himself. In doing so he has proved the truth of all that I have been saying; the business he has decided to enter is, of course, the consulting business!

Parkinson is very entertaining. The executive who cannot laugh along with him probably is too paranoid to be trusted with a responsible job. But most of today's blithe cartoonists of the organization would be impoverished for material were they not blessed with an enormous ignorance of the facts of organizational life. Let me put it as emphatically as I can. A company cannot function as an anarchy. It must be organized, it must be routinized, it must be planned in some way in the various stages of its operation. That is why we have so many organizations of so many different kinds. And to the extent that operations planning is needed, we get rigidity, order, and therefore some amount of conformity. No organization can have everybody running off uncoordinated in several different directions at once. There must be rules and standards.

Where there are enough rules, there will be damn fool rules. These can be mercilessly cartooned. But some rules which to an expert on ancient naval history look foolish are far from foolish if he bothers to become an expert in the problems of the business, or the government, or whatever group the particular organization is designed to deal with.

Conclusion

All this raises a seemingly frightening question. If conformity and rigidity are necessary requisites of organization, and if these in turn help stifle creativity, and furthermore if the creative man might indeed be stifled if he is required to spell out the details needed to convert his ideas into effective innovations, does all this mean that modern organizations have evolved into such involuted monsters that they must suffer the fearful fate of the dinosaur — too big and unwieldy to survive?

The answer to this is *no*. First, it is questionable whether the creative impulse would automatically dry up if the idea man is required to take some responsibility for follow-through.

The people who so resolutely proclaim their own creative energy will scarcely assert that they need a hothouse for its flowering. Secondly, the large organization has some important attributes that actually facilitate innovation. Its capacity to distribute risk over its broad economic base and among the many individuals involved in implementing newness are significant. They make it both economically and, for the individuals involved, personally easier to break untried ground.

What often misleads people is that making big operating or policy changes requires also making big organizational changes. Yet it is precisely one of the great virtues of a big organization that, in the short run at least, its momentum is irreversible and its organizational structure is, for all practical purposes, nearly impenetrable. A vast machinery exists to get a certain job done. That job must continue to get the toughest kind of serious attention, no matter how exotically revolutionary a big operating or policy change may be. The boat can and may have to be rocked, but one virtue of a big boat is that it takes an awful lot to rock it. Certain people or departments in the boat may feel the rocking more than others, and to that extent strive to avoid the incidents that produce it. But the built-in stabilizers of bigness and of group decision making can be used as powerful influences in *encouraging* people to risk these incidents.

Adding Flexibility

Finally, the large organization has an organizational alternative to the alleged "conservatizing" consequences of bigness. There is some evidence that the relatively rigid organization can build into its own structure certain flexibilities which would provide an organizational home for the creative but irresponsible individual. What may be required, especially in the large organization, is not so much a suggestion-box system as a specialized group whose function is to receive ideas, work them out, and follow them through in the necessary manner. This would be done after the group has evaluated each idea and, preferably, spoken at length with its originator. Then when the idea and the required follow-through are passed on to the appropriate executive, he will be more willing to listen. To illustrate:

• An organizational setup that approximates this structure has been established in the headquarters

Figure 6G (Cont.)

186

Marketing Department of the Mobil Oil Company.[9]

• A similar approach exists at the Schering Corporation under the name "Management R & D." Its purpose is to nurture and develop new ideas and methods of decision making.[10]

• Another suggestion which takes less solidly tangible organizational form in practice has been made by Murray D. Lincoln, president of Nationwide Insurance Co. He makes a plea for the notion of a company having a *Vice President in Charge of Revolution*.[11]

Beyond these, the problems and needs of companies differ. To this extent they may have to find their own special ways of dealing with the issues discussed in this article. The important point is to be conscious of the possible need or value of some system of making creativity yield more innovation.

Some companies have greater need for such

measures than others have. And, as pointed out earlier, the need hinges in part on the nature of the industry. Certainly it is easier to convert creativity into innovation in the advertising business than it is in an operating company with elaborate production processes, long channels of distribution, and a complex administrative setup.

For those critics of and advisers to U.S. industry who repeatedly call for more creativity in business, it is well to try first to understand the profound distinction between creativity and innovation, and then perhaps to spend a little more time calling on creative individuals to take added responsibility for implementation. The fructifying potentials of creativity vary enormously with the particular industry, with the climate in the organization, with the organizational level of the idea man, and with the kinds of day-in, day-out problems, pressures, and responsibilities of the man to whom he addresses his ideas. Without clearly appreciating these facts, those who declare that a company will somehow grow and prosper merely by having more creative people make a fetish of their own illusions.

[9] For a detailed discussion of how such a setup might operate and be organized, see my *Innovation in Marketing* (New York, McGraw-Hill Book Company, Inc., 1962), p. 159.
[10] See Victor M. Longstreet, "Management R & D," HBR July–August 1961, p. 125.
[11] New York, McGraw-Hill Book Company, Inc., 1960.

Figure 6G *(Cont.)*

2. What, in one sentence, is the point, claim, or thesis of the entire article?

_____

_____ .

> ● Creativity is not the miraculous road to business success, and may even be a hindrance to success.

3. What three points are given in the first section as an illustration of the author's thesis?

a. _____ .

b. _____ .

c. _____ .

> ● People who stress creativity as the road to business growth.
> a. confuse the generation of ideas with their implementation.
> b. do not understand the day-to-day problems of the executive.
> c. underestimate the complexity of business organization.

4. What is the "Great Illusion"?

_____

_____

_____ .

> ● The "Great Illusion" is an expansion of point *a* in question 3: the confusion between "the relatively easy process of being creative in the abstract and the infinitely more difficult process of being innovationist in the concrete."

5. Do you find the tone of the article acceptable—that is, has the author chosen words and expressions for their argumentative value rather than simply for their factual value, and if so, do you accept this procedure?

_____

_____

_____ .

● The author *does* seem to have chosen expression for their argumentative value ("relatively easy process of being creative," "great, original ideas," "judged more by their novelty"). Your acceptance of this procedure would probably depend upon whether you expect to agree with the selection or not.

6. Close-read as much of the section labelled "Conclusion" in Figure 6G as you need to in order to determine what the selection recommends as a way to reconcile creativity with the real problems of the executive and his business. Indicate below what you think the author's recommendations are.

_____

_____

_____.

● The author seems to recommend that the distinction between creativity and innovation be kept constantly in mind. He also seems to suggest that there is more opportunity for innovation in a large organization than critics suggest. (*Note:* With the exception of Parkinson, the author never identifies the critics he is refuting.)

Fill in the Loopholes

Finally, close-read any other sections of the article illustrated in Figure 6G that you think will be of value to you. If you have found the selection especially interesting, you might wish to close-read it from the beginning. However, for most purposes of understanding and retention, the procedure we have followed should be sufficient.

1. Has your attitude toward the selection been changed since you made a tentative decision after reading the introduction, and if so, in what way?

_____

_____

_____.

● This is an important step in the analysis of your critical reading. If your original attitude was based on a misunderstanding of the text, you must be more careful in forming opinions about material. If, however, you reacted for or against the material, and further reading has deepened your conviction, your procedure is probably working quite well.

SUMMARY

You have now applied critical reading to quite different types of material. The next step, of course, is application of the skill to your own day-to-day reading. In your own reading, you will have to adapt the skill to meet the requirements of your own business or profession. Despite minor adaptations, however, continue to follow the familiar sequence of skim-reading for main points, close-reading for significant details, and summarizing before attempting a critical evaluation.

The capacity for a temporary suspension of the critical attack until the content has been firmly grasped and condensed is one of the marks of a successful reader. Poor readers invariably begin to make critical judgments before they have really grasped the content—or make no critical judgments at all.

A very good practice source for critical evaluation can be found in newspaper editorials, which are usually both fact and interpretation. As you read them, ask if the facts are consistent with the interpretation given. Have the facts been obviously selected to fit the interpretation? Are facts and interpretations intermingled so that one improperly substitutes for the other?

But regardless of the type of reading material, your critical skill should be built into the general procedure given below:

1. What is the *author's position,* and what points does he introduce to support that position?
2. How does the *author's style* contribute to his argument?
3. What is *my background,* and what are my prejudices with regard to the topic? Am I reading the selection sympathetically?
4. Can I see any *problems* or *points* which the author has *omitted?*
5. Has this article *affected my opinion* and, if so, how?

With this general procedure before you, it should be clear that critical reading is not the *sole* property of English professors. Whenever your reading material involves judgment—on your part or the writer's—critical reading can and should be used. Yet, once more, let us remind you to think of it as a by-product of our previous reading techniques. When you have mastered skim-reading, and when you have practiced paragraph analysis and a structured approach to reading as a matter of course, the step toward incisive critical evaluation will not be that hard at all.

SKILL REMINDER

For critical reading, do this:

1. Understand the material before attempting to criticize it.
2. Notice the author's tone, point of view, and his main arguments.
3. Compare the material to other readings or to your own experiences in order to clarify similarities and differences.
4. Support your evaluation with specific evidence.

A TEST OF YOUR SKILLS
AND A REVIEW

We are now going to give you a fairly long reading selection that will allow you to put all your reading skills to work simultaneously. At the same time, it will serve as a test of your mastery of the skills. You will probably see right away why we have chosen this particular article for your comprehensive application.

Read the selection illustrated in Figure 7A and then answer the skill questionnaire and comprehension check for this section.

SKILL QUESTIONNAIRE

Skill I: Skim-Reading

1. Did you skim-read "The Importance of Structure"?
   ____Yes; ____No

2. Do you normally skim-read letters, articles, books, and book chapters?
   ____Yes; ____No

3. Give your definition of skim-reading.

   _____

   _____.

Skill II: Phrase Reading

1. Did you estimate the number of words in the selection so that you could be sure you were reading in phrases?
   ____Yes; ____No

2

THE IMPORTANCE OF STRUCTURE

THE first object of any act of learning, over and beyond the pleasure it may give, is that it should serve us in the future. Learning should not only take us somewhere; it should allow us later to go further more easily. There are two ways in which learning serves the future. One is through its specific applicability to tasks that are highly similar to those we originally learned to perform. Psychologists refer to this phenomenon as specific transfer of training; perhaps it should be called the extension of habits or associations. Its utility appears to be limited in the main to what we usually speak of as skills. Having learned how to hammer nails, we are better able later to learn how to hammer tacks or chip wood. Learning in school undoubtedly creates skills of a kind that transfers to activities encountered later, either in school or after. A second way in which earlier learning renders later performance more efficient is through what is conveniently called nonspecific transfer or, more accurately, the transfer of principles and attitudes. In essence, it consists of learning initially not a skill but a general idea, which can then be used as a basis for recognizing subsequent problems as special cases of the idea originally mastered. This type of transfer is at the heart of the educational process—the continual broadening and deepening of knowledge in terms of basic and general ideas.

Figure 7A

THE PROCESS OF EDUCATION

The continuity of learning that is produced by the second type of transfer, transfer of principles, is dependent upon mastery of the structure of the subject matter, as structure was described in the preceding chapter. That is to say, in order for a person to be able to recognize the applicability or inapplicability of an idea to a new situation and to broaden his learning thereby, he must have clearly in mind the general nature of the phenomenon with which he is dealing. The more fundamental or basic is the idea he has learned, almost by definition, the greater will be its breadth of applicability to new problems. Indeed, this is almost a tautology, for what is meant by "fundamental" in this sense is precisely that an idea has wide as well as powerful applicability. It is simple enough to proclaim, of course, that school curricula and methods of teaching should be geared to the teaching of fundamental ideas in whatever subject is being taught. But as soon as one makes such a statement a host of problems arise, many of which can be solved only with the aid of considerably more research. We turn to some of these now.

The first and most obvious problem is how to construct curricula that can be taught by ordinary teachers to ordinary students and that at the same time reflect clearly the basic or underlying principles of various fields of inquiry. The problem is twofold: first, how to have the basic subjects rewritten and their teaching materials revamped in such a way that the pervading and powerful ideas and attitudes relating to them are given a central role; second, how to match the levels of these materials to the capacities of students of different abilities at different grades in school.

18

Figure 7A (Cont.)

THE IMPORTANCE OF STRUCTURE

The experience of the past several years has taught at least one important lesson about the design of a curriculum that is true to the underlying structure of its subject matter. It is that the best minds in any particular discipline must be put to work on the task. The decision as to what should be taught in American history to elementary school children or what should be taught in arithmetic is a decision that can best be reached with the aid of those with a high degree of vision and competence in each of these fields. To decide that the elementary ideas of algebra depend upon the fundamentals of the commutative, distributive, and associative laws, one must be a mathematician in a position to appreciate and understand the fundamentals of mathematics. Whether schoolchildren require an understanding of Frederick Jackson Turner's ideas about the role of the frontier in American history before they can sort out the facts and trends of American history—this again is a decision that requires the help of the scholar who has a deep understanding of the American past. Only by the use of our best minds in devising curricula will we bring the fruits of scholarship and wisdom to the student just beginning his studies.

The question will be raised, "How enlist the aid of our most able scholars and scientists in designing curricula for primary and secondary schools?" The answer has already been given, at least in part. The School Mathematics Study Group, the University of Illinois mathematics projects, the Physical Science Study Committee, and the Biological Sciences Curriculum Study have indeed been enlisting the aid of eminent men in their various fields, doing so by means of summer proj-

19

Figure 7A (Cont.)

THE PROCESS OF EDUCATION

ects, supplemented in part by year-long leaves of absence for certain key people involved. They have been aided in these projects by outstanding elementary and secondary school teachers and, for special purposes, by professional writers, film makers, designers, and others required in such a complex enterprise.

There is at least one major matter that is left unsettled even by a large-scale revision of curricula in the direction indicated. Mastery of the fundamental ideas of a field involves not only the grasping of general principles, but also the development of an attitude toward learning and inquiry, toward guessing and hunches, toward the possibility of solving problems on one's own. Just as a physicist has certain attitudes about the ultimate orderliness of nature and a conviction that order can be discovered, so a young physics student needs some working version of these attitudes if he is to organize his learning in such a way as to make what he learns usable and meaningful in his thinking. To instill such attitudes by teaching requires something more than the mere presentation of fundamental ideas. Just what it takes to bring off such teaching is something on which a great deal of research is needed, but it would seem that an important ingredient is a sense of excitement about discovery—discovery of regularities of previously unrecognized relations and similarities between ideas, with a resulting sense of self-confidence in one's abilities. Various people who have worked on curricula in science and mathematics have urged that it is possible to present the fundamental structure of a discipline in such a way as to preserve some of the exciting sequences that lead a student to discover for himself.

20

Figure 7A (Cont.)

THE IMPORTANCE OF STRUCTURE

It is particularly the Committee on School Mathematics and the Arithmetic Project of the University of Illinois that have emphasized the importance of discovery as an aid to teaching. They have been active in devising methods that permit a student to discover for himself the generalization that lies behind a particular mathematical operation, and they contrast this approach with the "method of assertion and proof" in which the generalization is first stated by the teacher and the class asked to proceed through the proof. It has also been pointed out by the Illinois group that the method of discovery would be too time-consuming for presenting all of what a student must cover in mathematics. The proper balance between the two is anything but plain, and research is in progress to elucidate the matter, though more is needed. Is the inductive approach a better technique for teaching principles? Does it have a desirable effect on attitudes?

That the method of discovery need not be limited to such highly formalized subjects as mathematics and physics is illustrated by some experimentation on social studies carried out by the Harvard Cognition Project. A sixth-grade class, having been through a conventional unit on the social and economic geography of the Southeastern states, was introduced to the North Central region by being asked to locate the major cities of the area on a map containing physical features and natural resources, but no place names. The resulting class discussion very rapidly produced a variety of plausible theories concerning the requirements of a city—a water transportation theory that placed Chicago at the junction of the three lakes, a mineral resources theory that placed

21

Figure 7A (*Cont.*)

THE PROCESS OF EDUCATION

it near the Mesabi range, a food-supply theory that put a great city on the rich soil of Iowa, and so on. The level of interest as well as the level of conceptual sophistication was far above that of control classes. Most striking, however, was the attitude of children to whom, for the first time, the location of a city appeared as a problem, and one to which an answer could be discovered by taking thought. Not only was there pleasure and excitement in the pursuit of a question, but in the end the discovery was worth making, at least for urban children for whom the phenomenon of the city was something that had before been taken for granted.

How do we tailor fundamental knowledge to the interests and capacities of children? This is a theme we shall return to later, and only a word need be said about it here. It requires a combination of deep understanding and patient honesty to present physical or any other phenomena in a way that is simultaneously exciting, correct, and rewardingly comprehensible. In examining certain teaching materials in physics, for example, we have found much patient honesty in presentation that has come to naught because the authors did not have a deep enough understanding of the subject they were presenting.

A good case in point is to be found in the usual attempt to explain the nature of tides. Ask the majority of high school students to explain tides and they will speak of the gravitational pull of the moon on the surface of the earth and how it pulls the water on the moon's side into a bulge. Ask them now why there is also a bulge of less magnitude on the side of the earth opposite to the moon, and they will almost always be without a satisfactory

22

Figure 7A (Cont.)

THE IMPORTANCE OF STRUCTURE

answer. Or ask them where the maximum bulge of the incoming tide is with respect to the relative position of the earth and moon, and the answer will usually be that it is at the point on the earth's surface nearest to the moon. If the student knows there is a lag in the tidal crest, he will usually not know why. The failure in both cases comes from an inadequate picture of how gravity acts upon a free-moving elastic body, and a failure to connect the idea of inertia with the idea of gravitational action. In short, the tides are explained without a share of the excitement that can come from understanding Newton's great discovery of universal gravitation and its mode of action. Correct and illuminating explanations are no more difficult and often easier to grasp than ones that are partly correct and therefore too complicated and too restricted. It is the consensus of virtually all the men and women who have been working on curriculum projects that making material interesting is in no way incompatible with presenting it soundly; indeed, a correct general explanation is often the most interesting of all. Inherent in the preceding discussions are at least four general claims that can be made for teaching the fundamental structure of a subject, claims in need of detailed study.

The first is that understanding fundamentals makes a subject more comprehensible. This is true not only in physics and mathematics, where we have principally illustrated the point, but equally in the social studies and literature. Once one has grasped the fundamental idea that a nation must trade in order to live, then such a presumably special phenomenon as the Triangular Trade of the American colonies becomes altogether simpler to

23

Figure 7A (Cont.)

THE PROCESS OF EDUCATION

understand as something more than commerce in molasses, sugar cane, rum, and slaves in an atmosphere of violation of British trade regulations. The high school student reading *Moby Dick* can only understand more deeply if he can be led to understand that Melville's novel is, among other things, a study of the theme of evil and the plight of those pursuing this "killing whale." And if the student is led further to understand that there are a relatively limited number of human plights about which novels are written, he understands literature the better for it.

The second point relates to human memory. Perhaps the most basic thing that can be said about human memory, after a century of intensive research, is that unless detail is placed into a structured pattern, it is rapidly forgotten. Detailed material is conserved in memory by the use of simplified ways of representing it. These simplified representations have what may be called a "regenerative" character. A good example of this regenerative property of long-term memory can be found in science. A scientist does not try to remember the distances traversed by falling bodies in different gravitational fields over different periods of time. What he carries in memory instead is a formula that permits him with varying degrees of accuracy to regenerate the details on which the more easily remembered formula is based. So he commits to memory the formula $s = \frac{1}{2} gt^2$ and not a handbook of distances, times, and gravitational constants. Similarly, one does not remember exactly what Marlow, the commentator in *Lord Jim*, said about the chief protagonist's plight, but, rather, simply that he was the dispassionate onlooker, the man who tried to understand without judging what had led Lord Jim into

24

Figure 7A (Cont.)

THE IMPORTANCE OF STRUCTURE

the straits in which he found himself. We remember a formula, a vivid detail that carries the meaning of an event, an average that stands for a range of events, a caricature or picture that preserves an essence—all of them techniques of condensation and representation. What learning general or fundamental principles does is to ensure that memory loss will not mean total loss, that what remains will permit us to reconstruct the details when needed. A good theory is the vehicle not only for understanding a phenomenon now but also for remembering it tomorrow.

Third, an understanding of fundamental principles and ideas, as noted earlier, appears to be the main road to adequate "transfer of training." To understand something as a specific instance of a more general case—which is what understanding a more fundamental principle or structure means—is to have learned not only a specific thing but also a model for understanding other things like it that one may encounter. If a student could grasp in its most human sense the weariness of Europe at the close of the Hundred Years' War and how it created the conditions for a workable but not ideologically absolute Treaty of Westphalia, he might be better able to think about the ideological struggle of East and West—though the parallel is anything but exact. A carefully wrought understanding should also permit him to recognize the limits of the generalization as well. The idea of "principles" and "concepts" as a basis for transfer is hardly new. It is much in need of more research of a specific kind that would provide detailed knowledge of how best to proceed in the teaching of different subjects in different grades.

The fourth claim for emphasis on structure and prin-

25

Figure 7A (Cont.)

THE PROCESS OF EDUCATION

ciples in teaching is that by constantly reexamining material taught in elementary and secondary schools for its fundamental character, one is able to narrow the gap between "advanced" knowledge and "elementary" knowledge. Part of the difficulty now found in the progression from primary school through high school to college is that material learned earlier is either out of date or misleading by virtue of its lagging too far behind developments in a field. This gap can be reduced by the kind of emphasis set forth in the preceding discussion.

Consider now some specific problems that received considerable discussion at Woods Hole. One of them has to do with the troubled topic of "general science." There are certain recurrent ideas that appear in virtually all branches of science. If in one subject one has learned them well and generally, that achievement should make the task of learning them again in different form elsewhere in science much easier. Various teachers and scientists have raised the question whether these basic ideas should not be "isolated," so to speak, and taught more explicitly in a manner that frees them from specific areas of science. The type of idea can be easily illustrated: categorization and its uses, the unit of measure and its development, the indirectness of information in science and the need for operational definition of ideas, and so forth. With respect to the last, for example, we do not *see* pressure or the chemical bond directly but infer it indirectly from a set of measures. So too body temperature. So too sadness in another person. Can these and similar ideas be presented effectively and with a variety of concrete illustrations in the early grades in order to give the child a better basis for understanding their

26

Figure 7A (Cont.)

THE IMPORTANCE OF STRUCTURE

specific representation in various special disciplines later? Is it wise to teach such "general science" as an introduction to disciplinary sciences in the later grades? How should they be taught and what could we reasonably expect by way of easier learning later? Much research is needed on this promising topic—research not only on the usefulness of such an approach, but also on the kinds of general scientific ideas that might be taught.

Indeed, it may well be that there are certain general attitudes or approaches toward science or literature that can be taught in the earlier grades that would have considerable relevance for later learning. The attitude that things are connected and not isolated is a case in point. One can indeed imagine kindergarten games designed to make children more actively alert to how things affect or are connected with each other—a kind of introduction to the idea of multiple determination of events in the physical and the social world. Any working scientist is usually able to say something about the ways of thinking or attitudes that are a part of his craft. Historians have written rather extensively on this subject as far as their field is concerned. Literary men have even evolved a genre of writing about the forms of sensibility that make for literary taste and vigor. In mathematics, this subject has a formal name, "heuristic," to describe the approach one takes to solving problems. One may well argue, as it was argued at Woods Hole by men in widely differing disciplines, that it might be wise to assess what attitudes or heuristic devices are most pervasive and useful, and that an effort should be made to teach children a rudimentary version of them that might be further refined as they progress through school. Again, the

27

Figure 7A (Cont.)

THE PROCESS OF EDUCATION

reader will sense that the argument for such an approach is premised on the assumption that there is a continuity between what a scholar does on the forefront of his discipline and what a child does in approaching it for the first time. This is not to say that the task is a simple one, only that it is worthy of careful consideration and research.

Perhaps the chief arguments put forward in opposition to the idea of such efforts at teaching general principles and general attitudes are, first, that it is better to approach the general through the specific and, second, that working attitudes should be kept implicit rather than being made explicit. For example, one of the principal organizing concepts in biology is the persistent question, "What function does this thing serve?"—a question premised on the assumption that everything one finds in an organism serves some function or it probably would not have survived. Other general ideas are related to this question. The student who makes progress in biology learns to ask the question more and more subtly, to relate more and more things to it. At the next step he asks what function a particular structure or process serves in the light of what is required in the total functioning of an organism. Measuring and categorizing are carried out in the service of the general idea of function. Then beyond that he may organize his knowledge in terms of a still more comprehensive notion of function, turning to cellular structure or to phylogenetic comparison. It may well be that the style of thought of a particular discipline is necessary as a background for learning the working meaning of general concepts, in which case a general introduction to the

28

Figure 7A (Cont.)

THE IMPORTANCE OF STRUCTURE

meaning of "function" might be less effective than teaching it in the context of biology.

As for "attitude" teaching or even the teaching of heuristic in mathematics, the argument runs that if the learner becomes too aware of his own attitudes or approach, he may become mechanical or trick-oriented in his work. No evidence exists on the point, and research is needed before any effort is made to teach in this way. Work is now going on at Illinois on training children to be more effective in asking questions about physical phenomena, but much more information is needed before the issue is clear.

One hears often the distinction between "doing" and "understanding." It is a distinction applied to the case, for example, of a student who presumably understands a mathematical idea but does not know how to use it in computation. While the distinction is probably a false one—since how can one know what a student understands save by seeing what he does—it points to an interesting difference in emphasis in teaching and in learning. Thus one finds in some of the classic books on the psychology of problem solving (such as Max Wertheimer's *Productive Thinking*) a sharp line drawn between "rote drill" and "understanding." In point of fact, drill need not be rote and, alas, emphasis on understanding may lead the student to a certain verbal glibness. It has been the experience of members of the School Mathematics Study Group that computational practice may be a necessary step toward understanding conceptual ideas in mathematics. Similarly one may try to give the high school student a sense of styles by having him read contrasting authors, yet final insight into style may come

29

Figure 7A (Cont.)

THE PROCESS OF EDUCATION

only when the student himself tries his hand at writing in different styles. Indeed, it is the underlying premise of laboratory exercises that doing something helps one understand it. There is a certain wisdom in the quip made by a psychologist at Woods Hole: "How do I know what I think until I feel what I do?" In any case, the distinction is not a very helpful one. What is more to the point is to ask what methods of exercise in any given field are most likely to give the student a sense of intelligent mastery over the material. What are the most fruitful computational exercises that one can use in various branches of mathematics? Does the effort to write in the style of Henry James give one an especially good insight into that author's style? Perhaps a good start toward understanding such matters would be to study the methods used by successful teachers. It would be surprising if the information compiled failed to suggest a host of worthwhile laboratory studies on techniques of teaching—or, indeed, on techniques of imparting complex information generally.

A word is needed, finally, on examinations. It is obvious that an examination can be bad in the sense of emphasizing trivial aspects of a subject. Such examinations can encourage teaching in a disconnected fashion and learning by rote. What is often overlooked, however, is that examinations can also be allies in the battle to improve curricula and teaching. Whether an examination is of the "objective" type involving multiple choices or of the essay type, it can be devised so as to emphasize an understanding of the broad principles of a subject. Indeed, even when one examines on detailed knowledge, it can be done in such a way as to require an understand-

30

Figure 7A (Cont.)

THE IMPORTANCE OF STRUCTURE

ing by the student of the connectedness between specific facts. There is a concerted effort now under way among national testing organizations like the Educational Testing Service to construct examinations that will emphasize an understanding of fundamental principles. Such efforts can be of great help. Additional help might be given to local school systems by making available to them manuals that describe the variety of ways in which examinations can be constructed. The searching examination is not easy to make, and a thoughtful manual on the subject would be welcome.

To recapitulate, the main theme of this chapter has been that the curriculum of a subject should be determined by the most fundamental understanding that can be achieved of the underlying principles that give structure to that subject. Teaching specific topics or skills without making clear their context in the broader fundamental structure of a field of knowledge is uneconomical in several deep senses. In the first place, such teaching makes it exceedingly difficult for the student to generalize from what he has learned to what he will encounter later. In the second place, learning that has fallen short of a grasp of general principles has little reward in terms of intellectual excitement. The best way to create interest in a subject is to render it worth knowing, which means to make the knowledge gained usable in one's thinking beyond the situation in which the learning has occurred. Third, knowledge one has acquired without sufficient structure to tie it together is knowledge that is likely to be forgotten. An unconnected set of facts has a pitiably short half-life in memory. Organizing facts in terms of principles and ideas from which they may be

31

Figure 7A (*Cont.*)

inferred is the only known way of reducing the quick rate of loss of human memory.

Designing curricula in a way that reflects the basic structure of a field of knowledge requires the most fundamental understanding of that field. It is a task that cannot be carried out without the active participation of the ablest scholars and scientists. The experience of the past several years has shown that such scholars and scientists, working in conjunction with experienced teachers and students of child development, can prepare curricula of the sort we have been considering. Much more effort in the actual preparation of curriculum materials, in teacher training, and in supporting research will be necessary if improvements in our educational practices are to be of an order that will meet the challenges of the scientific and social revolution through which we are now living.

There are many problems of how to teach general principles in a way that will be both effective and interesting, and several of the key issues have been passed in review. What is abundantly clear is that much work remains to be done by way of examining currently effective practices, fashioning curricula that may be tried out on an experimental basis, and carrying out the kinds of research that can give support and guidance to the general effort at improving teaching.

How may the kind of curriculum we have been discussing be brought within the intellectual reach of children of different ages? To this problem we turn next.

32

Figure 7A (Cont.)

(The approximate length of the article is 4000 words. If you read it in ten minutes, your rate would be 400 WPM.)

2. Do you normally estimate the number of words and note the time elapsed when reading material of substantial length?

     ____Yes; ____No

3. Give your definition of phrase reading.

     _____

     _____.

Skill III: Paragraph Analysis

1. Did you note the function of paragraphs, especially key paragraphs, as you skim-read and later close-read the article?

     ____Yes; ____No

2. Do you normally look for guide and key words and try to expose the architecture of any selection as you read?

     ____Yes; ____No

3. Give your definition of paragraph analysis.

     _____

     _____.

Skill IV: Structuring Ideas

1. Did you make use of Bruner's frequent listing of major points and his recapitulations afterwards to fix the major ideas in your mind?

     ____Yes; ____No

2. Do you normally look for organizational aids and impose structure on material that is not well organized?

     ____Yes; ____No

3. Give your definition of structuring ideas.

     _____

     _____.

Skill V: Concentration

1. Both before and in the course of your reading, did you question, anticipate, and summarize for maximum command of the ideas?

   _____Yes; _____No

2. Do you normally attempt to apply an aggressive pattern of concentration techniques, especially when you find your attention less than what it might be?

   _____Yes; _____No

3. Give your definition of concentration.

   _____

   _____.

Skill VI: Critical Reading

1. Once you were sure of Bruner's main points, did you evaluate his ideas for their assumptions, their logic, and their validity as measured against your own experience?

   _____Yes; _____No

2. Do you normally make it a practice to find justifications in the text for your response to any written material?

   _____Yes; _____No

3. Give your definition of critical reading.

   _____

   _____.

NOW ANSWER THE FOLLOWING QUESTIONS ON THE SELECTION

1. The main theme of this selection is that

   _____a. A student should be directed to "do" certain things rather than to be expected to "understand" them.

   _____b. The curriculum of a subject should be based on the most fundamental understanding possible of the subject's underlying principles.

_____c. The understanding of fundamental principles is the main road to the continual broadening and deepening of knowledge.

2. Bruner feels that the following are best suited to design curricula for the elementary and secondary schools:

 _____a. The Physical Science and Study Committee.

 _____b. Ordinary elementary and secondary teachers.

 _____c. Our most able scholars and scientists.

3. Understanding fundamentals makes a subject more comprehensible in

 _____a. Physics and mathematics.

 _____b. Social studies and literature.

 _____c. Both a and b.

4. The most basic thing that can be said about the human memory is that

 _____a. Unless detail is placed in a structured pattern, it is rapidly forgotten.

 _____b. The general is recalled best through focus on the specific.

 _____c. Detailed material is conserved in memory by the use of complex mnemonic devices.

5. By a constant re-examination of the material taught in elementary and secondary schools, curriculum-makers will be able to:

 _____a. Make a dramatic separation between the kinds of material taught on each level.

 _____b. Narrow the gap between "advanced" knowledge and "elementary" knowledge.

 _____c. Eliminate recurrent ideas that appear at different levels.

    Answers: 1. b
        2. c
        3. c
        4. a
        5. b

TYPICAL READING PROBLEMS AND THEIR SOLUTIONS

As a further check on your reading development, we are going to present you with some common reading difficulties and then ask you to prescribe the skill, or skills, that best deals with them. During this exercise, you must keep in mind that the most effective approach combines techniques—even when one needs special stress.

1. Mr. A admits to you that, although he enjoys reading and reads a great deal, he finds it quite difficult afterwards to remember what he has read.

   Your Solution: _____

   _____.

2. Dr. B has a fine understanding, when he gets a chance to use it. His problem is that he reads so slowly he can only cover a very small amount of the reading he would like to do.

   Your Solution: _____

   _____.

3. Vice President C is very reluctant to admit it, but he would rather do anything than read the reports that pile up on his desk. The minute he opens one, he begins to think about golf.

   Your Solution: _____

   _____.

4. Mr. D feels that he has no mind of his own. He reads an article, is completely convinced by what it says, and then a day later finds himself convinced by an argument for just the opposite point of view.

   Your Solution: _____

   _____.

5. Mr. E's problem is comparatively minor, but quite annoying to him. He loves his newspaper, yet the only time in memory that he managed to read it as thoroughly as he wanted was one day when he had flu and couldn't go to the office.

   Your Solution: _____

   _____.

Answers: 1. Mr. A is probably trying to digest all the thousands of words he reads. He will find it far easier to remember what he has read—and to discuss his reading—when he distinguishes major points from minor ones. Paragraph analysis for a running summary and a structure—mental or written—will certainly help him. Stress Skills III and IV.

2. With a good understanding, Dr. B probably practices a structural approach to his reading, *unless* he must reread his material several times to comprehend it. His problem is probably word-by-word reading. Skimming will help him to sort out what he should read, but his real need is for training in the phrase-reading technique. Stress Skills I and II.

3. Vice President C's difficulty could be a complicated one indeed. He may be in the wrong job, although it is a little late to tell him that. The specific reading skill that will help him at this point is obviously concentration. If he can learn to visualize, he may find the material a little more interesting to him and, therefore, easier to face. In addition, skimming, questioning, anticipating, and summarizing can engage and sustain his interest and make the bulk of what he has to read more manageable. Stress Skills I and V.

4. Mr. D needs work on critical evaluation. Once he sees how an argument is built— through paragraph analysis—he will be prepared to judge it more in terms of its logic and its rhetorical devices than in terms of pure emotional impact. Stress Skills III and VI.

5. Mr. E may feel happier about his daily paper than he ever has once he learns to skim before he attempts a thorough reading. He still will not be able to read every word, but he *will* be able to cover the content of the entire paper, with time left over to read the articles that interest him most. Stress Skill I.

A REVIEW OF WORK IN THIS CHAPTER AND BOOK

If you were in any doubt about what skills to apply for these typical reading problems, go back over the table of contents to check on the skills available to you.

If three or more of the comprehension questions following your reading of Figure 7A were incorrect, you ought to think of a day or two of general review, with special attention to paragraph analysis, structuring, and concentration.

If you answered no to any of the questions in the skill questionnaire following the selection, or if you had difficulty in preparing a definition for any of the skills, return to the appropriate chapter for a review of the skill. As you re-examine the chapter, ask yourself whether you fully understood the theory and application of the skill in question.

If you feel that you have not yet used a skill often enough to be confident about it, set yourself exercises in your own reading that will duplicate the applications we have given you. Continue to work with the skill until it becomes an instinctive part of your reading attack.

From that point on, the major task is to make sure you apply your skills every day with the necessary variation for every possible type of reading matter. As your sense of command and confidence grows, and your reading rate increases to the point where you no longer have a huge reading backlog, you can be quite certain that this book has done its job.

EXTENDING YOUR SKILL

Reading skill is the product of a variety of physical and mental abilities. An analogy might be made to the field of athletics. In reading, as in golf, tennis, or swimming, proficiency comes only after a considerable amount of practice. Of course, many people feel that they can get along as they are and refuse to devote the attention necessary to achieve real competence in anything. They continue to play golf at the high scores and to bowl at low scores all their lives. They may take tips from their friends—tips that probably will increase their enjoyment and, to a lesser extent, their success. But tips will never enable them to catch up to the person who has learned a comprehensive pattern of skills for the game and has practiced them systematically.

You have a choice about the way you are going to handle your reading improvement. You can consider this book a source of "tips for better reading" and get a certain degree of improvement and added enjoyment from using it as such. Or, you can consider it a basic manual to be used systematically and consistently for developing your reading to "pro" caliber.

Here is a plan that will help you to extend systematically the basic skills in this book—a guide that will help you to integrate your skills and make them part of a concerted and powerful attack on any kind of reading material. Spend at least one full hour each day reading in a field *outside* that of your profession or business. (Consult the list at the end of this book for reading suggestions.)

For the first half of that hour, consciously experiment with your reading method. Always work with skills that already seem very helpful, and, at the same time, try to add others that haven't quite taken hold. Also, test different combinations of successful skills in one operation.

For the second half of the hour, relax and apply just the skills that seem most appropriate for the book that you are using. Perhaps you will spend ten minutes in a skim-reading, then cover the section again to check yourself.

Figure 8A

ONE-WEEK PLAN FOR SKILL EXTENSION

You may find this calendar useful during the hour each day that you practice reading skills. It can help to make your practice more systematic and your progress more dramatic. Before you start, consider the skills you wish to use during the coming hour and place a check after each one in the day's column. During the first half hour consciously experiment with your reading method, emphasizing specific techniques. During the second half hour, relax and enjoy your reading by using only those techniques which seem most appropriate for the book. Keep a record of the approximate time spent with each skill in the "time" column.

SKILLS TO PRACTICE	MONDAY		TUESDAY		WEDNESDAY		THURSDAY		FRIDAY		SATURDAY		SUNDAY	
	✓	time	✓	time	✓	time	✓	time	✓	time	✓	time	✓	time
I SKIM-READING														
II PHRASE READING														
III PARAGRAPH ANALYSIS														
IV STRUCTURING IDEAS														
V CONCENTRATION														
VI CRITICAL READING														
OTHERS:														
TOTAL PRACTICE TIME PER DAY														

The one-week plan on page 216 (Figure 8A) is a good way to program your practice sessions to be sure that you are actually covering the ground that you set out to cover. The plan will also help you to keep your skills from getting rusty in that crucial period between learning the theory of a skill and using it almost intuitively.

You may wonder why we urge you to practice on books *outside* your field, particularly when we have consistently stressed application of the skills to your own professional reading. You may be tempted to say—as many people do—"Why, I barely have time to get through the reading I must do, let alone anything else!"

If this was your reaction, the answer to this comment is a very simple one. When a man's reading is restricted solely to his own field, he usually develops inflexibility of reading habits. This limitation can very easily become a handicap because he has not readied himself for 'that situation which is just a little out of the ordinary. As you practice a variety of techniques on a variety of reading materials, you will be far better equipped to see how the skills covered in this book can be adapted and modified in ways that may not previously have occurred to you. And beyond that, we hope that these skills will develop confidence in your ability to read and heighten your satisfaction from what you have read, regardless of your present background.

In fact, you might deliberately look for difficult reading to use in that daily hour of outside reading. Perhaps there was a subject in school or college that you found almost impossible. Go back to it and try to deal with it again, using the resources these reading skills have provided.

We conclude our book with a list of selected readings in a variety of fields. These are suggestions and not a program to follow. There are areas in which you will probably never be much interested, even after sampling them. And there are other areas in which you will want to learn much more than you could from the few books we have listed. Strike out for yourself.

BIBLIOGRAPHY

SUGGESTED READINGS

Business and Economics

Benson, P. A., North, N. L., Ring, A. A., *Real Estate Principles and Practices.*

Black, E. R., *Diplomacy of Economic Development.*

Brainard, H. G., *Economics in Action.*

Cobleigh, I. U., *How to Make a Killing in Wall Street and Keep It.*

Dice, C. A. and Eiteman, W., *The Stock Market.*

Ellsworth, P. T., *International Economy.*

Hamilton, E. J., Rees, A. and Johnson, H. G., editors, *Landmarks in Political Economy* (2 vols.).

Hansen, A. H., *Guide to Keynes.*

Hazlitt, H., editor, *Critics of Keynesian Economics.*

Scott, W., Spriegel, W. and Clothier, R., *Personnel Management.*

Taylor, O., *History of Economic Thought.*

The Classics

Aristotle, *Ethics.*

Carroll, L., *Through the Looking Glass.*

Chaucer, G., *The Canterbury Tales.*

Dante, *The Divine Comedy.*

Dickens, C., *Bleak House.*

Fielding, H., *Tom Jones.*

Homer, *The Iliad, The Odyssey.*

Melville, H., *Moby Dick.*

Plato, *Selected Works.*

Poe, E. A., *Short Stories and Other Works.*

The Classics (Cont.)

Shakespeare, W., *Complete Works.*

Shaw, G. B., *Selected Plays and Prefaces.*

Sophocles, *Oedipus Rex.*

St. Augustine, *Confessions.*

Swift, J., *Gulliver's Travels.*

Fine Arts

Biancolli, L. and Bagar, R., *Victor Book of Operas.*

Brockway, W. and Weinstock, H., *Men of Music.*

Gardner, H., *Art Through the Ages.*

Gombrich, E. H., *The Story of Art.*

Hamlin, T. F., *Architecture Through the Ages.*

Taylor, F. H., *Fifty Centuries of Art.*

Wright, F. L., *The Future of Architecture.*

History

Baldwin, M. W. and Cole, C. W., *History of Europe.*

Beard, C. and Beard, M., *Basic History of the United States.*

Ceram, C. W., *Gods, Graves and Scholars.*

Coon, C. S., *The Story of Man.*

DeVoto, B., *Across the Wide Missouri.*

Morison, S. E., editor, *The Parkman Reader.*

Trevelyan, G. M., *History of England.*

Wells, H. G., *The Outline of History.*

Wissler, C., *Indians of the United States.*

Modern Life

Clarkson, R. E., *Herbs—Their Culture and Uses.*

Esquire, editors, *Esquire's Handbook for Hosts.*

Fisher, M. F. K., *The Art of Eating.*

Grossman, H. J., *Grossman's Guide to Wines, Spirits and Beers.*

Modern Life (Cont.)

Nelson, G. and Wright, H., *Tomorrow's House.*

Perry, E. K., *Crafts for Fun.*

Tangerman, E. J., *Whittling and Woodcarving.*

Wright, M. and Wright, R., *Guide to Easier Living.*

Philosophy and Religion

Aristotle, *Politics.*

Camus, A., *Resistance, Rebellion and Death.*

Durant, W., *The Story of Philosophy.*

Emerson, R. W., *Essays.*

James, W., *Varieties of Religious Experience.*

Machiavelli, N., *The Prince.*

Maritain, J., *An Introduction to Philosophy.*

Peterson, H., editor, *Essays in Philosophy.*

Thoreau, H. D., *Civil Disobedience.*

Plato, *Dialogues.*

Psychology and Medicine

English, O. S. and Pearson, G. H. J., *Emotional Problems of Living.*

Freud, S., *A General Introduction to Psychoanalysis.*

Fromm, E., *Escape from Freedom.*

Kinsey, A. C., *Sexual Behavior in the Human Male.*

Munn, N. L., *Psychology.*

Strecker, E. A., *Basic Psychiatry.*

Williams, J. F. and Geschickter, C., *Atlas of Human Anatomy.*

Poetry

Browning, E. B., *Sonnets from the Portuguese.*

Creekmore, H., editor, *A Little Treasury of World Poetry.*

Eliot, T. S., *Old Possum's Book of Practical Cats.*

Frost, R., *Complete Poems.*

Poetry (Cont.)

Nash, O., *Versus*.

Omar Khayyam, *The Rubaiyat*.

Quiller-Couch, A., *The Oxford Book of English Verse*.

Untermeyer, L., editor, *Modern American and Modern British Poetry*.

Williams, Oscar, editor, *A Little Treasury of American Poetry. A Little Treasury of Modern Poetry*.

Science

Asimov, I., *The Chemicals of Life*.

Einstein, A. and Infeld, L., *The Evolution of Physics*.

Glasstone, S., *Sourcebook on Atomic Energy*.

Hecht, S., *Explaining the Atom*.

Hoyle, F., *Nature of the Universe*.

Kendall, W. J., *Hi-Fi Handbook*.

Langewiesche, W., *Stick and Rudder*.

Ley, W. and Bonestell, C., *Conquest of Space*.

McDougal, et al., *Fundamentals of Electricity*.

Schneider, H. and Bendick, J., *Everyday Machines and How They Work*.

Shapley, H., editor, *A Treasury of Science*.

Index